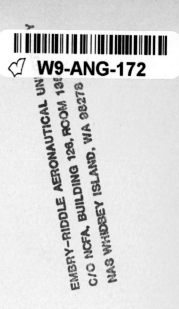

W9-ANG-172

EMBRY-RIDDLE AERONAUTICAL UNI
C/O NCFA, BUILDING 128, ROOM 13
NAS WHIDBEY ISLAND, WA 98278

STUDY GUIDE

 Houghton Mifflin Company

College Division, Western Region

925 E. Meadow Drive, Palo Alto, CA 94303   (415) 496-2100

ANDREA LOPEZ

Sales Representative

(800) 47-BOOKS (2-6657)
TOLL-FREE

(800) 732-3223
SOFTWARE HELP

Study Guide

Siropolis

SMALL BUSINESS MANAGEMENT

Fourth Edition

Robert J. Hughes

Richland College

HOUGHTON MIFFLIN COMPANY   BOSTON

Dallas   Geneva, Illinois   Palo Alto   Princeton, New Jersey

To Barbara Hughes

Copyright © 1990 by Houghton Mifflin Company. All rights reserved.

No part of this work may be reproduced or transmitted in any form or by any means, electronic or mechanical, including photocopying and recording, or by any information storage or retrieval system without the prior written permission of Houghton Mifflin Company unless such copying is expressly permitted by federal copyright law. Address inquiries to College Permissions, Houghton Mifflin Company, One Beacon Street, Boston, MA 02108

Printed in the U.S.A.

ISBN: 0-395-52999-9

ABCDEFGHIJ-HS-9876543210

CONTENTS

TO THE STUDENT

PURPOSE   The purpose of this study guide is to help you reinforce and evaluate your understanding of *Small Business Management* by Nicholas Siropolis. If your goal is to achieve a certain objective and you are willing to make a commitment to that objective because it is important to you, then you will have a chance for success. It takes a great deal of hard work, effort, and energy to be successful. Accordingly, if you want to make good grades, you must devote the time and hard work it takes to score well on examinations, exercises, and papers. This study guide can help you reach that objective.

FORMAT   The design of the study guide allows you to get fully involved in the learning process. Some learning experts have suggested that students must go over new information a number of times in order to comprehend thoroughly the ideas and concepts. This premise is the basis for the study guide's format. For each chapter in *Small Business Management,* the study guide offers the following:

Learning Objectives The learning objectives in the study guide are based on the main points of each chapter in the textbook. They provide an overview of what the chapter is about and enable you to anticipate important points in the chapter.

Chapter Review This exercise focuses on the main ideas presented in the textbook chapter. In the study guide, each of the major topics discussed in the textbook is first summarized and then followed by a list of its subtopics. Space is provided for you to record the main ideas for each subtopic.

Question for Mastery Questions for mastery are found in the textbook at the beginning of each chapter. These questions should be answered in the study guide. This exercise will give you an opportunity to test your comprehension of the information and an idea of what topics you need to review.

Definitions of Key Terms A thorough understanding of the concepts in any course depends on a working knowledge of the vocabulary. Writing down the definition for the important terms in each chapter will help you learn the language of business.

Questions There are true-false, multiple-choice, completion, and essay questions. True-false questions cover all major topics and subtopics in each chapter. They provide a review of the information in the entire chapter. Multiple-choice questions test all major topics. These questions require a different type of thought than the true-false questions. Here again, you are getting another general review of the chapter material. Completion questions focus on the summary in the textbook chapter review. All major points in the chapter are covered. Essay questions give you an opportunity to assimilate and to expand ideas about the major topics in the chapter.

The Difference Between Success and Failure This section is included in each chapter of the study guide to give additional information on a particular topic that is not included in the textbook. This information points out techniques that are helpful for succeeding in a small business.

Answer Key In this section you will find the answers to the objective questions included in each chapter. Use the key to evaluate your understanding in the chapter *only* after you have answered all the questions.

Robert J. Hughes

PART I

AN OVERVIEW OF SMALL BUSINESS

CHAPTER 1

Small Business in a Free Enterprise Society

Learning Objectives

After studying this chapter, you should understand

1.   Why small business has risen in prestige in recent years

2.   How small business is defined

3.   What roles small business plays in our economy

4.   What the relationship is between small business and big business

5.   Why small businesses succeed or fail

Chapter Review

As you read the chapter, complete the following outline with information from the text.

I.   **The Place of Small Business in History.** The first known piece of writing on small business appeared more than 4,000 years ago. It described how bankers loaned money at interest.

Small business flourished in almost all ancient cultures. List several of those cultures.

_____   _____

_____   _____

What effect did Hammurabi have on small business?

_____

_____

_____

© 1990 Houghton Mifflin Company. All rights reserved.   3

Although often ignored, it was largely through small business that civilization spread throughout the ancient world. What were four things that small businesses brought the have-nots?

_____   _____

_____   _____

Over the centuries that followed, the Roman Catholic Church held small businesspersons in low esteem. In particular the church condemned two practices. What were they?

_____

_____

A. **The Rising Status of Small Business.** During the 1980's, small business began to enjoy more esteem and prestige than ever before. Evidence to support this statement includes the White House Conferences on small business and the birth of dozens of publications devoted to small business.

II. **Definitions of Small Business.** *Small business* defies easy definition. Typically we apply the term to neighborhood stores; we apply the term *big business* to large corporations.

There are a number of common yardsticks used to define small business: (1) total assets, (2) owners' equity, (3) yearly sales revenues, and (4) number of employees. Each yardstick has points in its favor, but number of employees has more than any of the others. List four of them.

_____   _____

_____   _____

The number of employees we use to define a small business is 500. To qualify as a small business, then, a company must employ fewer than 500 people. It should also be independently owned and managed.

A. **The SBA's Definitions.** The Small Business Administration (SBA) is a federal agency that was created by Congress in 1953 to help small business thrive. To meet this goal, the SBA offers programs that help small businesses upgrade their managerial skills and borrow money. For businesses seeking loans, the SBA has drawn up definitions of smallness to fit just about every industry. The SBA does use different yardsticks and cutoff points for different industries. What are the broad definitions for the following industrial classifications (Exhibit 1.2)?

© 1990 Houghton Mifflin Company. All rights reserved.

Manufacturing _____

_____

Wholesaling _____

_____

Retailing _____

_____

Services _____

_____

These definitions are by no means hard and fast; they can be relaxed in some cases. Another rule that is sometimes used by the SBA is that a business qualifies as small if it does not dominate its industry.

III. **The Strengths of Small Business.** Returning to our definition of small business as a business that employs fewer than 500 people, let us place this number in focus. As shown in Exhibit 1.3, more than 99 percent of the nation's 19 million businesses are small. Further evidence of the importance of small business is the fact that small business employs roughly half the nation's workforce. In terms of sheer numbers of employees, then, small business far outstrips big business. But how well are small businesses doing in each of the following areas?

    A. **Financial Performance.** _____

_____

    B. **Innovation.** _____

_____

    C. **The Dependence of Big Business on Small Business.** Small businesses provide big businesses with many of the following:

        _____

        _____

        _____

    D. **Creation of New Jobs.** Small businesses create most of the nation's new jobs (Exhibit 1.6).

© 1990 Houghton Mifflin Company. All rights reserved.   5

E. Emergence of Women in Small Business. Women are assuming a significantly stronger role in the U.S. economy.

IV. The Weaknesses of Small Business. There are problems that are unique to small business. Many small businesses die in their infancy. In fact of the 600,000 new businesses launched each year in the United States, only half survive 18 months, and only one in five survives 10 years.

A. High Failure Rates. What role does ease of entry play in the high failure rates of small business?

_____

_____

_____

How do economists define freedom of opportunity?

_____

_____

According to Dun & Bradstreet, the major cause of business failure is bad management. Specifically, it lists the following reasons for business failures (Exhibit 1.10):

Incompetence (44 percent)
Lack of managerial experience (17 percent)
Unbalanced experience (16 percent)
Inexperience in line (15 percent)
Neglect (1 percent)
Fraud or disaster (1 percent)
Unknown (6 percent)

Although widely accepted, these failure rates may be open to question. The fact is no one knows the start-up rate or the failure rate of small businesses. In fact we don't even know what *failure* means. How do you define failure?

_____

_____

_____

© 1990 Houghton Mifflin Company. All rights reserved.

Is failure really failure? (Explain your answer.)

_____

_____

_____

B. **Lack of Managerial Expertness.** Often small businesses fail because they are not prepared to handle increased managerial demands. Why would an increase in the number of employees change the way a small-business owner must manage?

_____

_____

Why must small businesspersons rely on more sophisticated ways to plan and control when their businesses begin to grow?

_____

_____

Why do the presidents of large corporations have an advantage over small businesspersons in the area of professional management?

_____

_____

C. **Poor Minority Representation.** Historically minorities have been underrepresented in small business. Exhibit 1.11 compares minority-owned businesses to all businesses. What does it tell us about the current status of the following groups?

Blacks _____

_____

Hispanics _____

_____

Asian Americans _____

_____

© 1990 Houghton Mifflin Company. All rights reserved.

V. The Future of Small Business. In the future, small business probably will continue to spark progress in our economy. Discuss the effects the following elements will have on the future of small business.

Population growth _____

_____

_____

New technology _____

_____

_____

State and local governments _____

_____

_____

Our economy is likely to continue to become more scientific and therefore more complex. The rising flood of new knowledge, new managerial tools, and new managerial lifestyles will make obsolete many managerial practices as well as many products and services. And small businesspersons will have to be better prepared to master change. How will each of the following help small-business owners adapt to change?

Colleges and universities _____

_____

_____

The Small Business Administration _____

_____

_____

Big business _____

_____

_____

© 1990 Houghton Mifflin Company. All rights reserved.

Questions for Mastery

Questions for mastery are found in the textbook at the beginning of every chapter. Answer each question again to reinforce your understanding of the information.

1. Why has small business risen in prestige in recent years?

     _____

     _____

     _____

2. How is small business defined?

     _____

     _____

3. What roles does small business play in our economy?

     _____

     _____

     _____

4. What is the relationship between small business and big business?

     _____

     _____

     _____

5. Why do small businesses succeed or fail?

     _____

     _____

     _____

     _____

© 1990 Houghton Mifflin Company. All rights reserved.

Definitions of Key Terms

The following key terms are important in this chapter. In your own words, define each concept.

small business _____

_____

owners' equity _____

_____

return on owners' equity _____

_____

invention _____

_____

innovation _____

_____

total assets _____

_____

yearly sales revenues _____

_____

Small Business Administration (SBA) _____

_____

freedom of opportunity _____

_____

ease of entry _____

_____

© 1990 Houghton Mifflin Company. All rights reserved.

True-False Questions

Determine whether the following statements are true or false, then circle T or F. Correct answers are listed at the end of the study guide.

T   F   1.   So vital is small business that few, if any, parts of our economy could go on without its products and services.

T   F   2.   The first known piece of writing about small business appeared over 10,000 years ago and described how bankers loaned money at interest.

T   F   3.   Small business flourished in almost all ancient cultures.

T   F   4.   In 2100 B.C., Hammurabi, King of Babylon, drafted a code of 300 laws to protect consumers and small businesspersons, especially against fraud.

T   F   5.   The need to protect consumers is not as important today as it was in Hammurabi's time.

T   F   6.   Small business helped spread civilization to the four corners of the then-known world.

T   F   7.   During the Middle Ages, the Roman Catholic Church branded retailers as sinners because they did nothing to improve products yet charged higher prices than did the makers of those products.

T   F   8.   As a result of the first White House Conference on Small Business, Congress has passed over 150 recommendations that deal specifically with small business.

T   F   9.   Total assets are a firm's cash, inventory, land, machinery, and other resources.

T   F   10.   Owners' equity is the total investment made by investors in a business.

T   F   11.   Yearly sales revenues are the most common yardstick used to measure small business.

T   F   12.   The textbook defines a business as small if it employs fewer than 500 persons and is independently owned and managed.

T   F   13.   The qualification that a small business be independently managed rules out many franchises.

T   F   14.   The SBA was created by Congress in 1960.

T   F   15.   According to the SBA, a range of 100 to 1,000 employees is used to determine if a manufacturing business is small.

© 1990 Houghton Mifflin Company. All rights reserved.

T   F   16. According to the SBA, a range of $3.5 million to $13.5 million in sales revenues is used to determine if a retailing business is small.

T   F   17. The SBA's size guidelines can be relaxed in exceptional cases.

T   F   18. More than 99 percent of the nation's 19 million businesses are classified as small.

T   F   19. Small businesses employ roughly one-fourth of the nation's workforce.

T   F   20. On average, small manufacturers earn a lower return on owners' equity than do big manufacturers.

T   F   21. The very size of many big businesses may discourage innovation.

T   F   22. Small businesses provide big businesses with many of the services, supplies, and raw materials they need.

T   F   23. Big business, not small business, creates most new jobs.

T   F   24. Many small businesses die in their infancy.

T   F   25. Freedom of opportunity guarantees small-business owners the right to launch their own business ventures.

T   F   26. Seventeen percent of business failures are caused by lack of managerial experience.

T   F   27. According to Dun & Bradstreet, 75 percent of business failures are caused by bad management.

T   F   28. Forty-four percent of all business failures are caused by incompetence.

T   F   29. For small business, the future looks bright because of its ability to generate new ideas, new products, and new services that benefit consumers.

T   F   30. In the future, small-business failures will slow down.

© 1990 Houghton Mifflin Company. All rights reserved.

Multiple-Choice Questions

Write the letter of the correct answer in the blank to the left of the question. Correct answers are listed at the end of the study guide.

_____ 1. Which of the following statements is *true*?
   a. Small businesses did not flourish until the early 1900s.
   b. In 2100 B.C., Hammurabi, king of Babylon, drafted a code of 300 laws to protect consumers.
   c. The laws developed by Hammurabi were lost.
   d. The first known piece of writing on small business appeared more than 6000 years ago.

_____ 2. The Roman Catholic Church believed retailers were
   a. sinners because they did nothing to improve the products they sold.
   b. thieves because they charged interest on loans.
   c. very important contributors to the Roman economy.
   d. all of the above.

_____ 3. Total assets are
   a. everything sold during the calendar year.
   b. debts that are paid at the end of the month.
   c. the same thing as sales.
   d. cash, inventory, land, machinery, and other resources.

_____ 4. All of the following are common yardsticks used to measure small business *except*
   a. total assets.
   b. owners' equity.
   c. total expenses.
   d. yearly sales revenues.

_____ 5. A small business is one that is independently owned and managed and has fewer than _____ employees.
   a. 500
   b. 350
   c. 250
   d. 100

_____ 6. According to the Small Business Administration, a retailing business is small if its yearly sales revenues are _____ million.
   a. $1.0 to $10
   b. $1.0 to $15
   c. $2.5 to $11
   d. $3.5 to $13.5

© 1990 Houghton Mifflin Company. All rights reserved.

_____ 7. According to the Small Business Administration, a manufacturing business is small if its number of employees is between
  a. 50 and 1,500.
  b. 100 and 1,000.
  c. 500 and 1,000.
  d. 500 and 1,500.

_____ 8. According to the SBA, a service business is small if its yearly sales revenues are _____ million.
  a. $1.0 to $10
  b. $1.0 to $15
  c. $2.5 to $11
  d. $3.5 to $14.5

_____ 9. More than _____ percent of businesses in the United States are small.
  a. 85
  b. 90
  c. 94
  d. 99

_____10. Return on owners' equity is higher for
  a. a medium-sized manufacturer than a large wholesaler.
  b. a small manufacturer than a large manufacturer.
  c. a small retailer than a large retailer.
  d. none of the above

_____11. Which of the following statements is *true*?
  a. Their size allows big businesses to produce new products immediately.
  b. Small businesses are more innovative than large businesses.
  c. Size does not make a difference where innovations and new ideas are involved.
  d. Big businesses often suppress innovations.

_____12. According to a study by the SBA,
  a. there is no difference between the percentage of new jobs created by large businesses and small businesses.
  b. large businesses create most of the nation's new jobs.
  c. medium-sized businesses create most of the nation's new jobs.
  d. small businesses create most of the nation's new jobs.

_____13. About _____ businesses are incorporated each year.
  a. 300,000
  b. 450,000
  c. 600,000
  d. 750,000

© 1990 Houghton Mifflin Company. All rights reserved.

_____14. The primary reason that businesses fail is
    a.   limited resources.
    b.   lack of marketing research.
    c.   ease of entry.
    d.   poor bookkeeping methods.

_____15. According to Dun & Bradstreet, _____ is at the root of most business failures.
    a.   neglect
    b.   unbalanced experience
    c.   lack of managerial experience
    d.   incompetence

Completion Questions

Write your answer in the blanks provided in each question. Correct answers are listed at the end of the study guide.

1. Small business flourished in almost all ancient cultures. But their products and services were often shoddy. To help solve this problem, _____ drafted a code of _____ laws in _____ B.C.

2. In the Middle Ages, the Roman Catholic Church held small businesspersons in _____ esteem. The church branded retailers as _____ because they did nothing to improve products yet charged higher prices for them than did their makers. And until the nineteenth century, the church often spoke against the practice of charging _____ on loans.

3. The White House Conference on Small Business held in 1980 brought together _____ delegates from all 50 states. So influential was the conference that Congress has passed into law _____ of the 60 recommendations made there.

4. There are a number of common yardsticks used to measure small business. The most common are total _____, owners' _____, yearly sales _____, and number of _____.

5. In the textbook, we call a business small if it employs fewer than _____ employees, and is independently _____ and _____.

6. The SBA has drawn up definitions of smallness to fit virtually every industry. These definitions are by no means hard and fast, and they can be relaxed in exceptional cases. For example, in 1966 the SBA classified _____ _____ as a small business. The agency justified its action by applying a seldom-used test of smallness—that a business qualifies as small if it does not _____ its industry.

7. More than _____ percent of the nation's _____ million businesses are small. As further evidence of the importance of small business, small firms employ roughly _____ of the nation's workforce.

8. On average, small manufacturers earn a _____ return on _____ _____ than do large manufacturers.

9. Many small businesses die in their infancy. In fact of the _____ new businesses started each year in the United States, only _____ survive as long as _____ months, and only one in five survives as long as _____ years.

10. According to Dun & Bradstreet, the primary reason small businesses fail is because of _____ management, which often is manifested in heavy operating _____, slow-paying _____, _____ location, inventory difficulties, excessive fixed assets, and other problems.

11. A primary reason for the failure of small businesses is their inability to handle _____ managerial demands.

12. In the future, it is unlikely that small-business _____ will slow down. The example of successful small business will continue to attract the _____ as well as the qualified in increasing numbers. As our population expands, we can expect a steady _____ in the total number of small businesses.

Essay Questions

1. Typically we apply the term *small business* to so-called mom-and-pop stores, such as neighborhood groceries and restaurants, and we apply the term *big business* to such giants as IBM and General Motors. How would you define a small business?

2. More than 99 percent of the nation's 19 million businesses are small. Further evidence of its vitality is the fact that small business employs roughly half of the nation's workforce. What are other factors that point to the importance of small business in the U.S. economy?

3. Many small businesses die in their infancy. In fact of the 600,000 new businesses started each year in the United States, only half survive 18 months, and only one in five survives ten years. Why do so many small businesses fail?

The Difference Between Success and Failure

Before you go on to the next paragraph, stop for a moment and think of the name of a business—any business—that produces or sells a product or service.

Chances are you thought of a corporate giant like IBM or General Motors or AT&T. These are the businesses that seem to make the news and whose names stick in our minds. Yet they make up a very small portion of the total number of businesses in the United States today. By far the largest proportion of American businesses is small—extremely small compared to firms like General Motors.

This country's economic history is chock-full of stories of ambitious men and women who turned their ideas into business dynasties. The Ford Motor Company started with one man and a new method for industrial production. Macy's can trace its beginnings to a pushcart in the streets of New York. Both Xerox and Polaroid began as small firms with a better way to do a job.

Do most owners of small businesses dream of their firms growing into giant corporations managed by professionals while they serve on the board of directors? Or would they rather their firms stay small so they have the opportunity (and the responsibility) to do everything that needs to be done? The answers depend on the personal characteristics and motivation of the individual owner. For many, the advantages of remaining small far outweigh the disadvantages.

Advantages

1. Opportunities for personal relationships with customers and employees
2. Greater adaptability to change
3. Lower taxes
4. Fewer government regulations
5. Independence
6. Simplified record keeping

Disadvantages

1. Management not specialized
2. Shortage of working capital
3. Difficulty obtaining capital
4. Lack of extensive marketing research
5. Difficulty hiring and keeping top-quality employees
6. Difficulty keeping hours of operation competitive with those of large business

Every day, and in every part of the country, people are in the process of planning or opening new businesses. Many of these businesses may not succeed. Others represent well-conceived ideas developed by entrepreneurs who have the experience, the resources, and the determination to make their businesses succeed. As these well-prepared entrepreneurs pursue their individual goals, our society benefits in many ways from their work and creativity.

© 1990 Houghton Mifflin Company. All rights reserved.

CHAPTER 2

The Entrepreneur

Learning Objectives

After studying this chapter, you should understand

1. What an entrepreneur is

2. What the difference is between entrepreneurship and management

3. What the key traits are of successful entrepreneurs

4. What social conditions are conducive to the development of entrepreneurs

5. What the rewards and hazards are of being an entrepreneur

Chapter Review

As you read the chapter, complete the following outline with information from the text.

I. **Defining the Entrepreneur.** The *American Heritage Dictionary* defines *entrepreneur* as "a person who organizes, operates, and assumes the risk for business ventures."*

   A. **Henry Ford, Entrepreneur.** Describe Ford's early failures, the start of the Ford Motor Company, and the kind of man Ford was.

   Early failures _____

   _____

   _____

   The beginnings of the Ford Motor Company _____

   _____

   _____

*Copyright © 1985 by Houghton Mifflin Company. Reprinted by permission from *The American Heritage Dictionary, Second College Edition.*

© 1990 Houghton Mifflin Company. All rights reserved.

Henry Ford, the man _____

_____

_____

B. **Steven Jobs, Entrepreneur.** Describe Jobs's entrepreneurial vision, his relationship with Steven Wozniak, how the two started Apple Computer, and Jobs's success.

Jobs's entrepreneurial vision _____

_____

_____

_____

Relationship with Steven Wozniak _____

_____

_____

The beginnings of Apple Computer _____

_____

_____

_____

Jobs's success _____

_____

_____

C. **Pure Entrepreneurs.** Pure entrepreneurs launch their own ventures from scratch. They nurse them into successful businesses through hard work and their idea-producing ability. They display an instinct for opportunity and a sense of timing. Define *pure entrepreneur*.

_____

_____

_____

© 1990 Houghton Mifflin Company. All rights reserved.

Others qualify as entrepreneurs but not as pure entrepreneurs. They include those who take over a business after the founder retires, dies, or sells out, but who continue to build and innovate, and those who run a franchise independently of the franchisor.

D. **Entrepreneurship and Management.** Entrepreneurship is different from the traditional concept of an entrepreneur. Explain that difference.

_____

_____

_____

_____

Entrepreneurship is not the same thing as management. The first job of a manager is to make a business perform well. The manager takes given resources—personnel, money, machines, and materials—and orchestrates them into production. How is the job of an entrepreneur different from that of a manager?

_____

_____

_____

II. **Entrepreneurial Traits.** Although no two entrepreneurs are precisely alike, it is possible to predict the kinds of men and women who are most likely to succeed as entrepreneurs. List two of the reasons people choose to become entrepreneurs.

• _____

• _____

More than half of the nation's wage earners say they would rather work for themselves than for somebody else. Yet few become entrepreneurs. Explain what holds them back.

_____

_____

_____

In a study of successful entrepreneurs, David McClelland identified six key traits.

A. **Innovation.** Innovation becomes entrepreneurial only when carried into production to benefit consumers.

© 1990 Houghton Mifflin Company. All rights reserved.

B. **Reasonable Risk Taking.** Entrepreneurs are not gamblers, but they need to take reasonable risks to justify their efforts.

C. **Self-Confidence.** Entrepreneurs believe in themselves. How does this self-confidence translate into success?

_____

_____

D. **Hard Work.** Few people in our society work harder than entrepreneurs.

E. **Goal Setting.** According to psychologists, happiness means working toward reasonable goals, not necessarily achieving those goals. Is this definition of happiness applicable to entrepreneurs? (Explain your answer.)

_____

_____

_____

F. **Accountability.** Entrepreneurs want full credit for their success, but are willing to shoulder the blame for their failure. To measure their performance, entrepreneurs use two common yardsticks. What are they?

_____

_____

What two functions do profits perform for entrepreneurs?

- _____

- _____

III. **Developing Entrepreneurs.** The common traits we find among entrepreneurs stem from their social backgrounds, their ability to function individually or in groups, and the rewards and hazards of entrepreneurship.

A. **A Tradition of Entrepreneurship.** Psychologists say that entrepreneurs are likely to come from families in which parents set high standards for their children's performance, encourage habits of self-reliance, and avoid being strict disciplinarians.

© 1990 Houghton Mifflin Company. All rights reserved.

The need to achieve crops up in all ethnic groups, but is more likely to take an entrepreneurial form in groups with a tradition of entrepreneurship. Bias has also played a role in limiting entrepreneurial opportunities for certain ethnic groups. Today two forces are working to boost entrepreneurship among minorities. What are those forces?

_____

_____

B. **Individual Versus Group Achievement.** To this point, discussion in the textbook focuses on the individual achiever. Considering the individual nature of small business, is this natural? (Explain your answer.)

_____

_____

In what ways can working in a group help the entrepreneur?

_____

_____

_____

C. **Rewards and Hazards of Entrepreneurship.** There are both rewards and hazards to being an entrepreneur. List three of the rewards.

_____

_____

_____

When entrepreneurs fail, they suffer two personal losses. What are those losses?

_____

_____

IV. **On Self-Analysis.** For some reason, writers fail to offer advice on how best to pick oneself as boss. Most checklists are useless, but there are some factors that can help would-be entrepreneurs evaluate themselves. Discuss how the following can affect an entrepreneur's chance of success.

© 1990 Houghton Mifflin Company. All rights reserved.

The ability to appraise one's own capabilities _____

_____

_____

The willingness to impose personal discipline while risking one's own money _____

_____

_____

The willingness to gear a venture to the needs of customers _____

_____

_____

Questions for Mastery

Questions for mastery are found in the textbook at the beginning of every chapter. Answer each question again to reinforce your understanding of the information.

1. What is an entrepreneur? _____

_____

_____

_____

2. What is the difference between entrepreneurship and management? _____

_____

_____

3. What are key traits of successful entrepreneurs?

_____   _____

_____   _____

_____   _____

© 1990 Houghton Mifflin Company. All rights reserved.

4. What social conditions are conducive to the development of entrepreneurs? _____

    _____

    _____

5. What are the rewards and hazards of being an entrepreneur? _____

    _____

    _____

    _____

Definitions of Key Terms

The following key terms are important in this chapter. In your own words, define each concept.

entrepreneur _____

_____

pure entrepreneur _____

_____

innovation _____

_____

entrepreneurship _____

_____

management _____

_____

reasonable risk taking _____

_____

gamble _____

_____

© 1990 Houghton Mifflin Company. All rights reserved.

accountability _____

_____

profit _____

_____

True-False Questions

Determine whether the following statements are true or false, then circle T or F. Correct answers are listed at the end of the study guide

T   F   1.   Successful men and women come from such varied backgrounds that analysis of what it takes to create a successful business has been imprecise.

T   F   2.   An entrepreneur is a person who organizes, operates, and assumes the risk for business ventures.

T   F   3.   Henry Ford started his first business ventures in 1790.

T   F   4.   After failing twice, Ford raised $28,000 and launched the Ford Motor Company.

T   F   5.   In 1976, Steven Jobs joined forces with Hewlett-Packard and created the Apple computer.

T   F   6.   Pure entrepreneurs create ventures from the raw materials of their own ideas and hard work.

T   F   7.   Entrepreneurship is practiced in old businesses as well as new ones, and in big businesses as well as small ones.

T   F   8.   Entrepreneurship is the capacity for innovation, investment, and expansion in new markets, products, and techniques.

T   F   9.   *Management* and *entrepreneurship* mean the same thing.

T   F   10.   Studies at Harvard and MIT found that many entrepreneurs were unsuccessful in their previous employment.

T   F   11.   Although men and women become entrepreneurs for a variety of reasons, their desire for self-expression appears to be a common thread.

T   F   12.   Many would-be entrepreneurs refuse to take the fateful first step because they are afraid to risk their financial security.

© 1990 Houghton Mifflin Company. All rights reserved.

T F 13. Few small businesses fail during their first 18 months of operation.

T F 14. Generally entrepreneurs are not innovative.

T F 15. When forced to choose between a high-risk venture and a sure thing, most entrepreneurs would choose the sure thing.

T F 16. Entrepreneurs generally avoid ventures that are pure gambles.

T F 17. Often entrepreneurs lack the self-confidence necessary for success in a small-business venture.

T F 18. Many entrepreneurs are compulsive workers, especially when a crisis flares up.

T F 19. Many entrepreneurs find the goal-setting process is self-renewing.

T F 20. Return on investment and rate of profit growth are used to measure the success or failure of an entrepreneur.

T F 21. A small-business owner is guaranteed a profit because of the risk of opening a small business.

T F 22. Psychologists say that entrepreneurs are likely to come from families in which parents set high standards for their children.

T F 23. The need to achieve crops up in all ethnic groups but is more likely to take an entrepreneurial form in those with an entrepreneurial tradition.

T F 24. Asian Americans more than other groups rely on relatives or friends for business startup loans.

T F 25. Minorities have long been denied equal access to entrepreneurial opportunities.

T F 26. In some circumstances, entrepreneurs may achieve more when they work in a group rather than individually.

T F 27. Most entrepreneurs do not really care about the esteem of their friends and relatives.

T F 28. There is no such thing as a perfectly safe investment.

© 1990 Houghton Mifflin Company. All rights reserved.

Multiple-Choice Questions

Write the letter of the correct answer in the blank to the left of the question. Correct answers are listed at the end of the study guide.

_____ 1. The term *entrepreneur*
   a. means the same thing as *manager.*
   b. suggests spirit, zeal, and ideas.
   c. is the same thing as entrepreneurship.
   d. means the individual is guaranteed success.

_____ 2. Henry Ford's first two business ventures
   a. were an overnight success.
   b. involved electric trolley cars.
   c. were originally a partnership.
   d. folded because Ford mistook his market.

_____ 3. Steven Jobs and Steven Wozniak started Apple Computer
   a. in 1962.
   b. in New York with help from Hewlett-Packard.
   c. with less than $1,000.
   d. to compete for large organizational customers.

_____ 4. In the textbook, we define *pure entrepreneurs* as
   a. men and women who create ventures from the raw materials of their own ideas and hard work.
   b. those who run a business by a franchisor's rules.
   c. those who work for a large corporation.
   d. those who work for a small business.

_____ 5. All of the following qualify as entrepreneurs *except* those who
   a. start their own business from scratch.
   b. take over a business after the founder retires.
   c. run a franchise independently of the franchisor.
   d. are managers in large corporations.

_____ 6. Of all new businesses started, _____ fail within the first 18 months.
   a. one-fourth
   b. one-third
   c. one-half
   d. three-fourths

_____ 7. Reasonable risk taking means
   a. choosing a venture where the risk of failure is extremely high.
   b. avoiding a sure thing.
   c. looking for ventures where the odds are stacked against the entrepreneur.
   d. all of the above.

© 1990 Houghton Mifflin Company. All rights reserved.

_____ 8. Which of the following statements about entrepreneurship is *false?*
    a. They are paid overtime for when they work more than 40 hours.
    b. They seem to put in even longer hours than corporate executives.
    c. They are compulsive workers.
    d. They tend to work especially hard when a crisis flares up.

_____ 9. The process of setting and achieving goals
    a. is undertaken only by pure entrepreneurs.
    b. repeats itself among entrepreneurs.
    c. is unnecessary for entrepreneurs.
    d. is one of the hazards of entrepreneurship.

_____10. Profits are
    a. a reward for successful risk taking.
    b. guaranteed for the small-business owner.
    c. more a goal than a measure of entrepreneurial performance.
    d. the primary goal of every business.

_____11. Which of the following statements is *false?*
    a. Because they lack a tradition of entrepreneurship, most minorities tend to work for others rather than themselves.
    b. Prejudice has limited the entrepreneurial opportunities of many minority groups.
    c. In the 1990s we are likely to see little increase in the number of minorities entering the world of entrepreneurship.
    d. The federal government and colleges and universities are working to boost entrepreneurship among minority groups.

_____12. One reward of entrepreneurship is
    a. loss of ego.
    b. social rejection.
    c. a buildup of equity.
    d. loss of savings.

Completion Questions

Write your answer in the blanks provided in each question. Correct answers are listed at the end of the study guide.

1. An _____ is a person who organizes, operates, and assumes the risk for business ventures. The term *entrepreneur* suggests spirit, _____, and _____.

2. _____ entrepreneurs are men and women who create a venture from the raw materials of their own ideas and hard work. Other individuals who qualify as entrepreneurs, but not pure entrepreneurs, would include (1) those who take over a business after the founder retires, _____, or _____ out—but who continue to build and innovate; and (2) those who run a _____ independently of the franchisor.

© 1990 Houghton Mifflin Company. All rights reserved.

3. Although in the textbook we define entrepreneurs mostly as those who launch new ventures, _____ is far more widely practiced—in old businesses as well as new ones, in big businesses as well as small ones. Entrepreneurship is the capacity for _____, investment, and _____ in new markets, products, and techniques.

4. The first job of the manager is to make a business _____ well. The manager takes given resources—personnel, _____, _____, and materials—and orchestrates them into production.

5. Entrepreneurs enjoy a generally _____ than average level of success in their previous employment. This finding suggests that it is not _____ pressures that force successful people to become entrepreneurs. Clearly men and women become entrepreneurs for a variety of reasons. However, their desire for _____ appears to be a common thread. This desire helps explain why more than _____ of the nation's wage earners say they would rather work for themselves than for somebody else.

6. Many new businesses die in infancy. In fact _____ die within _____ months of birth. What is it, then, that makes for success instead of failure? To begin with, successful entrepreneurs are likely to be _____.

7. Successful entrepreneurs take _____ risks. They avoid ventures in which the _____ against them are high. At the same time, most entrepreneurs shun a _____ thing, because the satisfaction from such a task would be too small to justify their effort. However, even though entrepreneurs generally choose ventures that fall between the two extremes, they tend to go in the direction of _____ risk.

8. Entrepreneurs tend to be _____ workers, especially when a crisis flares up. According to one study, top executives work an average of _____ hours a week. Although we lack similar data on entrepreneurs, it is likely that they work even longer, especially during the first few years.

9. Psychologists often define happiness as striving toward meaningful goals, not necessarily the _____ of those goals. To entrepreneurs, merely choosing a new meaningful goal is _____.

10. Entrepreneurs generally want full credit for their success—or will assume full blame for their failure. To measure their performance, entrepreneurs may use any one of several yardsticks, among them return on _____ and rate of _____ growth. What they measure is profitability. Profits are really a measure of the _____ value of a company's contribution to users, distributors, and the public. Profits play another role, as a _____ for successful risk taking. Entrepreneurs deserve a _____ return on their investment because they risk failure.

11. Psychologists say that entrepreneurs are likely to come from families in which parents set _____ standards for their children's performance. The need to achieve crops up in all ethnic groups, but is more likely to take an entrepreneurial form in groups with a tradition of _____.

© 1990 Houghton Mifflin Company. All rights reserved.   30

12. In some circumstances, entrepreneurs may achieve more when they work in a _____ rather than individually. Group effort can help overcome the fear of _____.

13. Launching a new venture always carries a risk of _____. For the entrepreneur, that loss can be both financial and _____.

Essay Questions

1. What kinds of men and women are likely to start successful small businesses?

2. David McClelland of Harvard University found that entrepreneurs are likely to do well if they are innovative, reasonable risk takers, self-confident, hard workers, goal setters, and accountable. How important are these traits? Do you think other traits are also important? What are they?

3. There are signs that blacks and other minority groups may soon be entering the entrepreneurial world in record numbers. What forces are behind this change?

The Difference Between Success and Failure

Researchers have suggested a number of personal factors as reasons why individuals go into business. One is "entrepreneurial spirit"—the desire to create a new business. Others— independence, the desire to determine one's own destiny, the willingness to find and accept a challenge—also play a part. Background may come into play as well. In particular, researchers feel that people whose families have been in business (successfully or not) are most apt to start and run their own businesses. The age factor is important, too. People under 25 or over 40 are less likely to start their own businesses.

There also must be some motivation to start a business. One person may finally decide she has simply had enough of working and earning a profit for someone else. Another may lose his job for some reason and decide to start the business he has always wanted rather than look for another job. Still another person may have an idea for a new product or a new way to sell an existing product. Or the opportunity to go into business may arise suddenly, perhaps when a friend suggests a partnership. In 1951, Lillian Katz was a young housewife with a hard-working husband. An additional $50 a week in income would mean the difference between meeting expenses and living fairly well. Lillian paid $495 to advertise in *Seventeen* magazine, offering readers a matching belt and pocketbook. She received orders for $16,000 worth of goods. Today Katz owns and runs Lillian Vernon, a mail-order catalog firm with annual revenues of $100 million.*

---

*Richard Greene, "A Boutique in Your Living Room," *Forbes,* 7 May 1984, p. 86.

© 1990 Houghton Mifflin Company. All rights reserved.

In some people motivation develops more slowly as they gain the knowledge and ability required for success as a business owner. Knowledge and ability—especially management ability—are probably the most important factors involved. A new firm is built very much around the entrepreneur. The owner must be able to manage the firm's finances, its personnel (if there are any employees), and its day-to-day operations. He or she must handle sales, advertising, purchasing, pricing, and a variety of other business functions. The knowledge and ability to do so most often are obtained through experience working for other firms in the same area of business.

© 1990 Houghton Mifflin Company. All rights reserved.

CHAPTER 3

Opportunities and Trends

Learning Objectives

After studying this chapter, you should understand

1. What the major groups of industries are

2. What the flow of products and services is

3. Which industries offer the most promising entrepreneurial opportunities

4. What trends are likely to dominate the economy by the year 2000

5. What the hierarchy of technology is

Chapter Review

As you read the chapter, complete the following outline with information from the text.

Entrepreneurs energize our economy, thriving in almost every industry. Entrepreneurial opportunities, however, are greater in some industries than others.

I. **Major Groups of Industries.** There are four major industry groups: manufacturing, wholesaling, retailing, and services. Define them in your own words.

Manufacturing _____

_____

_____

Wholesaling _____

_____

_____

Retailing _____

_____

_____

Services _____

_____

_____

Each group differs in terms of personnel, money, materials, and machines (Exhibit 3.1). As a rule, a manufacturing business is the hardest to establish and a service business is the easiest.

Industry groups often overlap. And manufacturers, wholesalers, and retailers often are linked together to meet the needs of consumers. Service businesses reach out to all industry groups as well as consumers (Exhibit 3.2).

II. **Manufacturing.** Manufacturing lends itself to bigness because of the investment required in equipment, energy, and raw materials. It takes more money to start a manufacturing business.

Big business dominates the world of manufacturing. The nation's top 500 manufacturers account for two-thirds of the total sales revenues generated by manufacturers and three-fourths of the total workers employed in manufacturing.

With so much money at stake, the risks are much greater in manufacturing than in wholesaling, retailing, or services. But, often, so are the rewards. Many small manufacturers earn more than a 20 percent return on their investment. These high returns, however, tend to favor those industries that turn out a steady flow of ideas and products.

Most big businesses are aware of the innovations that flow from small manufacturers. In many cases, large businesses will buy into or buy out a promising small-business venture. A buyout can be advantageous for both the big business and the entrepreneur. Explore those advantages.

For the big business _____

_____

_____

For the entrepreneur _____

_____

_____

Because it is the parent of products, manufacturing offers more opportunities for innovation than any other industry.

III. **Wholesaling.** Small business dominates wholesaling. In fact businesses with fewer than 100 employees account for nearly 80 percent of all employees in wholesaling. This stems from the fact that wholesalers function mostly as caretakers; they need fewer employees for a given volume of business than do manufacturers or retailers. Why are wholesalers considered caretakers?

_____

_____

_____

Why is a long apprenticeship usually required before becoming a wholesaler?

_____

_____

Wholesaling is a balancing act. The entrepreneur is either smoothing the feathers of a retailer whose promised goods failed to arrive or chasing after suppliers and manufacturers who have failed to deliver.

Although small businesses dominate wholesaling, there are signs that larger companies are reshaping the industry. What effect is consolidation having in industry?

_____

_____

IV. **Retailing.** Small businesses with fewer than 100 employees account for more than 50 percent of all employees in retailing (Exhibit 3.3). Most of them have fewer than 5 employees. Moreover, there are hundreds of different kinds of retailers, ranging from wig shops to automobile agencies.

© 1990 Houghton Mifflin Company. All rights reserved.   35

Few retailers pursue innovation with regularity. Why do you think this is so?

_____

_____

_____

Specialty shops are especially attractive to retailing entrepreneurs. Explain why.

_____

_____

_____

Many entrepreneurs go into retailing with an eye to multiplying one store into many as quickly as possible. They do so primarily by selling franchises to investors. This allows them to expand without putting up too much of their own money.

V.   **Services.** Service ventures are generally the easiest to start. Many can be run from a home or storefront. List two examples:

_____

_____

These businesses require little, if any, investment; others require large investments. List two service businesses that would require a large initial investment.

_____

_____

Services hold a magnetic attraction for entrepreneurs. Unlike retailing, services are open to innovation. And no other industry group offers entrepreneurs a higher return on their investment of time.

Like retailing, services lend themselves to franchising. For many kinds of services, franchising is the least costly way to expand.

© 1990 Houghton Mifflin Company. All rights reserved.

Big business offers little threat to the survival of small service businesses. Why do you think this is so?

_____

_____

_____

What is the primary threat to small service businesses?

_____

How can those businesses counteract that threat?

_____

_____

There are many different kinds of service industries, some more accessible to entrepreneurs than others. In your own words, describe each of the following industry groups and their accessibility to entrepreneurs.

A. **Communications** _____

_____

_____

_____

B. **Construction** _____

_____

_____

_____

C. **Finance** _____

_____

_____

_____

© 1990 Houghton Mifflin Company. All rights reserved.

   D. Insurance _____

   _____

   _____

   _____

   E. Real Estate _____

   _____

   _____

   _____

   F. Transportation _____

   _____

   _____

   _____

   G. Utilities _____

   _____

   _____

   _____

VI. **A Look at the Future.** What will tomorrow be like? What products and services will consumers want in 10 or 20 years from now? Which industries will lend themselves to entrepreneurial adventure? The World Future Society describes several long-term trends that will have a major impact on the American economy in the twenty-first century (Exhibit 3.4). Describe those trends and what they mean for tomorrow's entrepreneurs.

© 1990 Houghton Mifflin Company. All rights reserved.

Societal trends _____

_____

_____

_____

_____

Technology trends _____

_____

_____

_____

_____

Educational trends _____

_____

_____

_____

_____

Trends in labor force and work _____

_____

_____

_____

_____

© 1990 Houghton Mifflin Company. All rights reserved.

Trends in values and concerns _____

_____

_____

_____

_____

Family trends _____

_____

_____

_____

In what industries lie the best opportunities for entrepreneurs in the future? There is no way to answer this question with precision. But it seems that entrepreneurs will be drawn to industries prepared for strong upward trends in affluence and leisure, individualism, urbanization, and technology. Describe the changes we can expect in these areas.

A. Affluence and Leisure _____

_____

_____

_____

_____

B. Individualism _____

_____

_____

_____

_____

© 1990 Houghton Mifflin Company. All rights reserved.

C.   Urbanization _____

_____

_____

_____

_____

D.   Technology _____

_____

_____

_____

_____

E.   General Outlook. How would you describe the general outlook for entrepreneurs between now and the year 2000?

_____

_____

_____

_____

Questions for Mastery

Questions for mastery are found in the textbook at the beginning of every chapter. Answer each question again to reinforce your understanding of the information.

1.   What are the major groups of industries?

_____

_____

_____

© 1990 Houghton Mifflin Company. All rights reserved.

2. What is the flow of products and services?

    _____

    _____

    _____

3. Which industries offer the most promising entrepreneurial opportunities?

    _____

    _____

    _____

4. What trends are likely to dominate the economy by the year 2000?

    _____

    _____

    _____

5. What is the hierarchy of technology?

    _____

    _____

    _____

Definitions of Key Terms

The following key terms are important in this chapter. In your own words, define each concept.

manufacturing _____

_____

wholesaling _____

_____

© 1990 Houghton Mifflin Company. All rights reserved.

retailing _____

_____

services _____

_____

venture capital _____

_____

franchising _____

_____

high-technology venture _____

_____

True-False Questions

Determine whether the following statements are true or false, then circle T or F. Correct answers are listed at the end of the study guide.

T   F   1.   Manufacturers convert raw materials into products.

T   F   2.   Manufacturers sell their products only to wholesalers or retailers.

T   F   3.   A wholesaler is someone who sells to retailers.

T   F   4.   As a product passes from the manufacturer to the wholesaler, the product is changed; this is why the wholesaler charges a higher price.

T   F   5.   Wholesalers provide fast delivery, credit financing, and other services to retailers.

T   F   6.   Retailers add value to a product by offering the consumer personal attention, wide selection, credit terms, and other services.

T   F   7.   Service firms sell personal skills to manufacturers, wholesalers, retailers, and consumers.

T   F   8.   As a rule, manufacturing businesses are the hardest to establish and retail businesses are the easiest.

© 1990 Houghton Mifflin Company. All rights reserved.

T   F   9.   The nation's top 500 manufacturers account for three-fourths of the total number of employees in manufacturing.

T   F   10.   Large businesses dominate the wholesaling industry.

T   F   11.   As caretakers, wholesalers buy products in bulk from manufacturers, store them in a place convenient to retailers, then sell them as retailers need them.

T   F   12.   One of the reasons entrepreneurs are attracted to wholesaling is the short apprenticeship required to learn the trade.

T   F   13.   Often wholesaling is a balancing act in which the entrepreneur is either smoothing the feathers of a retailer whose promised goods have failed to arrive or chasing after suppliers who have failed to deliver.

T   F   14.   Small businesses with fewer than 100 employees account for more than 50 percent of all employees in retailing.

T   F   15.   Most retailers have fewer than five employees.

T   F   16.   As a rule, retailers are more innovative than most small-business owners in other industries.

T   F   17.   Specialty shops are especially attractive to retailing entrepreneurs because they enable the entrepreneurs to focus their resources in depth on a narrow segment of a market.

T   F   18.   By selling franchises, entrepreneurs are able to expand without investing too much of their own money.

T   F   19.   Many service businesses can be run from a home or storefront.

T   F   20.   The service industry offers entrepreneurs a higher return of their investment of time than do other industries.

T   F   21.   Big business offers little threat to the survival of small service businesses.

T   F   22.   The greatest threat to the small service business is the consumer who turns do-it-yourselfer.

T   F   23.   The communications industry offers numerous opportunities for young entrepreneurs.

T   F   24.   Most construction contractors are small.

T   F   25.   The drawback to subcontracting is the amount of financing required to get started.

© 1990 Houghton Mifflin Company. All rights reserved.

T F 26. Venture-capital firms seek out old established businesses that have a proven background of managerial experience.

T F 27. Most of the nation's insurance companies are small.

T F 28. The insurance field offers no opportunities for the small-business owner.

T F 29. Entrepreneurs generally prefer residential real estate.

T F 30. The transportation industry is made up almost entirely of big business.

T F 31. The utility industry almost entirely shuts out the entrepreneur.

T F 32. Our store of knowledge is doubling every 20 years.

T F 33. By the year 2000, about half of all service workers will be involved in collecting, analyzing, synthesizing, storing, or retrieving information.

T F 34. The World Future Society predicts that the majority of families will depend on one income in the future.

T F 35. In the future, the number of working women will decrease from 63 percent to approximately 30 percent.

T F 36. Experts predict that over the next decade, automation, robotics, and computer applications will shorten the average workweek to 32 hours.

T F 37. With increased leisure time, fewer people will choose to moonlight by setting up their own businesses.

T F 38. Most of the companies founded in the future will be high-technology companies.

Multiple-Choice Questions

Write the letter of the correct answer in the blank to the left of the question. Correct answers are listed at the end of the study guide.

_____ 1. Which of the following statements is *false?*
  a. Some manufacturers sell their products directly to consumers.
  b. Service firms sell their products to manufacturers, wholesalers, retailers, and consumers.
  c. Retailers buy their products from service industries, then sell them to manufacturers and wholesalers.
  d. Wholesalers do not necessarily sell at big discounts.

© 1990 Houghton Mifflin Company. All rights reserved.

_____ 2. The industry group that adds value to a product by offering personal attention, wide selection, and credit terms is
a. manufacturing.
b. wholesaling.
c. retailing.
d. services.

_____ 3. As a rule, _____ businesses are the hardest to establish and services are the easiest.
a. manufacturing
b. wholesaling
c. retailing
d. construction

_____ 4. Small business dominates all of the following industries *except*
a. manufacturing.
b. wholesaling.
c. retailing.
d. services.

_____ 5. The nation's top 500 manufacturers account for _____ of the total sales revenues generated by manufacturers.
a. one-quarter
b. one-third
c. two-thirds
d. three-fourths

_____ 6. When a big business buys out a small business,
a. it may be investing profits or diversifying into something new.
b. the consumer always benefits.
c. the small-business owner usually loses a large portion of his or her investment.
d. the big business realizes capital gains.

_____ 7. Businesses with fewer than 100 employees account for nearly _____ percent of the employees in wholesaling.
a. 30
b. 50
c. 65
d. 80

_____ 8. The primary job of wholesalers is
a. producing a product.
b. caretaking.
c. selling to consumers.
d. changing the form of products.

© 1990 Houghton Mifflin Company. All rights reserved.

____ 9. Small businesses with fewer than 100 employees account for about _____ percent of the employees in retailing.
   a. 30
   b. 50
   c. 65
   d. 80

____10. Which of the following statements is *true?*
   a. Services are the easiest type of business to go into compared with the other major industrial groups.
   b. Services are not open to innovation.
   c. All service industries require little initial investment.
   d. Services are declining in importance.

____11. The greatest threat to small service businesses is
   a. big business.
   b. the consumer who turns do-it-yourselfer.
   c. manufacturers.
   d. wholesalers.

____12. Which of the following statements is *true?*
   a. Subcontracting requires a large investment for the beginning entrepreneur.
   b. Most construction contractors are large.
   c. General contracting holds the greatest attraction for pure entrepreneurs.
   d. None of the above is true.

____13. Commercial banking no longer holds much attraction for entrepreneurs because
   a. to start a bank, entrepreneurs must hold a master's degree in business administration.
   b. banks are not profitable.
   c. banks require too much capital to get started.
   d. government regulation limits their projected profits.

____14. Which of the following statements is *true?*
   a. Most experts expect high-technology businesses to decrease in number in the future.
   b. Of the 600,000 businesses started each year, approximately 15 percent are high-technology companies.
   c. High-technology companies spend four times as much for research as the average for all manufacturing companies.
   d. High-technology companies are supported by the growing workforce in medium-, low-, and no-technology companies.

© 1990 Houghton Mifflin Company. All rights reserved.

Completion Questions

Write your answer in the blanks provided in each question. Correct answers are listed at the end of the study guide.

1. Manufacturers convert raw materials into _____. This industry group lends itself to bigness because of the large investment required. The nation's top 500 manufacturers account for _____ of the total sales revenues generated by manufacturers and _____ of the total number of employees in manufacturing.

2. Wholesalers are _____ between manufacturers and retailers. Small business dominates wholesaling. In fact businesses with fewer than 100 employees account for nearly _____ percent of the number of employees in wholesaling. This high percentage stems from the fact that wholesalers are to a large degree _____; they need fewer employees for a given volume of business than do manufacturers or retailers.

3. Retailers buy products from either wholesalers or manufacturers and sell them to _____. Small businesses with fewer than 100 employees account for more than _____ percent of all employees in retailing. _____ shops are especially attractive to retailing entrepreneurs because these shops enable them to focus their resources in depth on a narrow segment of the market rather than spread those resources too thinly over a wider spectrum.

4. Service firms do not deal in a product; they sell personal _____ to manufacturers, wholesalers, and retailers, as well as to consumers. Of all the industry groups, services are the _____ to go into.

5. Magazines, newspapers, television, and radio are dominated by _____ business.

6. Most construction contractors are _____. And contrary to popular opinion, small business is the nation's biggest builder. _____ contracting holds the greatest attraction for pure entrepreneurs in construction, mostly because of the challenges it offers. _____ also attracts entrepreneurs, often because it requires little investment beyond tools and skill.

7. Finance is dominated by small business. Most of the nation's _____ commercial banks are small. But commercial banking no longer holds much attraction for entrepreneurs. It's too hard to get into.

8. Many entrepreneurs do make their mark in finance, but in venture capital, stock brokerage, mortgage lending, finance companies, and investment banking. Of these _____ capital probably has the strongest appeal for entrepreneurs. While banks _____ money, venture-capital firms _____ money.

9. In real estate, entrepreneurs generally prefer _____ sales rather than _____ sales. And they are likely to go in not as brokers but as _____. For example, the explosive growth of shopping centers after World War II was mostly the work of entrepreneurs. More than _____ shopping centers now dot the country.

10. Our store of knowledge is doubling every _____ years, or several times faster than in the 1920s. By contrast, in the Stone Age, the knowledge of primitive human beings doubled every _____ years.

Essay Questions

1. As a rule, manufacturing businesses are the hardest to establish and services are the easiest. Why is this so? Are there exceptions to this general rule?

2. Small business dominates wholesaling. In fact, businesses with fewer than 100 employees account for nearly 80 percent of the employees in wholesaling. This high percentage stems from the fact that wholesalers are mostly caretakers. What is a caretaker? How do wholesalers justify their place in the distribution flow?

3. Many entrepreneurs go into retailing with an eye to multiplying one store into many as quickly as possible. They do so chiefly by selling franchises. How does selling franchises help an entrepreneur expand?

4. Knowledge is now exploding so fast that industry leaders must look 5, 10, or 20 years ahead just to keep up. They can ill afford to sit on their hands. How will the changes predicted in the last part of Chapter 3 affect the small-business owner of the future?

5. By the year 2000, it is likely that entrepreneurs will be attracted to those industries that capitalize on upward trends in affluence and leisure, individualization, urbanization, and technology. Choose a product or service that you feel will be profitable in the year 2000. Could this product or service develop into a profitable small business? Explain your answer.

The Difference Between Success and Failure

Some industries, like auto manufacturing, require huge investments in machinery and equipment. Businesses in these industries are big from the day they start—if an entrepreneur or group of entrepreneurs can gather the capital required to start one.

By contrast, a number of industries require low initial investment along with some special skills or knowledge. It is these industries that tend to attract new businesses. Growing industries like computer software are attractive because of their sales and profit potential.

© 1990 Houghton Mifflin Company. All rights reserved.

Some businesses range from corner newspaper stands to plants that develop optical fibers. The owners of small businesses sell gasoline, flowers, and coffee to go. They publish magazines, haul freight, teach languages, and program computers. They make wines, movies, and high-fashion clothes. They build new homes and restore old ones. They fix appliances, recycle metals, and sell used cars. They drive cabs and fly planes. They make us well when we are sick, and they sell us the products of corporate giants.

The various kinds of businesses generally are grouped in three broad categories: service industries, distribution industries, and production industries. Within these categories, small businesses tend to cluster in the service industries and in retailing.

Service Industries

This category accounts for about 35 percent of all small businesses. Of these, about three-quarters provide nonfinancial services like medical and dental care; watch, shoe, and TV repairs; hair cutting and styling; restaurant meals; and dry cleaning. About 8 percent of small business firms offer financial services, among them accounting, insurance, and investment counseling.

Distribution Industries

This category includes retailing, wholesaling, transportation, and communications—industries that are concerned with the movement of goods from producers to consumers. Distribution industries account for approximately 42 percent of all small businesses. Of these, almost 75 percent are involved in retailing, the sale of goods directly to consumers. Clothing and jewelry stores, pet shops, bookstores, and grocery stores, for example, are all retailing firms. Slightly less than 25 percent of small distribution firms are wholesalers. Wholesalers purchase products in quantity from manufacturers, then resell them to retailers.

Production Industries

This last category includes construction, mining, and manufacturing industries. Only about 23 percent of all small businesses are in this group, mainly because these industries require relatively large initial investments. Small firms that do venture into production generally make parts and subassemblies for larger manufacturing firms or supply special skills to larger construction firms.

© 1990 Houghton Mifflin Company. All rights reserved.

PART II

STARTING A NEW VENTURE

CHAPTER 4

Search for a New Venture

Learning Objectives

After studying this chapter, you should understand

1. Why it is important to ask "what business should I be in?"

2. What the advantages and disadvantages are of buying an existing business

3. What key questions to ask when deciding to buy an existing business

4. What the advantages and disadvantages are of starting a new business from scratch

5. How to patent an invention

Chapter Review

As you read the chapter, complete the following outline with information from the text.

"A thousand-mile journey begins with but a single step." So must a new venture. The first step may be the decision to become an entrepreneur, and the next step may be to choose a product or service. The would-be entrepreneur must decide whether to buy an existing business or start from scratch.

I. **Choice of Product or Service.** Early on, the entrepreneur must ask: "What business should I be in?" Often entrepreneurs *think* they know what business they have chosen without closely analyzing their choice.

To choose a product or service, entrepreneurs must look closely at their own skills and at industry trends to see how well they mesh. Why are these two questions important for a beginning entrepreneur?

Do I really have what it takes to succeed with that product or service?

_____

_____

_____

© 1990 Houghton Mifflin Company. All rights reserved.

Chapter 4

Do I really want to run that kind of business, do that kind of work, be that kind of person?

_____

_____

_____

To succeed, an entrepreneur must master the activities that spell the difference between success and failure.

II. **Buying an Existing Business.** After choosing a product or service and making sure that the choice fits their skills and wants, entrepreneurs must decide whether to buy an existing business or to start a business from scratch. Lawyers and bankers often advise entrepreneurs to buy out a business rather than start from scratch. The reason is that existing businesses are much less risky. Why?

_____

_____

_____

A. **Understanding a Seller's Motives.** There are several valid reasons why small-business owners may want to sell an existing business. List three of them.

_____

_____

_____

But sellers commonly hide their true motives for selling. They often give good rather than real reasons for selling. In most cases, fear underlies their desire to sell. What kinds of fear would cause a small business owner to sell?

▪ _____

_____

▪ _____

_____

▪ _____

_____

• _____

_____

B. **Evaluating Industrial Aspects of a Business.** Financial evaluation of an existing business raises several questions: (1) How healthy is the seller's business? (2) How profitable has it been? and (3) How much is it worth?

1. **The Role of Financial Statements.** To help answer these questions, buyers should begin with the seller's financial statements. Many buyers blindly accept any financial statements bearing an accountant's signature. But remember that accountants are advisers; they cannot stop sellers from using accounting methods that best serve their own purposes.

   The idea that businesspeople can more or less choose the profit level of their business may seem odd. But this is precisely what owners have the right to do. List three ways in which owners can legally overstate or understate profits.

   • _____

   • _____

   • _____

2. **Auditing.** The buyer's first step in evaluating the financial aspects of a business should be to find out what adjustments need to be made to the seller's financial statements to estimate what the business is really worth. To do that, the buyer should get the seller's income statements and balance sheets for the past five years. Armed with these statements, the buyer should examine bills owed by customers; inventories; equipment; bank loans, bills owed to suppliers, and other debts; leases, licenses, franchises, and contracts; and public records. To carry out this audit, the buyer normally needs the help of two professionals—an accountant and a lawyer.

C. **Setting a Price.** Having thoroughly examined and questioned the financial records of the seller's business, the buyer must tackle the problem of pricing it. In pricing a business, the buyer can use either of two traditional approaches—earnings or assets.

1. **The Earnings Approach.** The earnings approach consists of two different methods of setting a price for an existing business. The capitalizing profits method assumes that the buyer is really buying a series of yearly profits. It requires the buyer to ask, what am I willing to pay for the chance to earn a certain profit each year for, say, the next 10 years? To use this method, the entrepreneur must estimate after-tax profits. The best way to estimate after-tax profits is to look at average yearly projected profits for the next five years, based

© 1990 Houghton Mifflin Company. All rights reserved.   55

on the buyer's belief that his or her superior managerial skills will boost profits. Why is this method better than looking at past profits or even projected profits on the basis of past profits?

_____

_____

_____

The capitalizing profits method relates after-tax profit to total investments. What limitation is inherent in the method?

_____

_____

The personal return method looks at return from the perspective of the buyer's personal gain. It assumes that the entrepreneur stands apart from the business and its profits. In what ways can an entrepreneur earn a personal return on investment?

_____

_____

_____

The capitalizing profits method stresses after-tax profits expressed as a percentage of total business investment. The personal return method stresses the buyer's personal return expressed as a percentage of personal investment.

2. **The Asset Approach.** The asset approach ignores future earnings, focusing instead on the seller's assets (buildings, equipment, inventories, accounts receivable). There are three traditional asset methods. Explain each of them.

Book value method _____

_____

_____

© 1990 Houghton Mifflin Company. All rights reserved.

Adjusted book value method _____

_____

_____

Selected assets method _____

_____

_____

D. **Negotiating a Price.** Once entrepreneurs have estimated what a business is worth, they must negotiate a price. Generally there is a wide gap between what the buyer believes the business is worth and what the seller believes the business is worth.

Although money is certainly a critical component of negotiations, there are nonfinancial factors that can also play a role in the negotiation process. List three of them.

_____

_____

_____

Even after the give-and-take of negotiations, the buyer and seller still may be miles apart on price. Their ability to agree hinges on their skills at the negotiating table and on how they see each other's strengths and weaknesses.

III. **Starting from Scratch.** Pure entrepreneurs are more likely to start a business from scratch. The risks are usually greater: New ventures are less likely to succeed than takeovers. But there are some practical reasons why entrepreneurs may choose to begin from scratch. List three of those reasons.

- _____

- _____

- _____

Entrepreneurs must evaluate the prospects of a new venture. To do that, they have to study their market to estimate such things as total market, share of market, and sales revenues. This means gathering information in a process called *marketing research*. Marketing research is the most important step in the preparation of a business plan.

© 1990 Houghton Mifflin Company. All rights reserved.

IV. Invention and the Entrepreneur. Many entrepreneurs are also inventors. Often they have to decide whether to apply for a patent, which grants exclusive rights to an invention. Because obtaining a patent takes time and money, entrepreneurs should weigh the pros and cons by answering the following questions: Is my product patentable?

_____

Do I need or want patent protection?

_____

Although entrepreneurs can get a patent themselves, the process is so complex that they would be wise to leave it to a patent attorney.

A. The Patenting Process. In your own words, summarize the steps required to obtain a patent.

1. **Making a Record** _____

    _____

    _____

2. **Making Sure the Invention Is Practical** _____

    _____

    _____

3. **Hiring a Patent Attorney** _____

    _____

    _____

4. **Having a Search Made** _____

    _____

    _____

5. **Preparing an Application** _____

    _____

    _____

© 1990 Houghton Mifflin Company. All rights reserved.

Once a patent is granted, the entrepreneur has the "right to exclude others from making, using, or selling the invention throughout the United States." Patent rights last 17 years.

Competitors may try to "design around" an invention. To avoid infringing on a patent, competitors need only eliminate a single element of the entrepreneur's patent claims.

Questions for Mastery

Questions for mastery are found in the textbook at the beginning of every chapter. Answer each question again to reinforce your understanding of the information.

1. Why is it important to ask "what business should I be in?"

   _____

   _____

   _____

2. What are the advantages and disadvantages of buying an existing business?

   _____

   _____

   _____

3. What key questions should you ask when deciding to buy an existing business?

   _____

   _____

   _____

4. What are the advantages and disadvantages of starting a new business from scratch?

   _____

   _____

   _____

© 1990 Houghton Mifflin Company. All rights reserved.

5. How do you patent an invention?

_____

_____

_____

_____

Definitions of Key Terms

The following key terms are important in this chapter. In your own words, define each concept.

audit _____

_____

earnings _____

_____

capitalizing profits _____

_____

personal return on investment _____

_____

perquisite _____

_____

asset approach _____

_____

book value _____

_____

adjusted book value _____

_____

selected assets method _____

_____

marketing research _____

_____

patent _____

_____

True-False Questions

Determine whether the following statements are true or false, then circle T or F. Correct answers are listed at the end of the study guide.

T   F   1. A vital first step for would-be entrepreneurs is to define their business with precision and brevity.

T   F   2. When choosing a product or service, entrepreneurs should rely more on personal skills than industry trends.

T   F   3. Would-be entrepreneurs must decide whether to buy an existing business or start from scratch.

T   F   4. Lawyers and bankers often advise entrepreneurs to buy an existing business rather than start from scratch.

T   F   5. The track record of an existing business surpasses the guesswork required to evaluate the prospects of a business started from scratch.

T   F   6. With careful evaluation of past records, it is possible to eliminate risk when purchasing an existing business.

T   F   7. Sellers commonly hide their true motives for selling.

T   F   8. If the accounting statements for an existing business bear an accountant's signature, there is no need to have the statements audited by another accountant.

T   F   9. A business owner may more or less select the profit level of a business by choosing different methods to report inventories.

T   F   10. The buyer's first step in evaluating the financial aspects of a business should be to determine the adjustments that must be made to the seller's financial statements.

© 1990 Houghton Mifflin Company. All rights reserved.   61

T   F   11. A financial statement that is more than a year old is of no value in evaluating an existing business.

T   F   12. To carry out an audit, the buyer normally needs the help of two professionals—an accountant and a banker.

T   F   13. In pricing an existing business, the buyer can use either of two traditional approaches: earnings or assets.

T   F   14. The asset approach requires the buyer to focus on the profit the assets can earn.

T   F   15. The capitalizing profits method assumes that the entrepreneur is buying a series of yearly profits.

T   F   16. Capitalizing profits is a popular earnings method, although its results often are misleading.

T   F   17. The best way to estimate after-tax profits for next year is to use the average yearly profits for the past five years.

T   F   18. Small-business owners often invest as little of their own money as possible.

T   F   19. The personal return method assumes that the entrepreneur stands separate and apart from the business and its profits.

T   F   20. Interest and dividends are types of perquisites.

T   F   21. The asset approach is popular because it is easier to use than the earnings approach.

T   F   22. Book value is the amount of profit an existing business made last year.

T   F   23. Market value is the difference between what a business has (assets) and what it owes (liabilities).

T   F   24. When the selected assets method is used, the buyer ends up buying just parts of the seller's business.

T   F   25. When negotiating a price, it is the buyer's job to tell which human factors matter most to the seller.

T   F   26. Pure entrepreneurs are more likely to start a business from scratch rather than buy out an existing business.

T   F   27. Newborn ventures are less likely to fail than takeovers.

© 1990 Houghton Mifflin Company. All rights reserved.

T   F   28.   When starting a business from scratch, entrepreneurs must do marketing research to learn about their customers.

T   F   29.   Marketing research is probably the most important step in the preparation of a business plan.

T   F   30.   Assuming the entrepreneur is willing and able to pay the money required to obtain a patent, it is just a matter of filling out the proper forms.

T   F   31.   All patent attorneys are listed in the *American Directory of Patent Attorneys*.

T   F   32.   It takes about six months from the time an application is filed with the Commissioner of Patents until the patent is received.

T   F   33.   A patent is granted for a period of 17 years.

T   F   34.   Once granted, a patent generally is renewed for an additional 17-year period.

T   F   35.   To avoid infringing on a patent, a competitor need only eliminate a single element of the patent claims.

Multiple-Choice Questions

Write the letter of the correct answer in the blank to the left of the question. Correct answers are listed at the end of the study guide.

_____ 1.   Once the decision to become an entrepreneur has been made, the next question the entrepreneur should answer is
    a.   Should I incorporate the business?
    b.   Should I advertise in newspapers or use television?
    c.   What business should I be in?
    d.   What city should the business be located in?

_____ 2.   A vital first step for would-be entrepreneurs is to
    a.   define their business with precision and brevity.
    b.   determine how much cash they can raise.
    c.   determine if their business should be a partnership.
    d.   contact the SBA.

_____ 3.   Lawyers often advise entrepreneurs to
    a.   start a business from scratch.
    b.   buy out an existing business.
    c.   buy a franchise.
    d.   take their money and put it in a bank.

© 1990 Houghton Mifflin Company. All rights reserved.

_____ 4. The track record of an existing business
   a. is of no value because it is past history.
   b. surpasses the guesswork required to evaluate the prospects of starting a new business from scratch.
   c. is easy to evaluate.
   d. eliminates risk.

_____ 5. Which of the following statements is *false?*
   a. Sellers commonly hide their true motives for selling.
   b. Sellers often fear that technology is too complex to cope with.
   c. Sellers often fear that their product or service is outdated.
   d. Fear seldom underlies the desire to sell a business.

_____ 6. Accounting practices in small family-owned businesses
   a. may vary widely.
   b. are consistent from one business to the next.
   c. are not a point of concern if an accountant has been involved.
   d. always use the fastest depreciation allowances.

_____ 7. Which of the following statements is *true?*
   a. With the help of a lawyer and an accountant, pricing a business is a relatively easy task.
   b. A host of factors, many of them immeasurable, strongly influences the price placed on a business.
   c. The asset approach is the best method for determining an accurate price for a business.
   d. In most cases, the buyer of an existing business just pays the seller the asking price.

_____ 8. A buyer expects a business to earn $20,000 a year and expects a 20 percent return on investment. Using the capitalizing profits method, the purchase price of the business should be
   a. $100,000.
   b. $200,000.
   c. $300,000.
   d. $400,000.

_____ 9. An entrepreneur expects a personal return of $35,000 on a personal investment of $140,000. The entrepreneur's personal return on investment is _____ percent a year.
   a. 4
   b. 12.5
   c. 25
   d. 50

© 1990 Houghton Mifflin Company. All rights reserved.

____10. The fastest way to price an existing business is
   a.   capitalizing profits.
   b.   personal return on investment.
   c.   book value.
   d.   none of the above.

____11. The difference between what a business owns and what it owes is called
   a.   book value.
   b.   market value.
   c.   adjusted market value.
   d.   earnings.

____12. All of the following are practical reasons for starting a business from scratch *except*
   a.   avoiding the ill effects of a prior owner's errors.
   b.   choosing your own banker, equipment, inventories, location, suppliers, and workers.
   c.   creating your own loyal customers.
   d.   taking advantage of the previous owner's experience.

____13. Probably the most important step in the preparation of a business plan is
   a.   determining how much profit is guaranteed.
   b.   completing marketing research on the characteristics of prospective customers.
   c.   determining if the business should be a sole proprietorship, partnership, or corporation.
   d.   choosing suppliers.

____14. Patenting a product is best described as
   a.   a process that takes time and money.
   b.   relatively easy.
   c.   something most entrepreneurs do for themselves.
   d.   always necessary for new inventions.

____15. Patent rights last for
   a.   10 years.
   b.   17 years.
   c.   17 years with an automatic extension.
   d.   34 years.

© 1990 Houghton Mifflin Company. All rights reserved.

Completion Questions

Write your answer in the blanks provided in each question. Correct answers are listed at the end of the study guide.

1. In the search for a new business venture, the first step may be the decision to become an _____. The next step may be to choose a _____ or service. Then the would-be entrepreneur must decide whether to _____ an existing business or to _____ a new business from scratch.

2. Lawyers and _____ often advise entrepreneurs to buy out a business rather than start from scratch. The reason is that existing businesses are much _____ risky.

3. Sellers commonly hide their true motives for selling. In most cases, though, _____ underlies their desire to sell.

4. To help answer questions about an existing business, buyers should begin with the seller's _____ statements. The buyer's first step in evaluating the financial aspects of a business should be to find out what _____ need to be made to the seller's financial statements. To do that, the buyer should get the income statements and balance sheets for the past _____ years.

5. To carry out an audit, the buyer normally needs the help of two professionals: an _____ and a _____.

6. The earnings approach requires the buyer to focus on _____, past or future. The _____ approach, on the other hand, requires the buyer to focus only on assets, without regard to their _____ power in the future.

7. The _____ profits method assumes that the individual buying a business is really buying a series of _____ profits.

8. The _____ return method assumes that the entrepreneur stands separate and apart form the business and its profits. This method stresses the _____ personal return expressed as a percentage of personal investment.

9. The buyer need only look at the seller's book value on the latest balance sheet to determine a firm's book value. Book value is the difference between what a business owns, commonly referred to as _____, and what a business owes, commonly referred to as _____.

10. Newborn ventures are _____ likely to succeed than takeovers. With a takeover, there are records to give some idea of how healthy and _____ the business is. But with a new venture, the best an entrepreneur can do is _____ what the profits will be.

11. When starting from scratch, entrepreneurs must put in a great deal of effort to get information about the _____ . Marketing _____ is probably the most _____ step in the preparation of a business plan.

12. Many entrepreneurs are also _____ . Patenting a product takes time and _____ . Although entrepreneurs can get patents themselves, the patenting process is so complex that they are wise to leave it to a patent _____ .

Essay Questions

1. Lawyers and bankers often advise entrepreneurs to buy out a business rather than start from scratch. Why?

2. The financial statements of an existing business show, at least on paper, the financial health of the firm. Armed with these statements, the prospective buyer should examine, with a skeptic's eye, all the information contained in them. What should the prospective buyer look for?

3. When starting from scratch, entrepreneurs must put in a lot of effort to get information about their markets. What questions should entrepreneurs ask to obtain this information?

The Difference Between Success and Failure

One reason new small businesses fail is lack of adequate financing. Most people who run small businesses realize all too quickly that they have only two sources for financing their operations: their own funds and those they can borrow. As a rule, commercial bankers feel small businesses present too high a risk to justify anything but short-term loans. Although it is not impossible to obtain long-term financing, it is difficult. The Small Business Administration offers guaranteed loans, but there are often many more applicants than available funds.

Where else can a small business turn for financial help? This is one of the most serious problems owners and managers face. Financing can't be taken for granted. Here are some suggestions that have helped many small firms avoid financial disaster:

1. *Don't start too soon.* If you don't have enough money to start the business, it's better to wait until you do. A business that starts with inadequate capital will in most cases encounter difficulty later on.

2. *Realize that finances are important and devote some time to financial planning.* For the experienced small-business owner, this might include learning from past mistakes.

3. *Develop a good bookkeeping system and maintain accurate records.* Use the information in your records to help you make good management decisions.

© 1990 Houghton Mifflin Company. All rights reserved.

Chapter 4

4. *Look for management help that you can afford.* Possible sources might include the Small Business Administration, college courses, or your banker.

5. *Maintain an emergency fund for the unexpected.* The size of the fund should be determined by your firm's needs. Remember, it is better to be safe than sorry.

Obviously these suggestions are just a starting point. Because each business is different, the success of an individual enterprise depends on how well the owner can adapt to changing financial conditions and needs.

CHAPTER 5

Franchising

Learning Objectives

After studying this chapter, you should understand

1. How important franchising is to the economy

2. What the different kinds of franchising systems are

3. What the advantages and pitfalls of franchising are

4. How a lawyer can help evaluate a franchise opportunity

5. How best to evaluate a franchise opportunity

Chapter Review

As you read the chapter, complete the following outline with information from the text.

Today, few business topics spark more controversy than franchising. Opinions about its place in the economy differ sharply: Some see franchising as the last frontier of the would-be entrepreneur; others see it as a fraud. The truth lies somewhere in between.

I. **The History and Definition of Franchising.** Contrary to popular opinion, franchising did not begin with the boom of fast-food franchises in the 1950s. Describe the early history of franchising.

_____

_____

_____

_____

There is no one best definition of *franchising*: Its meaning depends on the industry. But a typical franchise is simply an agreement between seller and buyer—an agreement that permits the buyer (franchisee) to sell the product or service of the seller (franchisor). How does the International Franchise Association define *franchise?*

_____

_____

_____

_____

For a fee, the franchisee gets a ready-made business and expert help that would otherwise be too costly. List nine areas in which franchises receive help.

_____   _____

_____   _____

_____   _____

_____   _____

_____

Franchising thrives because it merges the incentive of owning a small business with the management skills of big business. And personal ownership is one of the best incentives yet created to spur hard work.

What are the advantages of franchising (Exhibit 5.3)?

- _____

- _____

- _____

- _____

© 1990 Houghton Mifflin Company. All rights reserved.

What are the disadvantages of franchising (Exhibit 5.3)?

- _____

- _____

- _____

- _____

Franchising benefits not only the franchisee but also the franchisor. Franchising enables the franchisor to grow rapidly by using other people's (franchisees') money.

The International Franchising Association predicts that franchising will soon dominate retailing. Franchising is also strong in services, and to a lesser degree in manufacturing. According to the Department of Commerce, in 1988 how much did franchises earn in sales revenues?

_____

Because a larger organization (the franchisor) provides guidance and sets standards, the failure rate of franchises is low. According to the Department of Commerce, what percentage of franchises in this country were discontinued in 1988?

_____

Although the statistics sound good, a franchise is not a sure way to success. There are problems that a would-be franchisee should consider before plunking down the money.

II. **Kinds of Franchising Systems.** Franchise systems exist in all four major industry groups: manufacturing, wholesaling, retailing, and services. And they connect groups within and across industries. Give an example of a franchise system that connects each pair of groups below.

Manufacturer and manufacturer _____

_____

Manufacturer and wholesaler _____

_____

Manufacturer and retailer _____

_____

© 1990 Houghton Mifflin Company. All rights reserved.   71

Wholesaler and wholesaler _____

_____

Wholesaler and retailer _____

_____

Retailer and retailer _____

_____

Services and services _____

_____

III. Myths of Franchising

A. **The Myth of Instant Wealth.** The fast growth of franchising has spawned a number of myths. Perhaps the most popular is the promise of instant wealth. Describe this myth.

_____

_____

_____

B. **The Myth of Independence.** Another myth is that franchisees are independent businesspeople. In many cases this simply is not so. Explain why.

_____

_____

_____

IV. Selecting a Franchise.
In a real sense, franchisees do not start from scratch. When they buy a franchise, entrepreneurs generally receive a ready-made business with instructions on how best to run it.

© 1990 Houghton Mifflin Company. All rights reserved.

A. **First Steps.** Before buying a franchise, entrepreneurs should first make sure that the decision is sound. Describe the procedure that would-be entrepreneurs should follow to evaluate a franchise opportunity (Exhibit 5.5).

_____ _____

_____ _____

_____ _____

_____

B. **Reviewing the Checklist of Questions.** To do a thorough job of analyzing a franchise opportunity, entrepreneurs should go through a checklist like the one shown in Exhibit 5.6. Take a few minutes and answer the 25 questions in the checklist. Although the answers are pretty obvious, it's important to examine any "unexpected" responses to determine if problems may develop at a later date.

C. **Getting Disclosure Statements.** To evaluate a franchise opportunity, entrepreneurs should ask the franchisor for its disclosure statement. What three things should a disclosure statement allow an entrepreneur to do?

_____

_____

_____

All franchisors are now required by federal law to provide disclosure statements to entrepreneurs. What type of detailed information does the law require?

- _____

- _____

- _____

- _____

- _____

- _____

© 1990 Houghton Mifflin Company. All rights reserved.

D. **Hiring a Lawyer.** Entrepreneurs should rely on a lawyer to get through the fine print of the franchisor's disclosure statement, to inform them fully about their legal rights before the franchise contract is signed, and to advise them about their obligations to the franchisor. What is the lawyer's most creative role in franchise negotiations?

_____

_____

E. **Negotiating the Franchise Contract.** The contract is the backbone of any franchisor-franchisee relationship. Failure to understand its fine print can cause trouble for the entrepreneur later on. Especially important is an understanding of the conditions under which the franchisor can cancel a franchise contract. What are some of those conditions?

- _____
- _____
- _____
- _____
- _____
- _____

What is the length of most franchise agreements?

_____

What problems can develop if a franchisee decides to sell an existing franchise?

_____

_____

_____

_____

F. **Evaluating a Franchisor's Training Program.** Perhaps the most critical question to consider in evaluating a franchisor relates to the franchisor's training program. What is the primary goal of a training program?

_____

_____

The franchise contract should spell out how and where training will take place. For example, McDonald's offers training in several locations. Describe the kind of training that goes on at each of them.

Instruction at a training school _____

_____

Instruction at an existing franchisee's site _____

_____

Instruction at own site _____

_____

G. **Estimating the Costs to the Franchisee.** Entrepreneurs must carefully estimate what a franchise will cost. In your own words, describe the following.

Franchise fee _____

_____

Working capital _____

_____

Building and equipment costs _____

_____

Royalties _____

_____

A reputable franchisor will want the entrepreneur to put up at least half the money needed to get started, as equity capital.

© 1990 Houghton Mifflin Company. All rights reserved.

V.   Franchise Opportunities for Minorities. Until the mid-1960s there were few minority franchisees. Today more than 900 franchisors have declared their franchises open to all would-be entrepreneurs, regardless of race. To further the progress of minority men and women, the federal government supports franchising as a way of improving their economic opportunities.

VI.   Women in Franchising. Until the 1980s, few franchisees were women. Today the number of franchises owned by women is growing. According to *The Wall Street Journal*, how are franchisors helping women become franchisees?

_____

_____

_____

Questions for Mastery

Questions for mastery are found in the textbook at the beginning of every chapter. Answer each question again to reinforce your understanding of the information.

1.   How important is franchising to the economy?

_____

_____

_____

2.   What are the different kinds of franchising systems?

_____

_____

_____

3.   What are the advantages and pitfalls of franchising?

_____

_____

_____

_____

© 1990 Houghton Mifflin Company. All rights reserved.

4. How can a lawyer help evaluate a franchise opportunity?

_____

_____

_____

_____

5. How do you best evaluate a franchise opportunity?

_____

_____

_____

_____

Definitions of Key Terms

The following key terms are important in this chapter. In your own words, define each concept.

franchise _____

_____

franchisor _____

_____

franchisee _____

_____

disclosure statement _____

_____

franchise fee _____

_____

working capital _____

_____

royalties _____

_____

True-False Questions

Determine whether the following statements are true or false, then circle T or F. Correct answers are listed at the end of the study guide.

T   F   1.   Today, few business topics spark more controversy than franchising.

T   F   2.   Franchising started in the 1950s, when McDonald's began its aggressive franchising program.

T   F   3.   According to the National Federation of Independent Business, about 20 percent of the nation's 19 million businesses now operate under some kind of franchise agreement.

T   F   4.   Franchising accounts for 50 percent of all retail sales.

T   F   5.   The term *franchising* originally meant "to free from slavery."

T   F   6.   A typical franchise is simply an agreement between seller and buyer—an agreement that permits the buyer (franchisee) to sell the product or service of the seller (franchisor).

T   F   7.   Franchising thrives because it merges the incentive of owning a business with the management skills of big business.

T   F   8.   Even old-line companies like Sears and Montgomery Ward have joined the ranks of franchisors.

T   F   9.   The fee one manufacturer charges another manufacturer for the use of a patented process is called a *royalty*.

T   F   10.   Retail and service franchise systems operate much like manufacturer and wholesaler systems.

T   F   11.   Perhaps the most popular myth about franchising is the promise of instant riches.

T   F   12.   Franchisees are free to run their business as they see fit.

© 1990 Houghton Mifflin Company. All rights reserved.

T F 13. Franchisors encourage their franchisees to improve the way they do business.

T F 14. One franchisor describes the ideal franchisee as the sergeant type.

T F 15. Self-analysis is the first step in choosing a franchise.

T F 16. Although franchisors are not currently required by federal law to have a disclosure statement, a would-be entrepreneur should obtain this statement if one is available.

T F 17. It is vital for entrepreneurs to get the help of a lawyer familiar with the legal workings of franchising.

T F 18. When dealing with a reputable franchisor, there is no need to have oral promises included in the written contract.

T F 19. The contract is the backbone of any franchisor-franchisee relationship.

T F 20. Typically, franchisors reserve the right to cancel a franchise contract if the franchisee fails to reach revenue goals.

T F 21. The right to sell or transfer the franchise determines whether or not a franchisee is truly an independent owner of a business.

T F 22. All franchisees have the right to keep any profit made when a franchise is sold.

T F 23. Perhaps the most critical question to consider in evaluating a franchisor relates to the franchisor's training program.

T F 24. Entrepreneurs should make sure their franchise contract tells precisely how and where training will take place.

T F 25. A business plan is unnecessary when the business is a franchise.

T F 26. Working capital is the money needed to buy long-term assets.

T F 27. Some franchisors lease both building and equipment to franchisees, sparing franchisees the need to make a large initial cash outlay.

T F 28. Royalties for franchises range between 15 and 25 percent of revenues.

T F 29. Reputable franchisors want entrepreneurs to put up at least half the money needed to get started, as equity capital.

T F 30. The federal government actively supports the entry of minority men and women into franchising.

© 1990 Houghton Mifflin Company. All rights reserved.

Multiple-Choice Questions

Write the letter of the correct answer in the blank to the left of the question. Correct answers are listed at the end of the study guide.

_____ 1. Which of the following statements is *true?*
   a.   To its severest critics, franchising is a fraud.
   b.   Franchises never fail.
   c.   Franchisees are generally free to run their business as they see fit.
   d.   Franchisors encourage their franchisees to improve the way they do business.

_____ 2. Franchising
   a.   got is first real push in 1950s.
   b.   began in the early 1800s.
   c.   is profitable only in the fast-food industry.
   d.   is limited to retailing and service industries.

_____ 3. Franchising accounts for _____ percent of the nation's 19 million businesses.
   a.   5
   b.   10
   c.   15
   d.   20

_____ 4. Franchising accounts for _____ percent of all retail sales.
   a.   14
   b.   24
   c.   34
   d.   44

_____ 5. The help the typical franchisee gets from the franchisor
   a.   does not include marketing strategy.
   b.   is limited to management training.
   c.   would otherwise be too costly for the individual small businessperson.
   d.   ends with the purchase of the franchise.

_____ 6. All of the following are advantages of franchising for the franchisee *except*
   a.   proven business methods.
   b.   training.
   c.   established reputation.
   d.   continuing obligation.

_____ 7. One benefit of franchising for the franchisor is
   a.   rapid growth using other people's money.
   b.   the guaranteed success of each outlet.
   c.   guaranteed profits.
   d.   none of the above.

____ 8. According to the Department of Commerce, only ____ percent of all franchises in the country were discontinued in 1988.
   a. 2
   b. 4
   c. 6
   d. 8

____ 9. A franchise system between an automobile manufacturer and a dealership connects a manufacturer and
   a. another manufacturer.
   b. a wholesaler.
   c. retailer.
   d. a service industry.

____10. All of the following are forms of franchising arrangements *except*
   a. front-end franchises.
   b. conversion franchises.
   c. distributorships.
   d. piggyback franchises.

____11. The most creative role lawyers perform for would-be franchisees is
   a. reading the fine print in disclosure statements.
   b. advising them about their legal obligations to the franchisor.
   c. suggesting changes in the contract to protect their interests.
   d. arranging financing.

____12. Working capital is used
   a. to pay the initial franchise fee.
   b. to buy buildings.
   c. to purchase inventory.
   d. for all of the above.

____13. Royalties paid to a franchisor typically range between _____ percent of revenues.
   a. 0 and 10
   b. 0 and 15
   c. 5 and 20
   d. 10 and 25

____14. Which of the following statements is *false?*
   a. Until the mid-1960s, there were few minority franchisees.
   b. Franchising offers special promise to minority men and women.
   c. Franchise opportunities for minorities are decreasing.
   d. The federal government has been pushing franchising as a good way to improve the economic lot of minorities.

© 1990 Houghton Mifflin Company. All rights reserved.

Completion Questions

Write your answer in the blanks provided in each question. Correct answers are listed at the end of the study guide.

1. A typical _____ is simply an agreement between seller and buyer—an agreement that permits the buyer (_____) to sell the product or service of the seller (_____).

2. According to the National Federation of Independent Business, about _____ percent of the nation's 19 million businesses now run under some kind of franchise agreement, and franchising accounts for _____ percent of all retail sales.

3. In 1988 franchises earned sales revenues estimated at _____ billion.

4. According to the U.S. Department of Commerce, only _____ percent of all franchises in the country were discontinued in 1988.

5. A _____ is a fee one manufacturer receives when another manufacturer uses the first manufacturer's patented process.

6. Perhaps the most popular myth associated with franchising is the promise of instant _____.

7. Another myth associated with franchising is that franchisees are _____ businesspersons. One franchisor describes the ideal franchisee as the _____ type—midway between the general who gives the orders and the private who merely follows them.

8. To evaluate a franchise opportunity, entrepreneurs should ask the franchisor for its _____ statement. All franchisors are now required by _____ law to provide disclosure statements to would-be franchisees. The law requires that these statements give detailed information on _____ subjects.

9. The franchise _____ is the backbone of any franchisor-franchisee relationship. It is especially critical to ask, under what conditions can the _____ pull out of the franchise contract and what would it cost to pull out?

10. Typically, franchise rights run _____ to _____ years, with options to renew.

11. The _____ fee gives the franchisee the right to do business at a specific address or in a specific territory.

12. Money used to buy inventory, pay salespersons, and make lease payments is called _____ capital.

13. _____ usually range from zero to 15 percent of revenues.

© 1990 Houghton Mifflin Company. All rights reserved.

14. More than _____ franchisors have declared that their franchises are open to all would-be entrepreneurs, regardless of race.

Essay Questions

1. Today, few business topics spark more controversy than franchising. Opinions about its place in the economy differ sharply: Some see it as a fraud; others see it as the last frontier of the would-be entrepreneur. What are the advantages and disadvantages of franchising?

2. To do a thorough job of analyzing a franchise opportunity, entrepreneurs should go through a checklist like the one in Exhibit 5.6. Take a few moments to answer the 25 questions in the checklist. After completing it, describe your findings. Does franchising seem practical for you?

3. All franchisors are now required by federal law to provide disclosure statements to entrepreneurs. The law requires that these statements give detailed information on 20 subjects. What types of subjects are covered in a disclosure statement?

4. Entrepreneurs should make sure they understand what they stand to lose if the franchisor should decide to cancel the franchise contract. For what reasons could a franchisor cancel a franchise contract?

The Difference Between Success and Failure

Modern franchising is designed to provide a tested formula for success, along with ongoing advice and training. The success rate for businesses owned and operated by franchisees is significantly better than the success rate for other independently owned small businesses. According to the Department of Commerce, fewer than 5 percent of franchisee-owned outlets have been discontinued since 1971. Compared to the overall small-business failure rate of around 70 percent, this is an enviable record.

Nevertheless, franchising is not a guarantee to success for either franchisees or franchisors. Too-rapid expansion, inadequate capital or management skills, and a host of other problems can cause failure for both. Thus, for example the Dizzy Dean's Beef and Burger franchise is no longer in business.

Advantages

The franchisor gains fast and selective distribution of its products without incurring the high cost of constructing and operating its own outlets. The franchisor thus has more capital available to expand production and to use for advertising. At the same time, the franchisor can ensure, through the franchise agreement, that outlets are maintained and operated by its own standards. The franchisor also benefits from the fact that the franchisee, a sole proprietor in most cases, is

© 1990 Houghton Mifflin Company. All rights reserved.   83

likely to be very highly motivated to succeed. The success of the franchise means more sales, which translate into higher royalties for the franchisor.

The franchisee gets the opportunity to start a business with limited capital and to make use of the business experience of others. Moreover, an outlet with a nationally advertised name—for example, McDonald's, Dunkin' Donuts, or Avis—often is assured customers as soon as it opens. If business problems arise, the franchisor gives the franchisee guidance and advice. This counseling is primarily responsible for the very high degree of success enjoyed by franchises. In most cases, the franchisee does not pay for this kind of help. The franchisee also receives materials to use in local advertising and can take part in national promotional campaigns sponsored by the franchisor. McDonald's and its franchisees, for example, constitute one of the nation's top 20 purchasers of advertising. Finally, the franchisee may be able to minimize the cost of advertising, of supplies, and of various business necessities by purchasing them in cooperation with other franchisees.

Disadvantages[*]

Because the franchisor retains a great deal of control, the disadvantages of franchising mainly affect the franchisee. The franchisor can dictate every aspect of the business: decor, the design of employees' uniforms, types of signs, and all the details of business operations. All Burger King french fries taste the same because all franchisees have to make them the same way.

Franchise holders pay for their security. Usually there are a one-time franchise fee and continuing royalty and advertising fees, collected as a percentage of sales. Insty-Prints collects a nonrefundable $8,000 franchisee fee, then a royalty of 3 percent of gross sales (payable monthly) and an additional 2 percent of sales for advertising materials.

Franchise operators also work hard. They often put in 10- and 12-hour days, six days a week. And in some fields, franchise agreements are not uniform: One franchisee may pay more than another for the same service.

Even success can cause problems. Sometimes a franchise is so successful that the franchisor opens its own outlet nearby, in direct competition. A spokesman for one franchisor says his company "gives no geographical protection" to its franchise holders and thus is free to move in on them.

The International Franchise Association advises prospective franchise purchasers to investigate before investing and to approach buying a franchise cautiously. Franchises vary widely in approach as well as in products. Some, like Dunkin' Donuts and Baskin-Robbins ice cream stores, demand long hours. Others, like Command Performance hair salons, are earmarked for those who don't want to spend many hours at their store.

[*]This section is adapted from *The Wall Street Journal,* 3 November 1980, p. 27. Reprinted by permission of *The Wall Street Journal,* ©Dow Jones & Company, Inc. 1980. All Rights Reserved Worldwide.

© 1990 Houghton Mifflin Company. All rights reserved.

Where Do You Go to Investigate Franchising?

Several private and government groups publish materials about franchising. Some are listed here.

International Franchise Association
1350 New York Ave., NW
Suite 900
Washington, D.C. 20005

Superintendent of Documents
U.S. Government Printing Office
Washington, D.C. 20402

Council of Better Business Bureaus, Inc.
1515 Wilson Boulevard
Arlington, VA 22209

U.S. Office of Consumer Affairs
1009 Premier Building
Washington, D.C. 20201

Small Business Administration
1441 L Street N.W.
Washington, D.C. 20416

© 1990 Houghton Mifflin Company. All rights reserved.

CHAPTER 6

Developing a Business Plan

Learning Objectives

After studying this chapter, you should understand

1. Why a business plan should be written

2. How to prepare a business plan

3. Why marketing research is the most important step in the preparation of a business plan

4. What facts a prospective entrepreneur needs to gather

5. What the difference is between operating plans and financial plans

Chapter Review

As you read the chapter, complete the following outline with information from the text.

A business plan is an essential step in turning ideas for products or services into flourishing ventures. Planning forces entrepreneurs to anticipate several things. What are they?

- _____

- _____

- _____

- _____

I. **The Need for Planning.** Planning is decision making—deciding what to do, how to do it, and when to do it. It is vital for success. The very act of preparing a business plan forces entrepreneurs to think through the steps they must take. How does a business plan resemble a road map?

_____

_____

_____

© 1990 Houghton Mifflin Company. All rights reserved.

Why should an entrepreneur spend time drawing up a business plan?

_____

_____

_____

_____

The idea of a business plan is not new. Big businesses have long been turning them out yearly by the thousands, especially for marketing new products, buying existing businesses, or expanding into foreign markets. What is new is the growing use of business plans by entrepreneurs. Why are entrepreneurs beginning to realize the importance of business plans?

_____

_____

_____

List two reasons why outside pressures for business plans are healthy.

▪ _____

_____

▪ _____

_____

II. **Authorship of Business Plan.** Entrepreneurs themselves should prepare and write their business plan. Why?

_____

_____

In creating a business plan, which is more important—form or substance? (Explain your answer.)

_____

_____

_____

© 1990 Houghton Mifflin Company. All rights reserved.

How do bankers and investors react when they receive a business plan prepared by a professional consultant?

_____

_____

How many entrepreneurs actually prepare formal business plans?

_____

According to William Osgood, what functions does a business plan perform?

_____

_____

_____

_____

III. **Parts of a Business Plan.** A business plan should be a thorough objective analysis of both personal abilities and business requirements for a particular product or service. List six functions for which a business plan should define strategies.

_____   _____

_____   _____

_____   _____

What three questions should a business plan answer?

- _____

_____

- _____

_____

- _____

© 1990 Houghton Mifflin Company. All rights reserved.

There is no best way to begin, although Exhibit 6.2 suggests steps to take in developing a business plan. Exhibit 6.3 shows how these steps tie together but it does not show the backtracking that is part of the process, to refine the plan.

As they develop a business plan, entrepreneurs should keep complete notes—documenting all facts, backing all assumptions, and giving the authority for all opinions. Why is documentation necessary?

_____

_____

IV. **Getting the Facts.** The steps that follow can help entrepreneurs get the facts, opinions, and judgments they need to improve the quality of their business plans.

   A. **Step 1: Making the Commitment.** The commitment to go into business for oneself requires little fact finding. One must be sure that the desire to become an entrepreneur dwarfs the desire to work for somebody else.

   B. **Step 2: Analyzing Oneself.** Entrepreneurs should analyze their strengths and weaknesses honestly, paying special attention to their own business experience and education.

   C. **Step 3: Choosing a Product or Service.** This is a critical step. What is the general rule that entrepreneurs should follow in choosing a product or service?

   _____

   _____

   _____

   _____

   Why should entrepreneurs answer the question: What need will my product or service fill?

   _____

   _____

   _____

© 1990 Houghton Mifflin Company. All rights reserved.

Why should entrepreneurs answer the question: What is unique about my product or service?

_____

_____

_____

Why should entrepreneurs answer the question: What does my product or service offer customers that competing products or services do not offer?

_____

_____

_____

D. **Step 4: Researching the Market.** Marketing research is perhaps the most critical step of all. Entrepreneurs should spare no expense in their quest for facts. Why do entrepreneurs sometimes do a poor job of researching the market?

_____

_____

What are the four steps in the typical marketing research process?

- _____

- _____

- _____

- _____

In their search for facts, what question should entrepreneurs answer first?

_____

Why should entrepreneurs begin their search for facts with the local Chamber of Commerce?

_____

_____

© 1990 Houghton Mifflin Company. All rights reserved.

What other sources of information are available to entrepreneurs?

_____

_____

E.   **Step 5: Forecasting Sales Revenues.** After estimating the market potential, entrepreneurs should estimate the share of that market they can reasonably expect to gain. This involves making realistic assumptions that take into account the number and size of competitors and the amount of time it will take to achieve goals.

Expected market share should be expressed in terms of sales revenues. First-year sales should be estimated on a monthly basis; second-year sales should be estimated on a quarterly basis; and third-year sales should be estimated on a yearly basis. Why are revenue forecasts so important?

_____

_____

Revenue forecasts are based on assumptions and facts. Their accuracy hinges largely on the accuracy of the assumptions that support them.

F.   **Step 6: Choosing a Site.** Wise entrepreneurs balance personal preference with business logic. Too often, entrepreneurs jump at the first vacancy that comes along rather than base their choice on the results of marketing research. Remember that location is a critical decision that can mean the difference between success and failure.

G.   **Step 7: Developing a Production Plan.** Only entrepreneurs who intend to manufacture a product need a production plan. What is the most important question an entrepreneur in a production business should ask?

_____

What should the entrepreneur's answer to that question be based on?

_____

_____

© 1990 Houghton Mifflin Company. All rights reserved.

What three factors should the entrepreneur consider in arranging equipment in a manufacturing plant?

• _____

• _____

• _____

How are flow diagrams used in the production planning process?

_____

_____

_____

Entrepreneurs also should plan to control the waste, quality, and inventory of their product.

H. **Step 8: Developing a Marketing Plan.** This step forces entrepreneurs to spell out how they plan to create customers at a profit. What *five* factors should entrepreneurs combine to develop a marketing plan?

_____   _____

_____   _____

_____

I. **Step 9: Developing an Organizational Plan.** Entrepreneurs should define their organizations in terms of skills, not people. Why?

_____

_____

_____

Why should entrepreneurs include full-time professionals (say marketing researchers or accountants) in their plans even though they cannot afford to hire them?

_____

_____

© 1990 Houghton Mifflin Company. All rights reserved.

What does an organizational chart do?

_____

_____

J. Step 10: Developing a Legal Plan. Among other decisions, entrepreneurs must decide which legal form of organization is appropriate for their business venture. An attorney that specializes in small business should be consulted before this and other legal decisions are made.

K. Step 11: Developing an Accounting Plan. From the start, entrepreneurs must keep records in order to know how well their venture is doing and in what direction it is moving. The system should be designed by an accountant. List four characteristics of a good record keeping system.

- _____

- _____

- _____

- _____

L. Step 12: Developing an Insurance Plan. Entrepreneurs must protect themselves and their venture from any unforeseen events that may threaten their survival. What three questions should a program of risk management answer?

- _____

- _____

- _____

To make sure a risk management program is tailored to the needs of their venture, entrepreneurs should seek the help of an insurance agent and possibly a lawyer.

© 1990 Houghton Mifflin Company. All rights reserved.

M. **Step 13: Developing a Computer Plan.** Today's entrepreneurs should consider the use of a computer in their venture. List four elements that should be included in a computer plan.

- _____

- _____

- _____

- _____

When their knowledge about computers and software is limited, entrepreneurs should seek advice from a professional who focuses on small-business computer applications.

N. **Step 14: Developing a Financial Plan.** A financial plan ties together all the preceding steps by translating operating plans—production, marketing, organizational, and all other plans—into dollars.

1. **The Cash Budget.** Why is the cash budget the most important element of the overall financial plan?

_____

_____

_____

What questions should a cash budget ask?

- _____

- _____

- _____

- _____

© 1990 Houghton Mifflin Company. All rights reserved.

2. **The Balance Sheet and Income Statement.** What do balance sheets show potential investors and lenders?

_____

_____

_____

_____

Why should would-be entrepreneurs prepare two balance sheets?

_____

_____

What do income statements show potential investors and lenders?

_____

_____

_____

3. **The Profitgraph.** What does a profitgraph show?

_____

_____

_____

O. **Step 15: Writing a Cover Letter.** The cover letter is a selling tool, addressed mostly to investors and creditors. It summarizes what the entrepreneur has included in the business plan.

© 1990 Houghton Mifflin Company. All rights reserved.

Questions for Mastery

Questions for mastery are found in the textbook at the beginning of every chapter. Answer each question again to reinforce your understanding of the information.

1. Why write a business plan?

    _____

    _____

    _____

    _____

2. How do you prepare a business plan?

    _____

    _____

    _____

    _____

    _____

    _____

3. Why is marketing research the most important step in the preparation of a business plan?

    _____

    _____

    _____

    _____

© 1990 Houghton Mifflin Company. All rights reserved.

4. What facts does a prospective entrepreneur need to gather?

_____

_____

_____

_____

_____

5. What is the difference between operating plans and financial plans?

_____

_____

_____

_____

Definition of Key Terms

The following key terms are important in this chapter. In your own words, define each concept.

planning _____

_____

balance sheet _____

_____

income statement _____

_____

marketing plan _____

_____

business plan _____

_____

© 1990 Houghton Mifflin Company. All rights reserved.   98

market potential _____

_____

organizational chart _____

_____

cash budget _____

_____

profitgraph _____

_____

True-False Questions

Determine whether the following statements are true or false, then circle T or F. Correct answers are listed at the end of the study guide.

T   F   1.   A business plan is an essential step in turning ideas for a product or service into a flourishing venture.

T   F   2.   The very act of preparing a business plan forces entrepreneurs to think through the steps they must take to open a business.

T   F   3.   In many ways, a business plan resembles a road map.

T   F   4.   Outside pressures now force entrepreneurs to develop their businesses on paper before investing time and money in a venture that may have little chance of success.

T   F   5.   The outside pressure for a business plan flows mainly from accountants and the Internal Revenue Service.

T   F   6.   Investors and creditors benefit from a business plan because it gives them better information with which to decide whether to help finance the entrepreneur.

T   F   7.   When developing a business plan, the entrepreneur should remember that form is more important than substance.

T   F   8.   In most cases, the entrepreneur should hire an expert or outside consultant to develop a business plan.

T   F   9.   About 15 percent of all entrepreneurs prepare formal business plans.

© 1990 Houghton Mifflin Company. All rights reserved.

T F 10. It is far cheaper not to start an ill-fated business than to learn by experience what your business plan could have taught you at a cost of several hours of concentrated work.

T F 11. A business plan should define strategies for production, marketing, organization, legal aspects, accounting, and finance.

T F 12. When developing a business plan, entrepreneurs should document all facts, back all assumptions, and give the authority for all opinions.

T F 13. As a rule, it is foolish for entrepreneurs to choose a product or service they know little about.

T F 14. Of all the steps required to prepare a business plan, entrepreneurs do the best job of researching the market.

T F 15. In the quest for facts, the logical place to begin is with the question: Who are my customers?

T F 16. Entrepreneurs should begin their marketing research with a visit to the Small Business Administration.

T F 17. Market potential is the total dollar value of products or services now purchased by customers in the entrepreneur's marketing area.

T F 18. First-year sales forecasts should be estimated on a quarterly basis.

T F 19. Second- and third-year sales forecasts should be estimated on a yearly basis.

T F 20. The accuracy of a revenue forecast hinges largely on the accuracy of the assumptions that support it.

T F 21. Wise entrepreneurs must balance personal preference with business logic in choosing a location for their business.

T F 22. Only entrepreneurs who intend to manufacture a product need a production plan.

T F 23. When deciding how large a production facility should be, general practice is to use the third-year sales forecast or even the fifth-year sales forecast.

T F 24. A marketing plan is a combination of distribution, pricing, advertising, personal selling, and sales promotion.

T F 25. When starting a small business, the would-be entrepreneur should pick a lawyer who is an expert in new ventures and preferably has experience in the entrepreneur's industry.

© 1990 Houghton Mifflin Company. All rights reserved.

T   F   26. Generally, entrepreneurs should develop their own accounting system because a system developed by an accountant is too complex.

T   F   27. To protect themselves, entrepreneurs should develop a program of risk management before they launch a venture.

T   F   28. A financial plan and an accounting plan are the same thing.

T   F   29. A financial plan is a dollar expression of the entrepreneur's operating plans.

T   F   30. The cash budget helps entrepreneurs make sure money will be there when bills fall due.

T   F   31. If an entrepreneur already has adequate financial backing, a cash budget is unnecessary.

T   F   32. The dollar amounts of sales revenues and operating expenses are reported on the income statement.

T   F   33. The profitgraph shows how sales volume, selling price, and operating expenses affect profits.

Multiple-Choice Questions

Write the letter of the correct answer in the blank to the left of the question. Correct answers are listed at the end of the study guide.

_____ 1. Planning forces entrepreneurs to anticipate
   a.   the potential market for their venture.
   b.   potential costs of meeting the demands of their market.
   c.   potential pitfalls in organizing the operations of the venture.
   d.   all of the above.

_____ 2. Outside pressures for a business plan flow mainly from
   a.   creditors and investors.
   b.   accountants and lawyers.
   c.   the Internal Revenue Service.
   d.   local government agencies.

_____ 3. The most important product of the entrepreneur's preparation of a business plan is
   a.   the thinking that goes on to come up with the plan.
   b.   a polished report that is more form than substance.
   c.   a report that highlights the strengths of the future business and ignores its weaknesses.
   d.   none of the above.

© 1990 Houghton Mifflin Company. All rights reserved.

_____ 4. Which of the following statements is *true?*
    a. Half of all new businesses fail within the first six months of operation.
    b. The best way to enhance the chance of success in a business venture is to plan and follow through on that planning.
    c. Planning is unnecessary for the experienced entrepreneur.
    d. The business plan is useful only for creditors and investors.

_____ 5. When researching the market, entrepreneurs
    a. tend to spend too much money in their quest for facts.
    b. do a poor job because they rely on hearsay instead of facts.
    c. should begin their search for facts with the Census Bureau.
    d. do all of the above.

_____ 6. Entrepreneurs should estimate sales revenues over a _____ period.
    a. one-year
    b. two-year
    c. three-year
    d. five-year

_____ 7. Which of the following statements is *false?*
    a. Location is a critical decision that can mean the difference between success or failure.
    b. Entrepreneurs should choose a location on the basis of personal preference.
    c. Too often, entrepreneurs jump at the first vacancy that comes along.
    d. Suppliers, customers, or financial support may determine regional locations.

_____ 8. All of the following are parts of a marketing plan *except*
    a. distribution.
    b. sales promotion.
    c. personal selling.
    d. production.

_____ 9. Which of the following statements is *false?*
    a. An entrepreneur should seek the help of an insurance agent when determining a firm's insurance needs.
    b. An effective insurance program should specify where dollar losses may occur.
    c. An effective insurance program is too costly for most small businesses.
    d. A program of risk management should be developed before a venture is launched.

_____10. A cash budget indicates
    a. possible cash-flow problems.
    b. the amount of total assets.
    c. the amount of total liabilities.
    d. market potential.

© 1990 Houghton Mifflin Company. All rights reserved.

____11. Commercial banks, in particular, appreciate projected
    a. cash budgets.
    b. balance sheets.
    c. income statements.
    d. profitgraphs.

____12. A balance sheet shows
    a. cash expenditures over a specific period of time.
    b. assets, liabilities, and owners' equity.
    c. sales revenues and operating expenses.
    d. the breakeven point.

____13. A profitgraph shows entrepreneurs
    a. their liabilities at any given point in time.
    b. the ups and downs of cash flow.
    c. how much product they must sell before they begin to make a profit.
    d. none of the above.

____14. A cover letter
    a. is a vital part of a business plan.
    b. summarizes the balance sheet and income statement prepared in Step 14.
    c. is a selling tool addressed mostly to investors and creditors.
    d. is none of the above.

Completion Questions

Write your answer in the blanks provided in each question. Correct answers are listed at the end of the study guide.

1. The business plan is a _____ exercise. The very act of preparing a business plan forces entrepreneurs to _____ . In many ways, the business plan resembles a _____ map.

2. _____ pressures now force entrepreneurs to develop their businesses on paper before investing time and money in a venture that may have little chance of success. These pressures flow mainly from _____ and _____ whom the entrepreneur may approach for money.

3. The value of a business plan is in the _____ . The important part is the thinking that goes on to come up with it. If the entrepreneur thinks form is more important than _____ , then he or she is missing the point of the business plan.

4. Investors and bankers strongly advise against using outside _____ to help develop a business plan. A professionally prepared business plan is a _____ if the entrepreneur is not the guiding force behind it.

© 1990 Houghton Mifflin Company. All rights reserved.

5. Probably fewer than _____ percent of all entrepreneurs prepare a formal business plan. The remaining _____ percent plan in less structured ways.

6. Entrepreneurs should express their expected market share in terms of estimated _____ revenues. A good rule of thumb is to estimate sales revenues over a _____-year period. First-year sales should be estimated on a _____ basis; second-year sales should be estimated on a _____ basis; and third-year sales should be estimated on a _____ basis.

7. A marketing plan combines the following marketing tools. (1) distribution, (2) price, (3) advertising, (4) personal _____, and (5) sales _____.

8. A financial plan ties together all the preceding steps in the planning process by translating operating plans into _____. Another reason the financial plan is so important is that it enables the entrepreneur to communicate with investors and _____.

9. A financial plan should be made up of a _____ budget, two balance _____, an _____ statement, and a _____.

10. Entrepreneurs should prepare _____ balance sheets—one that projects the _____ of their first year of business and the other that projects the _____ of that first year.

11. An income statement summarizes both expected _____ revenues and expected _____ expenses. The difference between them equals profit or _____.

12. A _____ shows how sales volume, selling price, and operating expenses affect profits. It also tells entrepreneurs how much product they must sell before they begin to make a _____.

Essay Questions

1. In many ways, the business plan resembles a road map, telling entrepreneurs how best to get from A to Z. Entrepreneurs may think: Why should I spend time drawing up a business plan? If an entrepreneur asked you this question, how would you answer?

2. The plan outlined in Chapter 6 describes a 15-step process for constructing an effective business plan for a small business. Choose 5 of the steps and explain why they are important.

3. Investors and bankers strongly advise against using outside consultants to help develop a business plan. A professionally prepared business plan is a turnoff if the entrepreneur is not the guiding force behind it. Why?

The Difference Between Success and Failure*

You want to own and manage your own business. It's a good idea—provided you know what it takes and have what it takes. Starting a business is risky at best. But your chances of making it go will be better if you understand the problems you'll face and work out as many of them as you can before you start. Here are some questions to help you think through what you need to know and do. Check each question in the appropriate column. Where the answer is no, you have some work to do.

Before You Start

How about you?   Yes   No

1. Are you the kind of person who can get a business
   started and make it go?   ____   ____

2. Think about why you want to own your own business.
   Do you want to badly enough to keep you working long
   hours without knowing how much money you'll end up with?   ____   ____

3. Have you worked in a business like the one you want
   to start?   ____   ____

4. Have you worked for someone else as a foreman or
   manager?   ____   ____

5. Have you had any business training in school?   ____   ____

6. Have you saved any money?   ____   ____

How about the money?

1. Do you know how much money you will need to get your
   business started?   ____   ____

2. Have you counted up how much money of your own you can
   put into the business?   ____   ____

3. Do you know how much credit you can get from your
   suppliers—the people you will buy from?   ____   ____

4. Do you know where you can borrow the rest of the money
   you need to start your business?   ____   ____

*Adapted from "Checklist for Going into Business," Small Marketer's Aid no. 71 (Washington, D.C.: U.S. Small Business Adminstration, September 1977).

© 1990 Houghton Mifflin Company. All rights reserved.

How about the money? (cont.)   Yes   No

5. Have you figured out what net income per year you expect
   to get from the business? Count your salary and your
   profits on the money you put into the business.   ____   ____

6. Can you live on less than this so that you can use some
   of it to help your business grow?   ____   ____

7. Have you talked to a banker about your plans?   ____   ____

How about a partner?

1. If you need a partner with money or know-how that you
   don't have, do you know someone who will fit—someone
   you can get along with?   ____   ____

2. Do you know the good and bad points about going it alone,
   having a partner, and incorporating your business?   ____   ____

3. Do you know what licenses and permits you need?   ____   ____

4. Do you know what business laws you have to obey?   ____   ____

5. Have you talked to a lawyer about opening your business?   ____   ____

How about your customers?

1. Do most businesses in your community seem to be doing well? ____   ____

2. Have you tried to find out whether stores like the one
   you want to open are doing well in your community and in the
   rest of the country?   ____   ____

3. Do you know what kind of people will want to buy what you
   plan to sell?   ____   ____

4. Do people like that live in the area where you want to
   open your store?   ____   ____

5. Do they need a store like yours?   ____   ____

6. If not, have you thought about opening a different kind
   of store or going to another neighborhood?   ____   ____

© 1990 Houghton Mifflin Company. All rights reserved.

If you have answered all these questions carefully, you've done some hard work and serious thinking. That's good. But you probably have found some things you still need to know more about or do something about.

Do all you can for yourself, but don't hesitate to ask for help from people who can tell you what you need to know. Remember, running a business takes guts! You've got to be able to decide what you need, then go after it.

© 1990 Houghton Mifflin Company. All rights reserved.

CHAPTER 7

Legal Aspects

Learning Objectives

After studying this chapter, you should understand

1. What legal questions all small businesses face

2. How you find the right lawyer

3. How the legal forms of organization differ

4. How government regulations affect small businesses

5. What the key political issues affecting small businesses are

Chapter Review

As you read the chapter, complete the following outline with information from the text.

I. **The Need for Legal Advice.** To avoid breaking the law and to spot opportunities permitted by the law, entrepreneurs need expert legal help. In fact one of the first things entrepreneurs should do is get a lawyer. Some entrepreneurs feel they need a lawyer only when they are being sued or are suing someone else. A lawyer's more creative role is to advise entrepreneurs so that they need never go to court.

    A. **Choosing the Right Lawyer.** When should entrepreneurs begin the search for a lawyer?

    _____

    Describe the four guidelines entrepreneurs should use to find the right lawyer.

    • _____

    _____

    _____

    _____

© 1990 Houghton Mifflin Company. All rights reserved.

_____

_____

_____

• _____

_____

_____

_____

• _____

_____

_____

• _____

_____

_____

_____

It is wrong for entrepreneurs to sit back and leave all decision making to their lawyer. The lawyer's main job should be to advise and inform. Entrepreneurs should make the actual decisions based on the information provided by their lawyer.

B. **Understanding the Legalities of Franchising and Buyouts.** The need to find the right lawyer is just as pressing for entrepreneurs who buy a franchise or buy out an existing venture as it is for those who start from scratch. Why is a lawyer's help needed to purchase a franchise?

_____

_____

_____

© 1990 Houghton Mifflin Company. All rights reserved.

What role does a lawyer play in the purchase of an existing business?

_____

_____

_____

_____

II. **Legal Forms of Organization.** Choosing a legal form of organization ranks among the entrepreneur's most vital decisions. This choice affects a number of managerial and financial issues.

There is no one best form of organization. What are three specific factors mentioned in the text that may affect the choice of a legal form of organization?

- _____

- _____

- _____

A. Sole Proprietorships. Sole proprietorships are the most popular legal form of organization, accounting for 71 percent of all businesses. Briefly explain these advantages of the sole proprietorship.

Freedom _____

_____

_____

Simplicity _____

_____

_____

_____

Low startup costs _____

_____

_____

_____

Tax benefits _____

_____

_____

_____

Explain these disadvantages of the sole proprietorship.

Unlimited liability _____

_____

_____

_____

Lack of continuity _____

_____

_____

_____

Difficulty raising money _____

_____

_____

_____

© 1990 Houghton Mifflin Company. All rights reserved.

B. General Partnerships. A general partnership is really a sole proprietorship multiplied by the number of partners. What is the most striking positive feature of the general partnership?

_____

_____

List five things a partnership agreement should spell out.

- _____

- _____

- _____

- _____

- _____

Describe three advantages of the partnership form of ownership.

- _____

- _____

- _____

Describe three disadvantages of the partnership form of ownership.

- _____

- _____

- _____

C. Other Forms of Partnership. Entrepreneurs can avoid the problem of unlimited liability by forming a limited partnership. Why does a limited partner have limited liability?

_____

_____

_____

© 1990 Houghton Mifflin Company. All rights reserved.

Why are limited partnerships more complex to organize than general partnerships?

_____

_____

_____

_____

What is a family partnership?

_____

_____

What is a real estate investment trust (*REIT*)?

_____

_____

D. **Regular Corporations.** Corporations dominate the business world. They account for 90 percent of all revenues generated by the nation's businesses, yet they make up only 19 percent of the total number of businesses.

How did Chief Justice John Marshall define a corporation?

_____

_____

_____

By defining the corporation as a legal "person," the Supreme Court gave the corporation the right to engage in certain activities. What are those activities?

_____

_____

_____

_____

© 1990 Houghton Mifflin Company. All rights reserved.

Describe four advantages of the corporate form of ownership.

Limited liability _____

_____

_____

Continuity _____

_____

_____

Transfer of ownership _____

_____

_____

Ability to raise capital _____

_____

_____

What is the difference between preferred stock and common stock?

_____

_____

_____

_____

List four legal rights of common shareholders.

- _____

- _____

- _____

- _____

© 1990 Houghton Mifflin Company. All rights reserved.

Briefly describe these disadvantages of the corporate form of ownership.

Regulation _____

_____

_____

_____

Cost _____

_____

_____

_____

Record keeping _____

_____

_____

_____

Double taxation _____

_____

_____

_____

E. **S Corporations.** Entrepreneurs can avoid double taxation by forming an S corporation. An S corporation enjoys the advantages of a corporation without any of its drawbacks. To qualify as an S corporation, a business must meet four legal requirements. What are they?

- _____

_____

_____

- _____

- _____

_____

_____

- _____

_____

Once the venture gets under way, there are two more requirements. What are they?

- _____

_____

- _____

_____

F. **1244 Corporations.** To encourage investors to risk their money in small businesses, in 1958 Congress enacted Section 1244 of the U.S. Internal Revenue Code, creating the 1244 corporation. What specific advantage does the 1244 corporation offer wealthy investors?

_____

_____

To qualify as a Section 1244 corporation, a small business must meet four criteria. List them.

- _____

_____

- _____

_____

_____

- _____
_____

- _____
_____

III. Government Regulations and Paperwork. Few subjects spark more complaints among entrepreneurs than the rising tide of government regulations and the avalanche of paperwork they create. In the federal government alone, there are now more than 90 regulatory agencies issuing hundreds of new rules each year. Regulatory agencies exist not only at the federal level but also at local and state levels.

List three areas in which small business feels the effects of government regulations and paperwork.

- _____

- _____

- _____

The cost of government regulation is especially staggering to small businesses. Why?

_____

_____

Of course many regulations benefit both society and the entrepreneur. List six of these benefits.

- _____

- _____

- _____

- _____
_____

- _____
_____

© 1990 Houghton Mifflin Company. All rights reserved.

• _____

_____

Questions for Mastery

Questions for mastery are found in the textbook at the beginning of every chapter. Answer each question again to reinforce your understanding of the information.

1. What legal questions do all small businesses face?

_____

_____

_____

_____

2. How do you find the right lawyer?

_____

_____

_____

_____

_____

3. How do the legal forms of ownership differ?

_____

_____

_____

_____

_____

© 1990 Houghton Mifflin Company. All rights reserved.

4. How do government regulations affect small businesses?

_____

_____

_____

_____

5. What are the key political issues affecting small business?

_____

_____

_____

_____

Definitions of Key Terms

The following key terms are important in this chapter. In your own words, define each concept.

unlimited liability _____

_____

S corporation _____

_____

double taxation _____

_____

limited partnership _____

_____

family partnership _____

_____

preferred stock _____

_____

common stock _____

_____

1244 corporation _____

_____

sole proprietorship _____

_____

general partnership _____

_____

corporation _____

_____

limited liability _____

_____

corporate charter _____

_____

True-False Questions

Determine whether the following statements are true or false, then circle T or F. Correct answers are listed at the end of the study guide.

T   F   1.   One of the entrepreneur's first acts should be to get a lawyer.

T   F   2.   The only time a small-business owner needs a lawyer is when he or she is being sued.

T   F   3.   The best way to find a lawyer is to ask friends, neighbors, or relatives for recommendations.

T   F   4.   The American Legal Directory lists the backgrounds of lawyers.

© 1990 Houghton Mifflin Company. All rights reserved.

T   F   5. The main job of the lawyer should be to advise and to inform the entrepreneur.

T   F   6. When purchasing a franchise or an existing business, the entrepreneur does not need a lawyer because all the legal work has been done by somebody else.

T   F   7. Before buying an existing business, entrepreneurs should determine who is responsible for existing claims.

T   F   8. Choosing a legal form of organization is one of the entrepreneur's most important decisions.

T   F   9. The best form of organization depends on the entrepreneur's preferences and tax bracket, and on the venture's needs.

T   F   10. Sole proprietorships account for 50 percent of all businesses.

T   F   11. Sole proprietors are forbidden by current tax law from deducting operating losses from their ordinary income.

T   F   12. Unlimited liability means that the entrepreneur is personally liable for all debts incurred by his or her business.

T   F   13. When a sole proprietor dies, the small-business venture continues to operate for a period of 45 days.

T   F   14. Sole proprietors can raise money easier and faster than partnerships and corporations.

T   F   15. A general partnership is really a sole proprietorship multiplied by the number of partners.

T   F   16. Partnerships account for 16 percent of all businesses.

T   F   17. The most striking positive feature of a partnership is its ability to grow by adding talent and money.

T   F   18. A partnership can have no more than 12 general partners.

T   F   19. In a general partnership, each partner can earn profits that bear no relation to his or her investment.

T   F   20. A written partnership agreement must be filed at the county clerk's office in order to be valid.

T   F   21. The Internal Revenue Service taxes partners as individuals.

© 1990 Houghton Mifflin Company. All rights reserved.

T   F   22. In a partnership, only the partner who incurs a business debt is responsible for that debt.

T   F   23. When one partner dies or pulls out, a partnership legally dies.

T   F   24. Because the law regards a partnership as a close, intimate relationship, no partner can sell out without the consent of the other partners.

T   F   25. Entrepreneurs can avoid the problem of unlimited liability by forming a limited partnership.

T   F   26. In a limited partnership, only general partners must register in each state in which the partnership plans to do business.

T   F   27. Corporations account for 90 percent of all revenues generated by the nation's businesses.

T   F   28. In the eyes of the law, a corporation is an artificial being, invisible, intangible, and existing only in the contemplation of the law.

T   F   29. Limited liability is the major disadvantage of the corporation.

T   F   30. A small business is more likely to issue preferred stock than common stock.

T   F   31. Ownership interest does not give common shareholders the automatic right to act for the corporation or to share in its management.

T   F   32. Forming a corporation costs more than forming either a sole proprietorship or a partnership.

T   T   33. Entrepreneurs can avoid double taxation by forming an S corporation.

T   F   34. To qualify as an S corporation, a venture can have no more than 25 stockholders.

T   F   35. In the federal government alone, there are now more than 125 regulatory agencies.

© 1990 Houghton Mifflin Company. All rights reserved.

Multiple-Choice Questions

Write the letter of the correct answer in the blank to the left of the question. Correct answers are listed at the end of the study guide.

_____ 1. Which of the following statements is *true?*
   a.   Entrepreneurs need a lawyer only when they are being sued.
   b.   An entrepreneur should begin the search for a lawyer months before he or she launches a business.
   c.   Lawyers should be consulted only when the entrepreneur is going to sue someone.
   d.   The best source of information about prospective lawyers is the entrepreneur's friends and relatives.

_____ 2. An entrepreneur can check the backgrounds of lawyers by looking in the
   a.   *American Legal Directory.*
   b.   *Legal Guide to U.S. Attorneys.*
   c.   *Martindale and Hubbell Directory.*
   d.   Internal Revenue Code.

_____ 3. All of the following are advantages of the sole proprietorship *except*
   a.   freedom from regulation.
   b.   unlimited liability.
   c.   simplicity of form.
   d.   low startup costs.

_____ 4. The partnership agreement should spell out all of the following *except*
   a.   who invested what sums of money in the partnership.
   b.   who gets what share of the partnership profits.
   c.   where the partnership agreement should be filed.
   d.   how the partnership can be dissolved.

_____ 5. The biggest drawback of a partnership is
   a.   unlimited liability.
   b.   its organizational complexity.
   c.   double taxation.
   d.   voluntary association.

_____ 6. In a limited partnership, a limited partner is
   a.   personally liable for all debts of the partnership.
   b.   liable only for his or her original investment.
   c.   active in the management of the firm.
   d.   none of the above.

_____ 7. Corporations account for _____ percent of the total number of businesses in the United States today.
   a. 8
   b. 12
   c. 19
   d. 25

_____ 8. Because a corporation is an artificial being created in contemplation of the law, it can
   a. sue and be sued.
   b. buy, hold, and sell property.
   c. commit crimes and be tried and punished for them.
   d. do all of the above.

_____ 9. Which of the following statements is *true?*
   a. Common stock represents an ownership interest in the business.
   b. Common shareholders are guaranteed dividends.
   c. Most small corporations issue preferred stock.
   d. At a future date, the corporation must buy back common stock.

_____10. Common shareholders have the right to
   a. receive dividends before preferred shareholders.
   b. cast one vote per share at shareholders' meetings.
   c. purchase the company's products or services at a discount.
   d. act for the corporation.

_____11. All of the following are disadvantages of the corporate form of ownership *except*
   a. high legal startup costs.
   b. close regulation by the government.
   c. extensive recordkeeping.
   d. limited liability.

_____12. The most expensive type of organization to start up is the
   a. sole proprietorship.
   b. general partnership.
   c. limited cooperative.
   d. corporation.

_____13. An organization that was created to eliminate double taxation is the
   a. limited partnership.
   b. regulation corporation.
   c. S corporation.
   d. 1244 corporation.

© 1990 Houghton Mifflin Company. All rights reserved.

_____14. In an S corporation,
    a. no more than 60 percent of revenues can come from foreign nations.
    b. only individuals or estates are permitted to be shareholders.
    c. no more than 15 percent of sales revenues can come from dividends, rents, interest, royalties, annuities, or stock sales.
    d. stock must be issued for cash or property, not in exchange for services.

_____15. Which of the following statements is *false?*
    a. As a result of government regulations, small businesses are more productive.
    b. The cost of government regulations is staggering.
    c. Government regulations tend to discourage innovation and technology.
    d. Government regulations impose a hardship on small businesses because they have limited resources.

Completion Questions

Write your answer in the blanks provided in each question. Correct answers are listed at the end of the study guide.

1. One of the entrepreneur's earliest acts should be to get a _____. To find the right lawyer, the entrepreneur should seek out the names of lawyers that are held in high esteem by the _____ community. It is also possible to check the backgrounds of lawyers by looking in the *Martindale and* _____ *Directory*. Then the entrepreneur should narrow the list of names to those whose law firms are _____. When making the final choice, the entrepreneur should make sure that the lawyer's expert knowledge is accompanied by a reasonable match in _____ chemistry.

2. Sole proprietorships are the most popular form of organization, accounting for _____ percent of all businesses. _____ is the most striking feature of a sole proprietorship. Still another is _____ startup cost. The main disadvantages of a sole proprietorship are _____ liability, lack of _____, and difficulty _____ money.

3. A general partnership is the _____ popular form of business organization. As defined by the _____ Partnership Act, a partnership is a _____ association of two or more persons to carry on as co-owners of a business for profit. Unlimited _____ is the worst drawback of a partnership. By law, each partner may be held liable for debts incurred in the name of the _____.

4. The entrepreneur can avoid the problem of unlimited liability by forming a _____ partnership. Limited partners can invest their money without being held liable for debts made by _____ partners on behalf of the partnership.

5. A _____ partnership enables partners to split income among members of their families to avoid high taxes. Another type of partnership is called the real estate _____ trust, which enjoys both continuity of life and ease of ownership transfer.

© 1990 Houghton Mifflin Company. All rights reserved.

6. A corporation is an _____ being, invisible, intangible, and existing only in contemplation of the law. _____ liability is the most striking advantage of a corporation. This means investors' liability is limited to their _____ investment.

7. A corporation can issue common stock, _____ stock, or both. Preferred stockholders enjoy priority, or preference, over _____ shareholders as to dividends and _____ when a venture is liquidated.

8. Each common shareholder owns part of the corporation, as evidenced by stock _____. As owners, common shareholders have certain rights, which include (1) the right to elect the _____ of the corporation, (2) the right to cast one _____ per share at shareholders' meetings, (3) the right to receive _____ in proportion to their number of shares, and (4) the right to _____ their shares.

9. Legal requirements for receiving a corporate _____ differ from state to state. Because of its complexity, the corporation is the _____ expensive legal form of business. An attorney's help is needed to ensure that the founders observe every _____ requirement.

10. Typical issues that must be decided before obtaining a corporate charter include taxes, business fees, minimum number of _____, liabilities for _____, minimum sum contributed by the _____, and rules for issuing _____.

11. Entrepreneurs can avoid _____ taxation by forming an _____ corporation. In this type of organization, there can be no more than _____ shareholders. And there are other requirements that must be met before the Internal Revenue Service recognizes the S corporation.

12. To encourage investors to risk their money in small businesses, in 1958 Congress enacted Section _____ of the Internal Revenue Code. This law allows investment losses of up to _____ a year to be deducted from _____ income.

13. In the _____ government alone, there are now more than _____ regulatory agencies issuing hundreds of new rules each year.

14. Small business suffers the effects of government regulations and paperwork on competition and _____, innovation and _____, and growth and capital _____.

Essay Questions

1. Entrepreneurs should get the right lawyer months before they plan to launch their venture. They should choose a lawyer with the same care they would a surgeon. What guidelines would you use to choose the right lawyer for a business?

© 1990 Houghton Mifflin Company. All rights reserved.

2. In the words of the SBA, no one legal form of organization, or for that matter no combination of two or more of them, is suited to each and every small business. Choose the sole proprietorship, partnership, or corporation, and describe its advantages and disadvantages.

3. All partnerships begin with an agreement of some kind—written, spoken, or even unspoken. But the wise entrepreneur insists on a written agreement. What type of information should be in a written agreement? What type of information should be in a partnership agreement? Why should the agreement be in writing?

4. In the words of Chief Justice Marshall, a corporation is "an artificial being, invisible, intangible, and existing only in contemplation of the law." What does this definition enable corporations to do?

The Difference Between Success and Failure

Small-business owners face at least two problems related to material covered in this chapter. First, they generally are not lawyers, nor do they usually have an attorney as an employee or on retainer. But legal advice can be well worth the cost of a consultation, which ranges from $75 to $150 an hour. One way to determine whether the advice is worth the cost is to look at the consequences of not seeking legal advice. Is the risk really worth it?

Second, the question "Should I incorporate?" often is asked by small-business owners. There is no clear-cut answer. The decision may be clouded by many factors, but the concept of limited liability is the primary reason small-business owners choose to incorporate.

Limited liability is a definite advantage. In a corporation, the owner's personal wealth is protected from the firm's creditors. Of course, creditors realize this fact and often are reluctant to loan money to a small corporation. Naturally creditors are concerned about repayment. In effect, the corporation is now responsible for its own actions and debts because of the limited-liability concept. In the case of business failure, the bankruptcy courts may seize a corporation's assets and sell them to pay creditors, but the courts usually cannot touch the personal possessions of shareholders.

To determine if it is a good idea to incorporate for liability reasons, the small-business owner must consult an attorney. If the attorney and the entrepreneur decide to incorporate, several other decisions must be made before and during the incorporation process.

Where to Incorporate

A business is allowed to incorporate in any state it chooses. Most small and medium-sized businesses are incorporated in the state where they do the most business. However, the founders of larger corporations or of those that do business nationwide may compare the benefits provided to corporations by various states. Some states are more hospitable than others, offering low taxes and other benefits to attract new firms.

© 1990 Houghton Mifflin Company. All rights reserved.

An incorporated business is called a *domestic* corporation in the state in which it is incorporated. In all other states where it does business, it is called a *foreign* corporation. Sears, Roebuck and Company, for example, is incorporated in New York, where it is a domestic corporation. In the remaining forty-nine states, it is a foreign corporation.

The Corporate Charter

Once a "home state" has been chosen, the incorporators submit articles of incorporation to the secretary of state. If the articles of incorporation are approved, they become the firm's corporate charter. A corporate charter is a contract between the corporation and the state, in which the state recognizes the formation of the artificial person that is the corporation. Usually the charter (and thus the articles of incorporation) includes the following information:

1. The firm's name and address
2. The incorporators' names and addresses
3. The purpose of the corporation
4. The maximum amount of stock and the type of stock to be issued
5. The rights and privileges of shareholders
6. How long the corporation will exist (usually without limit)

Each of these key details is a product of decisions that the incorporators must make when they organize the firm—before the articles of incorporation are submitted to the secretary of state.

Organizational Meeting

In the last step in forming a corporation, the original stockholders meet to elect their first board of directors. (Later, directors will be elected or re-elected at the corporation's annual meetings.) The board members are directly responsible to the stockholders for the way they operate the firm.

© 1990 Houghton Mifflin Company. All rights reserved.

CHAPTER 8

Location

Learning Objectives

After studying this chapter, you should understand

1. Why site location is important

2. How site location differs in importance among industries

3. How you should select a site for a wholesale, retail, or service business

4. What role marketing research plays in site selection

5. How you should select a site for a manufacturing plant

Chapter Review

As you read the chapter, complete the following outline with information from the text.

A saying common in retailing circles is "the three most important factors in retailing success are location, location, and location." Location is critical in retailing; it also plays a vital role in manufacturing, services, and wholesaling.

I. **The Varying Importance of Location.** Location is more vital in some industries than in others. What characteristics make location more important for some businesses and less important for others?

- _____

  _____

- _____

  _____

- _____

  _____

Why is location unimportant for these businesses?

Management consultant _____

_____

_____

_____

Antique furniture repair _____

_____

_____

_____

Why is location very important to the success of a supermarket?

_____

_____

_____

II. **Marketing Research in Site Selection.** Marketing research is one of the entrepreneur's most important activities. Focusing as it does on the quest for facts about markets, marketing research is indispensable in site selection. Only through this research can the entrepreneur carry off the site-selection process (Exhibit 8.1). That process involves choosing a geographical region, a city within that region, an area within that city, and a specific site within that area.

Few entrepreneurs go through a logical process of site selection. Instead they permit personal preference to influence their decision where to locate. Personal preference is a factor that should be weighed in choosing a location, but entrepreneurs should not allow their biases to take the place of objective research.

Marketing research provides information that is useful before and after a venture begins. What type of information is available from the following sources?

© 1990 Houghton Mifflin Company. All rights reserved.

The federal government _____

_____

_____

_____

_____

Trade associations _____

_____

_____

_____

Chambers of Commerce _____

_____

_____

_____

"Survey of Buying Power" _____

_____

_____

_____

III. **Selecting a Wholesale, Retail, or Service Location**

A. **Locating a Wholesale, Retail, or Service Business.** The process of site selection varies for each product or service. What factors should entrepreneurs consider in the following areas?

© 1990 Houghton Mifflin Company. All rights reserved.   133

City _____

_____

_____

_____

_____

Area within the city _____

_____

_____

_____

_____

Specific site within the area _____

_____

_____

_____

_____

_____

_____

Choosing the best location calls for painstaking attention to detail. No fact should go ignored. Entrepreneurs must narrow their choices down to the most likely sites, then dig out the facts about each of them.

B. **Locating a Manufacturing Plant.** So far, discussion has centered on locating a retail store or a service firm. The process of deciding where to locate a manufacturing plant is more complex and requires painstakingly thorough marketing research.

In choosing a location for a plant, how should entrepreneurs balance the following factors?

© 1990 Houghton Mifflin Company. All rights reserved.

Potential sales revenues _____

_____

_____

Manufacturing costs _____

_____

_____

Transportation costs _____

_____

_____

Questions of markets and costs are by no means the only ones that entrepreneurs should answer. In what ways do the following factors influence the location decision for a manufacturing plant?

Labor force _____

_____

_____

Community size _____

_____

_____

_____

Transportation _____

_____

_____

Water pollution _____

_____

_____

© 1990 Houghton Mifflin Company. All rights reserved.

Air pollution _____

_____

_____

Land _____

_____

_____

_____

Fuel and power _____

_____

_____

Taxes _____

_____

_____

Financing opportunities _____

_____

_____

In the real world, symmetrical markets and purchase areas are the exception. This means entrepreneurs must do an exhaustive analysis to measure the attractiveness of likely sites. How does return on investment affect a location decision for a manufacturing plant?

_____

_____

_____

© 1990 Houghton Mifflin Company. All rights reserved.

What are the differences between locating a plant and selecting a store or office location?

_____

_____

_____

_____

_____

_____

C. **Location Criteria Used by High-Technology Companies.** There is little question that high-technology companies will continue to fuel the nation's economy. List twelve factors that high-technology companies look for in selecting a plant site (Exhibit 8.7).

_____   _____

_____   _____

_____   _____

_____   _____

_____   _____

_____   _____

Which area of the United States is expected to have the most high-technology development in the immediate future?

_____

D. **The Role of Shopping Centers and Industrial Parks.** Even in those industries where location matters, the choice of location is less and less within the domain of the entrepreneur. What is the marked trend toward shopping centers and industrial parks?

_____

_____

_____

_____

How many shopping centers and industrial parks are there in the United States today?

_____

As a result of this trend, the developer, not the entrepreneur, often selects location.

Developers of shopping centers and industrial parks must now go to great lengths to justify their proposals. Why are communities more selective now than they were a few years ago?

_____

_____

_____

_____

Questions for Mastery

Questions for mastery are found in the textbook at the beginning of every chapter. Answer each question again to reinforce your understanding of the information.

1. Why is site selection important?

_____

_____

_____

2. How does site selection differ in importance among industries?

_____

_____

_____

_____

3. How should you select a site for a wholesale, retail, or service business?

_____

_____

_____

_____

_____

4. What role does marketing research play in site selection?

_____

_____

_____

5. How should you select a site for a manufacturing plant?

_____

_____

_____

_____

© 1990 Houghton Mifflin Company. All rights reserved.

Chapter 8

Definition of Key Terms

The following key terms are important in this chapter. In your own words, define each concept.

industrial park _____

_____

developer _____

_____

ecological concerns _____

_____

marketing research _____

_____

buying power _____

_____

shopping center _____

_____

return on investment _____

_____

census tract _____

_____

True-False Questions

Determine whether the following statements are true or false, then circle T or F. Correct answers are listed at the end of the study guide.

T   F   1.   One of the most important factors in the success of a retail store is location.

T   F   2.   Location is more important in some industries than others.

© 1990 Houghton Mifflin Company. All rights reserved.

T   F   3. In general, location is more important for a service business than a retailing business.

T   F   4. Most entrepreneurs go through a logical process in choosing a site.

T   F   5. Entrepreneurs often allow personal preference to influence their decision on where to locate.

T   F   6. Personal preference should not be a factor in choosing a location.

T   F   7. The Census Bureau provides population characteristics by census tract for all cities of 25,000 or more inhabitants.

T   F   8. Each census tract has an average population of 4,000 to 5,000.

T   F   9. The "Survey of Buying Power" is published quarterly by *Sales and Marketing Management* magazine.

T   F   10. Census information is furnished by the Census Bureau every ten years.

T   F   11. The process of deciding where best to locate a manufacturing plant is more complex than choosing a location for a retail or a service firm.

T   F   12. To find the right location for a manufacturing plant, an entrepreneur must balance three factors: potential sales revenues, manufacturing costs, and transportation costs.

T   F   13. When choosing a site for a manufacturing plant, one yardstick that entrepreneurs should use is return on investment.

T   F   14. Choice of region or community is far more important to retailers than to manufacturers.

T   F   15. Relocating a manufacturing plant can mean financial collapse.

T   F   16. High-technology companies will continue to fuel the nation's economy.

T   F   17. According to the Joint Economic Committee of Congress, easy access to raw materials is the most important criterion in considering an area as a possible site for a high-technology plant.

T   F   18. Because all labor costs in the United States are about the same, affordable labor is not a factor in determining a location for a high-technology plant.

T   F   19. According to the Joint Economic Committee of Congress, the Midwest is expected to have the most high-technology development in the immediate future.

© 1990 Houghton Mifflin Company. All rights reserved.

T F 20. New England and the Far West, which now have the highest intensity of high-technology firms, may not be able to maintain their positions because of labor costs, taxes, and the cost of living.

T F 21. The choice of location is less and less within the domain of the entrepreneur.

T F 22. In 1989 there were more than 37,000 shopping centers in the United States.

T F 23. In 1989 there were more than 4,5000 industrial parks in the United States.

T F 24. The location of an industrial park is dictated by ecological concerns as well as by access to transportation and markets.

T F 25. The developer of an industrial park just has to buy vacant land, then develop it.

T F 26. Many communities are now trying to stem the unbridled growth of shopping centers and industrial parks.

Multiple-Choice Questions

Write the letter of the correct answer in the blank to the left of the question. Correct answers are listed at the end of the study guide.

_____ 1. Of the following industries, location is most important in
   a. antique furniture repair.
   b. management consulting.
   c. tax preparation.
   d. retail food sales.

_____ 2. In selecting a location, an entrepreneur should first choose a(n)
   a. geographical region.
   b. city within that region.
   c. area within that city.
   d. specific site within that area (except for shopping centers).

_____ 3. Which of the following statements is *true?*
   a. When choosing a shopping center location, the entrepreneur has as much say in site selection as the developer of the center.
   b. Few entrepreneurs go through a logical process of site selection.
   c. Personal preference is more important than other factors in site selection.
   d. All of the above are true.

_____ 4. The Census Bureau publishes census data for all cities of _____ or more inhabitants.
   a. 20,000
   b. 30,000
   c. 40,000
   d. 50,000

_____ 5. Each census tract has an average population of
   a. 2,000 to 3,000.
   b. 3,000 to 4,000.
   c. 4,000 to 5,000.
   d. 5,000 to 6,000.

_____ 6. The "Survey of Buying Power" is updated
   a. monthly.
   b. quarterly.
   c. semiannually.
   d. yearly.

_____ 7. The "Survey of Buying Power" is published by
   a. *Advertising Age.*
   b. *Sales and Marketing Management.*
   c. the U.S. Bureau of the Census.
   d. the National Chamber of Commerce.

_____ 8. Which of the following statements is *true?*
   a. Marketing research is perhaps the entrepreneur's most important marketing activity.
   b. Choosing the best location calls for painstaking attention to detail.
   c. Among the most fertile sources of information for the entrepreneur is the federal government.
   d. All of the above are true.

_____ 9. When locating a manufacturing plant, a would-be entrepreneur must
   a. find a broker who will find the right piece of real estate.
   b. balance three factors: potential sales revenues, manufacturing costs, and transportation costs.
   c. seek the least expensive location.
   d. ignore the location of rivals.

_____10. When entrepreneurs are faced with a choice of manufacturing sites, they should use _____ as a financial yardstick.
   a. return on expenses
   b. return on total assets
   c. return on investment
   d. return on total liabilities

© 1990 Houghton Mifflin Company. All rights reserved.

____11. According to the Joint Economic Committee of Congress, the most important factor in choosing a new manufacturing site is
   a. affordable labor.
   b. affordable cost of living.
   c. limited regional regulatory controls.
   d. academic institutions that can provide research support.

____12. Factors identified as important by high-technology firms when choosing a new plant site include all of the following *except*
   a. labor productivity.
   b. a favorable tax climate.
   c. an accessible transportation system.
   d. a guaranteed profit return.

____13. In 1989 there were more than _____ shopping centers in the United States.
   a. 20,000
   b. 25,000
   c. 26,000
   d. 28,000

____14. In 1989 there were more than _____ industrial parks in the United States.
   a. 3,500
   b. 4,000
   c. 4,500
   d. 5,000

____15. Which of the following statements is *true?*
   a. A developer is guaranteed success if he or she constructs an industrial park in the Sunbelt.
   b. Many communities have passed laws forcing developers to meet specific requirements regarding air and water pollution.
   c. Within a generation or two, most consumers will be shopping in downtown areas.
   d. The trend toward shopping centers and industrial parks has increased the role of the entrepreneur in site-location decisions.

Completion Questions

Write your answer in the blanks provided in each question. Correct answers are listed at the end of the study guide.

1. In order to select a location, an entrepreneur must choose a _____ region, a _____ within that region, an _____ within that city, and a _____ site within that area.

2. The U.S. Bureau of the _____ provides population characteristics by census tract for all cities of _____ or more inhabitants. Each census tract has an average population of _____ to _____.

3. The "Survey of _____ Power" is published by *Sales and* _____ *Management* magazine. This survey gives data on population, income, and certain categories of _____ sales for major metropolitan areas. The survey is updated on a _____ basis.

4. To find the right location for a manufacturing plant, an entrepreneur should try to balance three site factors: potential _____ revenues, _____ costs, and transportation costs.

5. There is little question that _____-technology companies will continue to fuel the nation's economy. According to the Joint Economic Committee of Congress, _____ labor is the most important criterion in considering an area as a possible site for a high-technology plant. Also the committee predicts that the _____ region of the United States will have the most high-technology development in the immediate future. New England and the Far West, which now have the highest intensity of high-technology firms, may not be able to maintain their positions because of _____ costs, taxes, and the _____ of living.

6. The choice of location is less and less within the domain of the entrepreneur. The main reason is the marked trend toward shopping centers and industrial parks. In 1989 there were more than _____ shopping centers and _____ industrial parks in the United States.

7. Many communities are now trying to slow the growth of shopping centers and industrial parks, creating conflicts between developers and entrepreneurs who claim their right to free _____ and the communities that claim their right to remain residential.

Essay Questions

1. Location is more vital in some industries than others. Certain characteristics of businesses determine the importance of location. What are they? How would they affect a decision to locate a high-fashion clothing store?

2. In many cases, entrepreneurs are still free to choose a geographical region, a city within that region, an area within that city, and a specific site within that area. What types of questions should an entrepreneur ask to determine the best region, city, area, and specific site for a boat dealership?

3. To find the right location for their plant, entrepreneurs should try to balance three site factors: potential sales revenues, manufacturing costs, and transportation costs. What other factors should would-be manufacturers consider?

© 1990 Houghton Mifflin Company. All rights reserved.   145

The Difference Between Success and Failure*

Different stores have different location requirements. You would not put a toy store in a retirement village or start a garden supply store in a rental apartment district. The customers you serve, the things they buy, the way they reach your store, the adjacent stores, the neighborhood—all bear on the location. These factors must be related to the types and characteristics of shopping centers when you are considering a shopping center as a site.

For merchants making a decision whether to locate in a shopping center, the advantages of the site must be related to the limitations placed on them as tenants. In a shopping center, tenants are part of a merchant team. As such, they must pay their pro rata share of the budget for the team effort. They must keep certain store hours, light their windows, and place their signs within established rules.

Types of Shopping Centers

Each planned shopping center is built around a major tenant. Centers are classed, in part, according to their leading tenant. According to tenant makeup and size, there are three types: neighborhood, community, and regional.

1. *Neighborhood.* The supermarket or the drugstore is the leading tenant in a neighborhood center. This is the smallest type of shopping center. It caters to the convenience needs of a neighborhood.

2. *Community.* Variety or junior department stores lead in the next bigger type—the community center. Here you find room for more specialty shops, and the need for wider price ranges, for greater style assortments, and for more impulse-sale items.

3. *Regional.* The department store, with its prestige, is the leader in the regional center—the largest type of shopping center. When you find that a second or third department store also is locating in the center, you know the site has been selected to draw from the widest possible market area. You will find, too, that smaller tenants are picked to offer a range of goods and services approaching the appeal once found only downtown.

Other Factors To Consider

Suppose that the owner-developer of a shopping center asks you to be a tenant. In considering the offer, you would need to determine what you can do in the center. What rules will affect your operation? In exchange for your adhering to the rules, what will the center do for you?

Even more important, you must consider the trade area, the location of your competition, and the location of your space in the center. These factors help determine how much business you can expect to do. Other factors to consider include:

---

*Adapted from "Factors in Considering a Shopping Center Location," Small, Marketer's Aid no. 143 (Washington, D.C.: U.S. Small Business Administration, reprinted July 1978).

© 1990 Houghton Mifflin Company. All rights reserved.

1. *Your space.* Determine where your space will be. Your location in the center is important. Do you need to be in the main flow of customers as they pass between the stores with the greatest customer pull? Who will your neighbors be? What will their effect be on your sales?

    The amount of space is also important. Using your experience, you can determine how much space you will need to handle the sales volume you expect to have in the shopping center. And, of course, the amount of space will determine your rent.

2. *Total rent.* Most shopping center leases are negotiated. Rental expense may begin with a minimum guarantee that is equal to a percentage of gross sales. Typically, this is between 5 and 7 percent of gross sales, but it varies by type of business and other factors.

    This guarantee is not the end. In addition, you may have to pay dues to the center's merchant association. And you may have to pay for maintenance of the common areas or contribute to an advertising fund.

3. *Finishing out.* Generally the owner furnishes bare space; you do the finishing out at your own expense. In completing your store to suit your needs, you pay for light fixtures, counters, shelves, painting, and floor coverings. In addition, you may have to install your own heating and cooling units. Your lease should be long enough to pay out your finishing-out expense.

Whether a small retailer can get into a particular shopping center depends on the market and management. A neighborhood shopping center may need just one children's shoe store, for example; a regional center may expect enough business for several. The management aspect is simple to state: Developers and owners of shopping centers look for successful retailers.

© 1990 Houghton Mifflin Company. All rights reserved.

CHAPTER 9

Financing

Learning Objectives

After studying this chapter you should understand

1. Why a financial plan is necessary

2. How to estimate the amount of money needed to launch a new venture

3. What the difference is between equity capital and debt capital

4. What the various ways of raising money are

5. How federal agencies like the SBA help entrepreneurs finance their ventures

Chapter Review

As you read the chapter, complete the following outline with information from the text.

Without money, the entrepreneur's dreams may never become a reality. This is why entrepreneurs should understand how to estimate the amount of money they need, then how to go about raising that money.

I. **Estimating Money Needs.** Before they can estimate how much money they need, entrepreneurs must know what they plan to do. Why is a business plan important in determining how best to launch a new business?

    _____

    _____

    _____

© 1990 Houghton Mifflin Company. All rights reserved.

The centerpiece of the business plan is the cash budget, which translates operating plans into dollars. So vital are cash budgets that few investors or creditors will entertain a request for money without one. What three questions does the cash budget help bankers answer?

- _____

- _____

- _____

A. **The Price of Failing to Budget.** Although budgeting is widely practiced by individuals, government, and big business, it is little used by entrepreneurs. What is one reason many entrepreneurs shy away from the budgeting process?

_____

_____

B. **Preparing a Budget.** Before they can begin to develop a cash budget, entrepreneurs must first spell out their operating plans, defining production, marketing, staffing, accounting, and legal goals.

What are the two limitations of budgeting?

- _____

_____

_____

_____

_____

- _____

_____

_____

_____

Although it is rough, the revenue forecast is the single most important estimate entrepreneurs can make. Most of the other estimates they must make are based on the revenue forecast. Having forecast revenues, entrepreneurs next must estimate the cost of the fixed and current assets they will need to support those revenues.

© 1990 Houghton Mifflin Company. All rights reserved.

1. **Fixed Assets.** Fixed assets are resources whose benefits last more than one year. List four examples of fixed assets.

   _____   _____

   _____   _____

   Fixed assets can be tangible or intangible. Give an example of each and explain the difference.

   _____

   _____

   _____

2. **Current Assets.** Current assets are resources whose benefits last less than a year. List three common current assets.

   _____   _____

   _____

   Read through the home furnishings store example in Chapter 9 of your text, then answer the following questions.

   What is the cost of the building at year zero?

   _____

   What is the cost of inventory at year zero?

   _____

   What is the cost of the parking lot at year zero?

   _____

   What is the cost of fixtures, office equipment, and a delivery truck at year zero?

   _____

   What is the total amount of current assets at year zero?

   _____

© 1990 Houghton Mifflin Company. All rights reserved.

What is the total amount of fixed assets at year zero?

_____

What is the amount of other assets at year zero?

_____

What is the estimate for monthly cash expenses?

_____

What is the expected profit margin for Home Furnishings Store, Inc.?

_____

How much of a cushion did the entrepreneur add to her estimates to allow for cash-flow problems and unexpected bills?

_____

What is the total amount this entrepreneur must raise to launch her business?

_____

Entrepreneurs use cost figures to draft a cash budget. Besides the cash budget, entrepreneurs should prepare beginning and ending balance sheets, and an income statement. Most of the figures in these financial statements come from the cash budget.

II. **Equity Capital Versus Debt Capital.** Once entrepreneurs have estimated how much money they need to finance their venture, they then must decide what fraction of this money should come from investors as equity capital and from creditors as debt capital.

The ratio of debt capital to equity capital is a controversial topic. What is the position of commercial bankers on this topic? Why?

_____

_____

_____

_____

How do entrepreneurs feel about this topic? Why?

_____

_____

_____

_____

Entrepreneurs find it generally is safer to finance a new venture with more investors' money than creditors' money. Why?

_____

_____

_____

_____

III. **Sources of Money: Equity Capital.** One of the most puzzling questions for entrepreneurs is where best to raise money. There are a bewildering variety of sources ranging from private to governmental (Exhibit 9.6). We begin by looking at sources of equity capital (investors' money).

    A.   **Venture-Capital Firms.** Most venture-capital firms refuse 80 percent of applicants after less than a day's study. Why?

        _____

        _____

        In your own words, define each of the following venture-capital firms.

        Traditional partnerships _____

        _____

        _____

        _____

© 1990 Houghton Mifflin Company. All rights reserved.   153

Professionally managed pools _____

_____

_____

Investment banking firms _____

_____

_____

Insurance companies _____

_____

_____

_____

A popular misconception about venture-capital firms is that they invest in mom-and-pop shops. They do not (Exhibit 9.7). What types of firms do they invest in?

_____

_____

_____

B. **Small Business Investment Companies.** SBICs are another source of equity capital. When did they originate?

_____

What was the purpose of the Small Business Investment Act?

_____

_____

_____

© 1990 Houghton Mifflin Company. All rights reserved.

C. **Big Business.** Still another source of equity capital is big business. Many of the nation's major corporations have formed departments that seek out promising entrepreneurs to invest in. List two of their motives for investing in small business.

- _____

_____

- _____

_____

D. **Other Sources.** Other sources of equity include entrepreneurs themselves and their friends and relatives.

IV. **Sources of Money: Debt Capital.** Now we turn to ways of raising debt capital. Many entrepreneurs believe that banks regularly lend money to ventures that have yet to earn their first dollar, and that the SBA regularly lends money to unborn ventures. Both beliefs are erroneous. In fact most bankers reject the loan applications of would-be entrepreneurs unless certain conditions are met. What are three of those conditions?

- _____

_____

_____

- _____

_____

_____

- _____

_____

_____

© 1990 Houghton Mifflin Company. All rights reserved.   155

A. **Private Lenders.** There are many private lenders, ranging from commercial banks to storefront finance companies, from insurance companies to relatives. Of these, commercial banks offer entrepreneurs the most help. Besides lending money, what other services do banks offer small-business owners?

_____ \qquad _____

_____ \qquad _____

_____

Commercial bankers are as indispensable to entrepreneurs as lawyers. Entrepreneurs should strike up a working relationship with a banker months before they launch a new venture.

Commercial banks make two major kinds of loans.

1. **Short-Term Loans.** What is a short-term loan?

_____

What are short-term loans used for?

_____

_____

2. **Long-Term Loans.** What is a long-term loan?

_____

What are long-term loans used for?

_____

_____

B. **Supplier Credit.** Entrepreneurs with good credit ratings also can use supplier credit to ease their financing problems.

© 1990 Houghton Mifflin Company. All rights reserved.

C. **Government Lenders.** There are many government lenders, not only at the federal level, but also at state and local levels. Of all these lenders, the SBA offers entrepreneurs the most help. What three criteria must a business meet to qualify for SBA help?

- _____

  _____

  _____

- _____

  _____

- _____

  _____

  _____

In your own words, describe the following SBA loan programs.

1. **Guaranteed Loans** _____

   _____

   _____

   _____

   _____

2. **International Trade Loans** _____

   _____

   _____

   _____

© 1990 Houghton Mifflin Company. All rights reserved.   157

3. **Direct Loans** _____

_____

_____

4. **Displaced Business Loans** _____

_____

_____

_____

5. **Regulatory Compliance Loans** _____

_____

_____

6. **Solar and Other Energy Conservation Loans** _____

_____

_____

_____

7. **Local Development Companies (LDCs)** _____

_____

_____

_____

8. **Women's Business Ownership Loans** _____

_____

_____

_____

© 1990 Houghton Mifflin Company. All rights reserved.

9. **Pollution Control Loans** _____

_____

_____

_____

10. **Handicapped Assistance Loans** _____

_____

_____

V. **Special Programs for Minority Entrepreneurs.** Since the late 1960s, a number of special programs have surfaced to help minority-group members become entrepreneurs. Describe the objectives of these two programs.

A. **Economic Opportunity Loan Program** _____

_____

_____

_____

_____

B. **MESBIC Program** _____

_____

_____

_____

_____

_____

© 1990 Houghton Mifflin Company. All rights reserved.

Questions for Mastery

Questions for mastery are found in the textbook at the beginning of every chapter. Answer each question again to reinforce your understanding of the information.

1. Why is a financial plan necessary?

   _____

   _____

   _____

2. How do you estimate the amount of money needed to launch a new venture?

   _____

   _____

   _____

   _____

3. What is the difference between equity capital and debt capital?

   _____

   _____

   _____

   _____

4. What are the various ways of raising money?

   _____

   _____

   _____

   _____

   _____

   _____

© 1990 Houghton Mifflin Company. All rights reserved.

5. How do federal agencies like the SBA help entrepreneurs finance their ventures?

_____

_____

_____

_____

_____

Definitions of Key Terms

The following key terms are important in this chapter. In your own words, define each concept.

budgeting _____

_____

fixed assets _____

_____

current assets _____

_____

secured loan _____

_____

SBIC _____

_____

MESBIC _____

_____

accounts receivable _____

_____

© 1990 Houghton Mifflin Company. All rights reserved.

supplier credit _____

_____

cash budget _____

_____

equity capital _____

_____

debt capital _____

_____

unsecured loan _____

_____

self-liquidating loan _____

_____

short-term loan _____

_____

long-term loan _____

_____

True-False Questions

Determine whether the following statements are true or false, then circle T or F. Correct answers are listed at the end of the study guide.

T   F   1.   Without money, the entrepreneur's dream may never become a reality.

T   F   2.   For most entrepreneurs, preparing a business plan is unnecessary because they know what they want to do and how to finance their business.

T   F   3.   The centerpiece of the business plan is the income statement.

T   F   4.   Although planning is widely practiced among individuals, government, and big business, entrepreneurs do the best job of planning.

© 1990 Houghton Mifflin Company. All rights reserved.

T F 5. Before they can begin to develop a cash budget, entrepreneurs must first spell out their operating plans.

T F 6. A budget can be no better than the estimates on which it is based.

T F 7. Budgets can account for the effects of intangible qualities and unpredictable events.

T F 8. A forecast of sales revenues should be estimated on a monthly basis for the first year.

T F 9. Fixed assets are resources that benefit the entrepreneur for no more than three years.

T F 10. A building is an example of an intangible asset.

T F 11. Current assets are resources whose benefits last less than a year.

T F 12. Accounts receivable are bills owed by customers who buy on credit.

T F 13. After the cash budget is prepared, an entrepreneur also should prepare beginning and ending balance sheets and an income statement.

T F 14. Entrepreneurs have two sources of financing: debt capital and equity capital.

T F 15. Commercial bankers generally recommend that entrepreneurs and their investors put in at least two dollars for every dollar they borrow.

T F 16. Investors' money bears the first impact of loss.

T F 17. Entrepreneurs find that it is generally safer to finance a new venture with more creditors' money than investors' money.

T F 18. Almost all loans require the borrower to meet a repayment schedule that demands both repayment of the loan and payment of interest.

T F 19. Investors' money involves a definite promise to repay.

T F 20. Investors are guaranteed a return or dividend.

T F 21. On average, venture-capital firms fund just 2 of every 100 loan requests.

T F 22. Venture-capital firms generally drop small-business loan requests because they are not accompanied by a business plan.

T F 23. A popular misconception about venture-capital firms is that they invest in mom-and-pop shops.

© 1990 Houghton Mifflin Company. All rights reserved.   163

T F 24. Venture-capital firms usually invest in firms that promise to grow rapidly.

T F 25. The purpose of the Small Business Investment Act was to encourage private investors to finance entrepreneurs.

T F 26. Some SBICs act like commercial banks, choosing to make loans rather than buy shares of stock.

T F 27. Most venture capital comes from the entrepreneur's own resources or from family and friends.

T F 28. Both commercial banks and the SBA regularly loan money to unborn ventures.

T F 29. It is unnecessary to develop a working relationship with a banker before there is a need to borrow money.

T F 30. Commercial banks prefer to make short-term loans—that is, loans that fall due within one year.

T F 31. Short-term loans generally are used to finance the purchase of equipment.

T F 32. Short-term loans are sometimes called *self-liquidating loans.*

T F 33. Generally, long-term loans are repaid from profits.

T F 34. Supplier credit is a form of long-term debt capital.

T F 35. To qualify for SBA help, businesses must be independently owned and operated, and cannot dominate their fields.

T F 36. Under the SBA's guaranteed loan program, the SBA can guarantee up to 100 percent of the loan amount.

T F 37. Under the direct loan program, loans cannot exceed $500,000.

T F 38. Local development companies (LDCs) are profit or nonprofit corporations founded by local citizens who want to boost their community's economy.

T F 39. Women's business ownership loans guarantee loans of up to $50,000 to women.

T F 40. The most that can be borrowed under the economic opportunity loan program is $200,000.

T F 41. Individuals or companies can form a MESBIC by putting up at least $150,000 of their own money.

© 1990 Houghton Mifflin Company. All rights reserved.

Multiple-Choice Questions

Write the letter of the correct answer in the blank to the left of the question. Correct answers are listed at the end of the study guide.

_____ 1. The cash budget helps the banker answer all of the following questions *except*
   a. How much money do you need?
   b. How will you spend the money?
   c. How soon will you pay us back?
   d. How much profit will you make?

_____ 2. Before entrepreneurs can begin to develop a cash budget, they first must
   a. spell out their operating plans.
   b. determine how much money they can borrow.
   c. calculate the amount of profit they would like.
   d. find an investor willing to finance their business.

_____ 3. Which of the following statements is *true?*
   a. Budgeting is an exact science.
   b. All budgets depend on estimates of what will happen in the future.
   c. A budget is unnecessary if the entrepreneur has enough money.
   d. Budgets aren't really needed if the small business is showing a profit.

_____ 4. All of the following are fixed assets *except*
   a. buildings.
   b. land.
   c. accounts receivable.
   d. trucks.

_____ 5. Assuming a profit margin of 45 percent, the entrepreneur would realize a gross profit of _____ on every $100 worth of sales.
   a. $35
   b. $45
   c. $55
   d. Given the above information, it is impossible to tell.

_____ 6. Which of the following statements is *true?*
   a. Creditors' money involves a definite promise to repay.
   b. Investors must be repaid, but over a long period of time.
   c. Dividends must be paid to stockholders, but repayment is not guaranteed.
   d. None of the above is true.

© 1990 Houghton Mifflin Company. All rights reserved.

_____ 7. A venture-capital firm formed by wealthy families to manage money aggressively by investing in small businesses is called a(n)
    a.   traditional partnership.
    b.   professionally managed pool.
    c.   investment banking firm.
    d.   family cooperative.

_____ 8. Venture-capital firms generally invest in
    a.   low-risk industries.
    b.   low-technology industries where money is needed to innovate.
    c.   idea-rich, high-technology industries.
    d.   other financial firms that lend money to entrepreneurs.

_____ 9. According to Figure 9.7, the largest portion of venture-capital funds were invested in the _____ industry.
    a.   communications
    b.   consumer related
    c.   energy
    d.   genetic engineering

_____10. The best source of funding for entrepreneurs is
    a.   venture-capital firms.
    b.   banks.
    c.   the government.
    d.   themselves and family and friends.

_____11. According to the National Federation of Independent Business, approximately _____ percent of entrepreneurs use personal savings when starting a business from scratch.
    a.   50
    b.   60
    c.   75
    d.   80

_____12. According to the National Federation of Independent Business, approximately _____ percent of entrepreneurs buying an existing business use personal savings.
    a.   37
    b.   50
    c.   67
    d.   84

© 1990 Houghton Mifflin Company. All rights reserved.

___13. Which of the following statements is *false?*
  a. Entrepreneurs are more likely to get loans from a bank if they are willing to put up their personal holdings as security.
  b. A bank may be willing to lend money to a would-be entrepreneur if a wealthy friend agrees to cosign the bank note.
  c. Banks make a practice of lending money to would-be entrepreneurs.
  d. A would-be entrepreneur may find it easier to get a construction loan from a commercial bank than to borrow money to finance the opening of a new store.

___14. Under the SBA guaranteed loan program, the loan amount cannot exceed
  a. $100,000.
  b. $250,000.
  c. $500,000.
  d. $750,000.

Completion Questions

Write your answer in the blanks provided in each question. Correct answers are listed at the end of the study guide.

1. The centerpiece of the business plan is the _____ budget. Without this budget, entrepreneurs have no way of estimating _____ needs. So vital is this budget that few investors or _____ will entertain a request for money without one.

2. Before they can begin to develop a cash budget, entrepreneurs must first spell out their _____ plans, defining their production, marketing, staffing, accounting, and legal goals. There are two limitations of budgeting. First, budgets can be no better than the _____ of what the future holds. Second, budgets cannot account for the effects of _____ qualities or unpredictable events.

3. _____ assets are resources that benefit the entrepreneur for more than one year; _____ assets are resources whose benefits last less than a year.

4. Bankers are in the business of _____ depositors' money, not risking it. Investors are in the business of _____ money. If losses occur, _____ money bears the first impact of loss. The greater the amount of investors' money, then, the greater the likelihood that a bank will recover its loan.

5. Almost all loans require the borrower to meet a _____ schedule that demands not only repayment of the loan but also payment of _____. Failure to meet this twin obligation could force the entrepreneur's venture into _____.

6. _____ money does not involve a definite promise to repay. Nor are investors entitled to a return on their investment—unless, of course, the venture makes a profit and declares a _____.

© 1990 Houghton Mifflin Company. All rights reserved.

7. Venture-capital firms generally invest in ventures that promise to grow _____. They lend to favor idea-rich, high-technology industries like _____ hardware and software.

8. In 1989 there were more than _____ Small Business Investment Companies (SBICs). All SBICs have one thing in common: a willingness to assume _____ for a share of owners' _____. Some SBICs act like commercial banks—choosing to make _____ rather than buy stock—but they are the exception, not the rule.

9. Many of the nation's major corporations have formed departments that seek out promising entrepreneurs to _____ in. Their motives are mixed, ranging from a desire to put their money to work earning more money to a desire to identify candidates for future _____.

10. According to one study, _____ capital is more likely to be raised, not from venture-capital firms, but from entrepreneurs themselves or their _____ and family.

11. Many entrepreneurs believe that banks and the SBA regularly lend money to _____ ventures. This belief is _____.

12. As a rule, commercial banks like to see a _____ turnover of loans. So they tend to make _____-term loans—that is, loans that fall due within _____ year. These loans are called self-_____ loans.

13. Long-term loans help satisfy the entrepreneur's _____ need for money. Long-term loans run for more than one year and generally are repaid from _____.

14. To qualify for SBA help, businesses must (1) be _____ owned and operated and not dominant in their fields, (2) be unable to get _____ financing on reasonable terms, and (3) qualify as _____ according to the SBA's size standards.

15. Any individual or company can form a MESBIC by putting up at least _____ of their own money. After investing most of this sum in minority ventures, the MESBIC can increase its original investment _____ through a combination of federal and private financing. Like SBICs, MESBICs can either buy _____ in minority ventures or lend them money.

Essay Questions

1. What are the advantages and disadvantages of the budgeting process?

2. Once entrepreneurs have estimated how much money they need to finance their venture, they must decide what fraction of this money should come from investors and what fraction should come from creditors. Assume that you are a small-business owner who would like to start a manufacturing business. You need $375,000. How would you obtain financing?

© 1990 Houghton Mifflin Company. All rights reserved.

3. The commercial banker is as indispensable to entrepreneurs as the lawyer. It makes sense, then, for entrepreneurs to strike up a working relationship with a banker months before they launch a venture. How would you develop a working relationship with a banker?

The Difference Between Success and Failure[*]

Small businesses seem to be constantly in need of money for one reason or another. An owner may have enough capital to start and operate the business. But then he or she may require more money to finance increased operations during peak selling seasons, to pay for required pollution-control equipment, to mop up after a flood, or to finance an expansion.

Banks are reluctant to loan money to small businesses because of their high failure rate. Typical reasons bankers cite for turning down small-business loans include (1) no collateral, (2) too much existing debt, (3) unstable sales, (4) too many expenses, and (5) not enough personal investment.

When all else fails, the SBA makes loans available to applicants who meet the following credit requirements:

1. Good character
2. Ability to operate a business successfully
3. Enough money in the business so that, with an SBA loan, the owner can operate the business on a sound financial basis
4. Past earnings record and future prospects that indicate the ability to repay the loan
5. Sufficient funds from personal resources to withstand possible losses

The Guaranteed Loan Program

Most of the SBA's business loans actually are made by private lenders, but repayment is guaranteed in part by the SBA. That is, the SBA may guarantee that it will repay up to 90 percent of the loan if the borrowing firm cannot repay it. Guaranteed loans can be as large as $750,000, and repayment can take up to 25 years. The average size of an SBA-guaranteed business loan is $102,000, and its average duration is about 8 years.

Other Factors to Consider

To apply for SBA loan assistance, a company must:

1. Prepare a current financial statement.
2. Prepare an earnings statement for the previous full year.
3. Prepare a current personal financial statement of the owner or each partner or stockholder owning 20 percent or more of the corporate stock.

---

[*]A portion of this material was adapted from U.S. Small Business Administration, *SBA Business Loans*, (Washington, D.C.: Office of Public Information, March 1978).

© 1990 Houghton Mifflin Company. All rights reserved.   169

4. List collateral to be offered as security for the loan, with an estimate of each item's present market value.
5. State the amount needed and explain the exact purposes for which it will be used.
6. Apply for a bank loan and, if turned down, ask the bank to make the loan under the SBA's Loan Guarantee Plan.
7. If a guaranteed loan is not available, write or visit the nearest SBA office.

The procedure for obtaining a loan to start a business is basically the same except that more importance is placed on projected sales and expenses.

© 1990 Houghton Mifflin Company. All rights reserved.

CHAPTER 10

Organizational Planning

Learning Objectives

After studying this chapter, you should understand

1. Why organizational planning is important

2. How to define skill needs

3. What kinds of help professionals can provide

4. How to build a staff and fulfill skill needs

5. What kinds of help are available from private and government sources

Chapter Review

As you read the chapter, complete the following outline with information from the text.

Major corporations employ hundreds of knowledge workers. In contrast, would-be entrepreneurs generally cannot afford the luxury of expert help. They often have no recourse but to stand alone. How can entrepreneurs fill their needs for skilled but knowledgeable support? Help does exist, often for no fee. To make the most of this help, entrepreneurs should first ask themselves two questions: What skills do I need to launch my venture successfully? And how can I get the help of individuals armed with those skills?

I.   **The Need for Organizational Planning.** In this complex age, few entrepreneurs are equipped with all the business skills they need to survive on their own. Since World War II, simplicity has given way to complexity. No longer can entrepreneurs be their own troubleshooters, lawyers, bookkeepers, financiers, tax experts, and systems analysts.

To survive and grow, entrepreneurs need help and should be able to identify precisely what kinds of help they need. To do so, they must plan their organization before they launch their venture.

© 1990 Houghton Mifflin Company. All rights reserved.

Why is organizational planning circular in nature?

_____

_____

_____

What is the key role of the organizational plan in a small-business venture?

_____

_____

_____

II. **Defining Skill Needs.** An organization is any team of people who work together to meet goals.

Entrepreneurs should define their organization in terms of skills, not individuals. Why should entrepreneurs plan their organizations as if they could afford the skills they need?

_____

_____

_____

Entrepreneurs should set meaningful goals that are measurable. Why are specific goals important?

_____

_____

_____

Why do you think goals should be measurable?

_____

_____

_____

© 1990 Houghton Mifflin Company. All rights reserved.

A good place to begin establishing an organization is with the business plan discussed in Chapter 6. Entrepreneurs must decide which of the fifteen steps they can complete themselves. Then they can choose other professionals (lawyers, accountants) to help them complete the remaining steps in the plan.

Why are bankers a better source of information about professionals than the Chamber of Commerce?

_____

_____

What basis does the Chamber of Commerce use to judge professionals?

_____

III. **Finding the Right Professionals.** In their quest for help, entrepreneurs should seek professionals who work in their industry. This allows entrepreneurs to profit from the professionals' experience with similar problems in other businesses in the industry.

Describe how these five types of professionals help entrepreneurs start a business.

Accountant _____

_____

Lawyer _____

_____

Banker _____

_____

Insurance agent _____

_____

_____

Computer consultant _____

_____

© 1990 Houghton Mifflin Company. All rights reserved.

Describe how these five types of professionals help entrepreneurs on an ongoing basis.

Accountant _____

_____

_____

Banker _____

_____

_____

_____

Lawyer _____

_____

Insurance agent _____

_____

_____

Computer consultant _____

_____

_____

IV. **Building a Staff.** Accountants, lawyers, bankers, insurance agents, and computer consultants provide entrepreneurs with outside professional help. But many entrepreneurs also need inside help. Why is inside help not a problem in some small businesses?

_____

_____

© 1990 Houghton Mifflin Company. All rights reserved.

A. **Job Descriptions.** Once the need for employees becomes apparent, entrepreneurs should prepare an organizational plan complete with job descriptions. What five things should a job description spell out (Exhibit 10.3)?

- _____
- _____
- _____
- _____
- _____

By using job descriptions, what type of "disease" can entrepreneurs avoid?

_____

_____

_____

Job descriptions are one aspect of the organizational plan. Entrepreneurs also should define the personal qualifications needed for above-average performance in each position. Why?

_____

_____

_____

B. **Organizational Charts.** No organizational plan is complete without an organizational chart. What does the organizational chart trace?

_____

_____

© 1990 Houghton Mifflin Company. All rights reserved.

In your own words, define the following terms.

Line-staff organization _____

_____

_____

_____

_____

Line authority _____

_____

_____

_____

Staff authority _____

_____

_____

_____

Line organization _____

_____

_____

Functional organization _____

_____

_____

_____

© 1990 Houghton Mifflin Company. All rights reserved.

In a small business, what problems does the functional organization create?

_____

_____

_____

1. **Switching Organizational Forms.** The line organization is a practical choice for ventures that start small. But once they begin to grow beyond ten employees, entrepreneurs should consider switching to a line-staff form of organization.

    What types of problems does a switch from a line organization to a line-staff organization involve?

    _____

    _____

    _____

    How can entrepreneurs avoid these problems?

    _____

    _____

    _____

    _____

2. **Limitations of Organizational Charts.** Entrepreneurs also should be aware of the limitations of organizational charts. Few businesses run precisely the way their organizational charts indicate. Why?

    _____

    _____

    _____

    How often should organizational charts be updated in a growing business?

    _____

© 1990 Houghton Mifflin Company. All rights reserved.   177

How does preparing an organizational chart help entrepreneurs crystallize their thinking?

_____

_____

_____

_____

C. **Finding the Right Employees.** Many entrepreneurs have difficulty finding and hiring new employees. The problems here often stem from entrepreneurs' failure to look beyond the printed word of their job descriptions. Experience is important, but so are four other characteristics. What are they?

- _____

- _____

- _____

- _____

Why is flexibility so important among first employees?

_____

_____

_____

Why is it important for entrepreneurs to develop a chemistry with new employees?

_____

_____

_____

© 1990 Houghton Mifflin Company. All rights reserved.

Finding employees is by no means easy. Discuss each of the hiring methods listed below.

Newspaper ads _____

_____

_____

_____

Notices on college bulletin boards _____

_____

_____

_____

Employment agencies _____

_____

_____

_____

Word of mouth _____

_____

_____

_____

D.   **Delegation of Authority.** Few entrepreneurs enjoy delegating authority. Why?

_____

_____

At the very least, entrepreneurs should delegate enough authority to get work done, to allow key employees to take initiative, and to keep things going in their absence.

© 1990 Houghton Mifflin Company. All rights reserved.

V. Fulfilling Skill Needs: Boards of Directors. Potentially, boards of directors offer entrepreneurs a wealth of help, especially as problem solvers. Elected by shareholders, the directors are legally responsible for the venture and have full authority. In theory, directors perform three functions. What are they?

- _____

_____

- _____

_____

- _____

_____

A. Myths About Boards of Directors. Studies show that more than 90 percent of all boards fail to perform. What two myths are exploded by Professor Mace's study?

- _____

_____

_____

_____

- _____

_____

_____

© 1990 Houghton Mifflin Company. All rights reserved.

In contrast, how is Ray Peterson, president of Industrial Fabricating Company, using his board of directors?

_____

_____

_____

_____

_____

_____

B. **Finding the Right Board Members.** Of course, some boards do perform well, especially as problem solvers.

What type of people should the entrepreneur choose as board members?

_____

_____

_____

_____

Why should a board of directors be small?

_____

_____

_____

© 1990 Houghton Mifflin Company. All rights reserved.   181

VI. Fulfilling Skill Needs: Management Consultants

A. The Value of Management Consultants. Giving advice to management about management has grown into a $7-billion-a-year industry. Yet opinions vary widely about the worth of management consultants. Why are entrepreneurs unhappy with management consultants?

_____

_____

_____

_____

What are two complaints management consultants make about entrepreneurs?

▪ _____

_____

▪ _____

_____

How can entrepreneurs see to it that they get their money's worth from management consultants?

_____

_____

_____

B. Finding the Right Consultants. How can entrepreneurs check a consultant's credentials? Testimonial letters generally are worthless. Reputations belong only to the big firms whose high fees are beyond the reach of most entrepreneurs. And unlike medicine and law, management consulting is not a profession.

The Association of Consulting Management Engineers (ACME) warns entrepreneurs to watch for four unprofessional practices when choosing a management consultant. What are they?

▪ _____

_____

© 1990 Houghton Mifflin Company. All rights reserved.

  ■ _____

_____

  ■ _____

_____

  ■ _____

_____

What five questions should entrepreneurs ask before deciding on a particular consultant?

  ■ _____

_____

  ■ _____

_____

  ■ _____

_____

  ■ _____

_____

  ■ _____

_____

VII. Fulfilling Skill Needs: The Federal Government. Exhibit 10.8 lists sources of help for entrepreneurs. Heading the list is the SBA. Since it was founded in 1953, the SBA has helped hundreds of thousands of entrepreneurs.

Most entrepreneurs have the mistaken view that all the SBA does is lend money or guarantee repayment of loans made by commercial banks. More important are the SBA's efforts to help entrepreneurs prepare themselves for the job of managing a small business.

A. SBA Management-Counseling Programs. The SBA offers entrepreneurs four major management counseling programs to upgrade their management skills and help them get federal contracts. In your own words, describe each of these programs.

© 1990 Houghton Mifflin Company. All rights reserved.

1. **SCORE Program** _____

_____

_____

_____

_____

_____

2. **ACE Program** _____

_____

_____

_____

_____

_____

3. **SBI Program** _____

_____

_____

_____

_____

_____

4. **SBDC Program** _____

_____

_____

_____

_____

_____

© 1990 Houghton Mifflin Company. All rights reserved.

B. Cooperation Among SBA Programs. These four counseling programs often work jointly in the best interest of the entrepreneur. They also work together to offer certain educational programs. List those programs.

- _____

- _____

- _____

How does the SBA's minority enterprise program operate?

_____

_____

_____

_____

VIII. Fulfilling Skill Needs: Trade Associations. The purpose of trade associations is to help their members survive and grow. They are uniquely qualified to do so because they offer expert help and guidance related directly to their members' industry.

How many trade associations are there in the United States?

_____

Many trade associations offer skilled help in research, finance, labor relations, tax issues, regulations, and marketing. They also offer entrepreneurs expert guidance in six areas. What are those areas?

- _____

- _____

- _____

- _____

- _____

- _____

© 1990 Houghton Mifflin Company. All rights reserved.

Are trade associations worth the cost of membership? (Explain your answer.)

_____

_____

_____

IX. **Small-Business Networks.** Another excellent source of help that now enjoys widespread popularity is networking. How does the process work?

_____

_____

_____

How have women and minority entrepreneurs found networking to be an effective problem-solving tool?

_____

_____

_____

_____

Questions for Mastery

Questions for mastery are found in the textbook at the beginning of every chapter. Answer each question again to reinforce your understanding of the information.

1. Why is organizational planning important?

_____

_____

_____

_____

2. How do you define skill needs?

_____

_____

_____

_____

_____

_____

3. What kinds of help can professionals provide?

_____

_____

_____

_____

_____

4. How do you build a staff and fulfill skill needs?

_____

_____

_____

_____

_____

_____

_____

© 1990 Houghton Mifflin Company. All rights reserved.   187

5. What kinds of help are available from private and government sources?

    _____

    _____

    _____

    _____

    _____

    _____

Definitions of Key Terms

The following key terms are important in this chapter. In your own words, define each concept.

functional organization _____

    _____

line organization _____

    _____

delegation of authority _____

    _____

SCORE _____

    _____

ACE _____

    _____

SBI _____

    _____

SBDC _____

    _____

networking _____

_____

organization _____

_____

job description _____

_____

organizational chart _____

_____

line authority _____

_____

staff authority _____

_____

board of directors _____

_____

ACME _____

_____

True-False Questions

Determine whether the following statements are true or false, then circle T or F. Correct answers are listed at the end of the study guide.

T   F   1. Organizational planning is circular in nature.

T   F   2. Most entrepreneurs are quite good at organizational planning and use it as a planning tool.

T   F   3. An organization is any team of people who work together to meet common goals.

T   F   4. Because of the limited nature of most small businesses, entrepreneurs usually can afford to purchase the skills they need.

© 1990 Houghton Mifflin Company. All rights reserved.   189

T   F   5. Entrepreneurs should define their organization in terms of skills, not individuals.

T   F   6. All the small-business owner's goals should be precise and measurable.

T   F   7. When choosing professionals to help start a business, the best source of information about them is the Better Business Bureau.

T   F   8. Accountants, lawyers, bankers, insurance agents, and computer consultants provide entrepreneurs with outside professional help.

T   F   9. Owners of small businesses have no need for job descriptions because they know what everyone is supposed to do.

T   F   10. Job descriptions should spell out who does what, who has what authority, and who reports to whom.

T   F   11. Job descriptions save entrepreneurs from organizational muddle.

T   F   12. Typically, entrepreneurs allow their organizations to evolve naturally, with everybody reporting to them or with some employees reporting to two or more bosses.

T   F   13. Entrepreneurs should define the personal qualifications needed for average performance in each worker's position.

T   F   14. No organizational plan is complete without an organizational chart.

T   F   15. Line positions give the people in them the right to lead those under them on the organizational chart.

T   F   16. The power of staff positions usually stems from the right to hire and fire employees.

T   F   17. Staff authority is the power of knowledge that one person has over another.

T   F   18. Line positions are charged with getting out the product and with closing the sale.

T   F   19. The line organization is common in ventures with fewer than ten employees.

T   F   20. The functional organization is probably the most practical type of organization for most small businesses.

T   F   21. Veteran jobholders in a small business tend to treat workers in newly created staff positions as intruders.

T   F   22. An entrepreneur should draft job descriptions only as the business begins to grow and it becomes apparent that there is a need for a new employee.

© 1990 Houghton Mifflin Company. All rights reserved.

T F 23. Few ventures run precisely the way their organizational charts indicate.

T F 24. To be effective, an organizational chart must communicate.

T F 25. The board of directors is appointed by the corporation's president.

T F 26. In theory, the board of directors sets policy on paying dividends.

T F 27. If a venture is a sole proprietorship or a partnership, entrepreneurs do not have to form a board.

T F 28. Studies show that more than 90 percent of all boards fail to perform.

T F 29. A myth exploded by Professor Mace's study is that board members set goals and ask wise, probing questions.

T F 30. Entrepreneurs should choose corporate boards that have between 10 and 15 members.

T F 31. In working with a management consultant, the first thing entrepreneurs should do is figure out what they want to know.

T F 32. The best way to check a consultant's credentials is to ask for testimonial letters.

T F 33. ACME stands for the Association of Consulting Management Engineers.

T F 34. All members of the SCORE program are retired executives who enjoyed successful careers in small or big businesses.

T F 35. Counselors in the ACE program are paid a nominal fee.

T F 36. The SBI program draws on talents available at colleges and universities.

T F 37. SBDCs are designed to draw together all the various disciplines—including technical and professional schools—of a university and make their knowledge available to small businesses.

T F 38. The primary goal of the SBA's minority enterprise program is to provide financing for minority entrepreneurs.

T F 39. The purpose of trade associations is to help their members survive and grow by providing expert help and guidance related directly to their members' industry.

T F 40. *Broadcasting* is a term that describes entrepreneurs getting together regularly to discuss mutual problems and opportunities.

© 1990 Houghton Mifflin Company. All rights reserved.   191

Multiple-Choice Questions

Write the letter of the correct answer in the blank to the left of the question. Correct answers are listed at the end of the study guide.

_____ 1. The small-business owner should define his or her organization in terms of
   a. skills.
   b. financial resources.
   c. people.
   d. profits.

_____ 2. The best source of information about the professionals an entrepreneur needs to start a business is the
   a. Better Business Bureau.
   b. National Federation of Independent Businesses.
   c. Chamber of Commerce.
   d. commercial banker.

_____ 3. Before opening a business, entrepreneurs need
   a. an accountant to prepare monthly income statements.
   b. a lawyer to advise on legal matters.
   c. a banker to help finance expansion.
   d. all of the above.

_____ 4. Accountants, lawyers, bankers, insurance agents, and computer consultants
   a. are sources of inside help.
   b. are necessary during the planning stage of a business, but are not needed once the business is in operation.
   c. should give entrepreneurs help on a continuing basis.
   d. are too expensive for the typical small-business owner to use as a source of outside help.

_____ 5. A job description spells out
   a. who does what.
   b. who has what authority.
   c. who reports to whom.
   d. all of the above.

_____ 6. The authority that gives people the right to lead because they have the power to hire and fire is called _____ authority.
   a. line
   b. staff
   c. attitudinal
   d. limited

© 1990 Houghton Mifflin Company. All rights reserved.

_____ 7. People in _____ positions have the power of knowledge.
   a.   line
   b.   staff
   c.   attitudinal
   d.   limited

_____ 8. In the line organization,
   a.   everyone has a staff function.
   b.   every jobholder reports to a single boss.
   c.   a jobholder may report to two or more bosses.
   d.   staff and line functions are divided equally among workers.

_____ 9. Which of the following statements is *true?*
   a.   Today, finding employees is an easy task for entrepreneurs.
   b.   For most entrepreneurs, there is one best hiring method.
   c.   Advertisements in local newspapers force entrepreneurs to screen all applicants.
   d.   Generally, employment agencies do not charge small-business owners the full fee for finding employees.

_____10. In theory, board members have the power to
   a.   choose the president and other officers of the venture.
   b.   delegate power to run the day-to-day affairs of the venture.
   c.   set policy on paying dividends, on financing major spending, and on executive pay.
   d.   do all of the above.

_____11. Studies show that _____ percent of all boards fail to perform.
   a.   50
   b.   70
   c.   85
   d.   90

_____12. Which of the following statements is *true?*
   a.   Management consultants are decreasing in number because of the cost of using them.
   b.   Entrepreneurs can make better use of management consultants by focusing on what they need to know.
   c.   In most cases, management consultants simply solve problems by putting their expert knowledge to practical use.
   d.   All of the above are true.

_____13. The _____ program consists of retired volunteers who have been successful in either small or large businesses.
   a.   ACE
   b.   SCORE
   c.   SBI
   d.   SBDC

© 1990 Houghton Mifflin Company. All rights reserved.

_____14. Which of the following statements is *true?*
    a. There are more than 4,500 trade associations in this country today.
    b. Trade associations are designed to provide fellowship to the people in a particular industry.
    c. The costs of belonging to a trade association are reasonable.
    d. Trade associations are of no practical value because they meet on average, just once a month.

Completion Questions

Write your answer in the blanks provided in each question. Correct answers are listed at the end of the study guide.

1. Organizational planning is _____ in nature. Despite the need for it, organizational planning is ignored by many _____. They fail to see how _____ it really is.

2. An _____ is any team of people who work together to meet common goals. Entrepreneurs should define their organization in terms of _____, not of individuals. There is a catch, though. Usually they cannot afford to hire all the full-time personnel they need. Even so, entrepreneurs should plan their organization as if they _____ afford them.

3. Before starting a business, entrepreneurs generally need the following kinds of professional help: (1) an _____ to set up the books, (2) a _____ to advise on legal matters, (3) a _____ to advise on financial matters, (4) an _____ agent to make sure the venture is protected, and (5) a _____ consultant to advise on computer uses.

4. A job _____ should spell out who does what, who has what authority, and who reports to whom. Job descriptions help entrepreneurs avoid _____ muddle.

5. In addition to job descriptions, entrepreneurs should define the _____ qualifications needed for _____-average performance in each position.

6. No organizational plan is complete without an organizational _____. This kind of chart traces lines of _____ and authority between jobs.

7. In a line-staff organization, each jobholder reports to a _____ boss. Line positions give the people in them the right to lead those under them because they have the power to _____ and fire. People in staff positions exercise their expert _____ to help line managers solve marketing and production problems.

8. In the _____ organization, every jobholder reports to a single boss; no one has a _____ function. In the _____ organization, a jobholder may report to two or more bosses.

© 1990 Houghton Mifflin Company. All rights reserved.

9. Few ventures run precisely the way their _____ charts indicate. In a growing venture, organizational charts soon become dated. For this reason, wise entrepreneurs update their organizational charts at least _____ a year.

10. _____ by shareholders, the directors are _____ responsible for the venture and have full authority.

11. In theory, directors (1) choose the _____ and other officers of the venture, (2) _____ power to run the day-to-day affairs of the venture, and (3) set policy on paying _____, on financing major spending, and on executive pay.

12. One myth about boards of directors is that their members select the _____. Another is that board members set _____ and ask wise, probing questions.

13. According to ACME, when choosing a consultant, entrepreneurs should watch for the following unprofessional practices: (1) high-pressure _____ that promises quick, sure results; (2) _____ surveys offered cold at a fixed fee; (3) requests for _____ in advance; and (4) offers to consult at a _____ fee until results are shown.

14. Since it was founded in _____, the SBA has helped hundreds of thousands of entrepreneurs. The SBA offers four major management-counseling programs: (1) the _____ program, (2) the _____ program, (3) the _____ program, and (4) the _____ program.

15. There are more than _____ trade associations in this country. They offer expert help in such wide-ranging subjects as research, finance, labor relations, taxes, government regulations, and marketing. Generally, membership dues are a _____ of 1 percent of the venture's yearly sales revenues.

16. _____ is a term that applies to entrepreneurs getting together regularly to discuss mutual problems and opportunities. In particular, women and minority entrepreneurs have found networking to be an _____ problem-solving tool.

Essay Questions

1. In their quest for help, entrepreneurs should look for professionals who can provide the advice needed to open a small-business venture. What type of professional help do would-be entrepreneurs need? Where can entrepreneurs get information about professionals who may be able to give them that help?

2. Line authority is the power of authority that one person has over another. Staff authority is the power of knowledge that one person has over another. What are some of the problems that can develop when an entrepreneur switches from a line organization to a line-staff organization? How can the entrepreneur avoid these problems?

© 1990 Houghton Mifflin Company. All rights reserved.

3. Testimonial letters about management consultants generally are worthless. Reputations belong only to the big firms, whose high fees are beyond the reach of most entrepreneurs. And unlike medicine and law, management consulting is not a profession. How can entrepreneurs check a consultant's credentials?

The Difference Between Success and Failure

One of the hardest things for a small-business owner to do is to delegate. *Delegation* is the assigning of part of a small-business owner's work and power to a subordinate. No owner can do everything alone, so delegation is vital to the completion of the owner's work. Delegation also is important in developing the skills and abilities of subordinates. It allows those who are being groomed for higher-level positions to play increasingly important roles in decision making.

Steps in Delegation

Three steps generally are involved in the delegation process. First, the small-business owner must *assign responsibility*. *Responsibility* is the duty to do or perform a task. Along with assigning responsibility the owner must *grant authority*. *Authority* is the power, within the organization, to accomplish an assigned job or task. This might include the power to obtain specific information, order supplies, authorize relevant expenditures, and make certain decisions. Finally, the owner must *create accountability*. *Accountability* is the obligation of a subordinate to accomplish an assigned job or task.

Notice that accountability is created, not delegated. Suppose you are responsible for performing a job. You, in turn, delegate part of the work to a subordinate. You still remain accountable to the owner for getting the job done properly. If your subordinate fails to complete the assignment, you—not the subordinate—will have to account for what has become "your" failure.

Barriers to Delegation

There are several reasons why small-business owners may be unwilling to delegate work. One is that the person who delegates remains accountable for the work. Many small-business owners are reluctant to delegate simply because they want to be sure that the work gets done properly. In other words, they just don't trust their subordinates. Another reason for reluctance to delegate stems from the opposite situation. Some small-business owners are afraid that a subordinate can do the work better than they can. Finally, some owners don't delegate because they are so disorganized that they simply can't plan and assign work in an effective way.

© 1990 Houghton Mifflin Company. All rights reserved.

PART III

MANAGING THE ONGOING VENTURE

CHAPTER 11

Accounting

Learning Objectives

After studying this chapter, you should understand

1. What the uses of accounting are

2. What a good accounting system should do

3. How income statements and balance sheets differ

4. What the limitations of accounting are

5. What the importance of cash flow is

Chapter Review

As you read the chapter, complete the following outline with information from the text.

I. **The Uses of Accounting.** Although it is the accountant who designs the entrepreneur's accounting system, it is the entrepreneur who needs the information supplied by that system to plan and control the venture. Who else uses the information supplied by an accounting system (Exhibit 11.1)?

- _____

- _____

- _____

What problems do entrepreneurs tend to blame their failures on?

- _____

- _____

- _____

- _____

- _____

A well-designed accounting system can help entrepreneurs spot these problems early and head them off.

It is not enough for an accounting system to be well designed and carefully run. The entrepreneur must take action based on the information generated by the system. Otherwise the system is useless.

A. **Elements of a Good Accounting System.** An accounting system is more than journals and ledgers and worksheets. What should a good accounting system do?

- _____

_____

_____

- _____

_____

- _____

_____

- _____

_____

- _____

_____

There is no such thing as one best accounting system for all businesses, big or small. Any system can work as long as it performs the functions listed above.

As a general rule, the bigger the venture, the more complex the accounting system.

B. **The Need for an Accountant.** No matter how simple their venture, entrepreneurs should call in an accountant to help design an accounting system. Designing a good system, especially as a venture begins to grow, takes professional skill.

© 1990 Houghton Mifflin Company. All rights reserved.

Today no entrepreneur should launch a venture without an accountant's help. The services accountants perform are vital. Their role should not be passive. Accountants can do much more than prepare tax returns. List six of their more creative functions.

- _____

_____

- _____

_____

- _____

_____

- _____

_____

_____

- _____

_____

- _____

_____

Entrepreneurs should find the right accountant months before they plan to launch a venture. List three guidelines entrepreneurs should use in choosing an accountant.

- _____

_____

- _____

_____

- _____

_____

© 1990 Houghton Mifflin Company. All rights reserved.

The CPA designation means that the accountant is a college graduate who has passed a qualifying state test. Only a CPA can certify—or *legally* guarantee—the truth of financial statements.

C. **Accounting for a Purpose.** Accounting is not an end in itself. It should never be done for its own sake. What are four objectives of accounting?

- _____

- _____

- _____

- _____

An accounting system should help entrepreneurs answer two questions: Is my venture earning a profit? And what is my venture worth?

D. **Kinds of Accounting Systems.** Entrepreneurs can choose two kinds of accounting systems. Describe them.

Cash system _____

_____

_____

Accrual system _____

_____

_____

Which system is the better accounting system for a small business? (Explain your answer.)

_____

_____

_____

_____

© 1990 Houghton Mifflin Company. All rights reserved.

II. Financial Statements: The Income Statement

A. **A Summary of Operating Performance.** The income statement tells entrepreneurs how well they are doing, whether they have earned a profit or not. How often should entrepreneurs prepare an income statement?

_____

In an income statement, profits are what remain after operating expenses have been deducted from sales revenues. Profits are the net effect of two opposing flows of money. What are those flows?

- _____

_____

_____

- _____

_____

_____

How does an income statement for a retailing, wholesaling, or manufacturing business differ from an income statement for a service business?

_____

_____

How does the financial flow of revenues differ for a business that sells a product compared to a business that sells a service (Exhibit 11.3)?

_____

_____

_____

_____

B. **The Income Statement as an Instrument of Control.** In all businesses, control is simply a means by which entrepreneurs can check their progress against their goals.

The process traces the entire cycle of planning and control. Entrepreneurs begin the year by translating their operating plans into dollars (budget); they end the year by measuring their actual performance (income statement), then comparing it with budgeted performance. These comparisons signal potential problems.

III. Financial Statements: The Balance Sheet

A. **A Summary of Financial Health.** The income statement summarizes how well a venture has done over time; the balance sheet summarizes its financial health at one point in time.

What types of information should the balance sheet tell entrepreneurs?

- _____

_____

- _____

_____

- _____

_____

- _____

_____

Read the Corrales Mens's Shoes example in Chapter 11 of the text, then answer the following questions.

How much money did Corrales deposit in the bank to start his shoe business?

_____

How much money did he borrow from the bank?

_____

How many pairs of shoes did Corrales buy from a supplier on February 3?

_____

How many pairs of shoes did he sell on February 4?

_____

© 1990 Houghton Mifflin Company. All rights reserved.

How did sales on February 4 affect the store's balance sheet?

_____

_____

How are the store's income statement and balance sheet related?

_____

_____

_____

_____

Although the balance sheet tells Corrales that his worth is $20,000, this is true only on paper. He cannot know the true worth of the venture until he tries to sell out. The store could be worth more or less than $20,000, depending on what a prospective buyer is willing to pay for it.

B. **Relationship Between Assets and Equities.** Accountants generally define a balance sheet as a statement that lists liabilities and owners' equities on one side and assets on the other. What do the right- and left-hand sides of the balance sheet describe?

Right-hand (equities) side _____

_____

Left-hand (assets) side _____

_____

Assets and equities always balance because all assets of a venture must be claimed by someone—either investors or creditors. And because the dollar amount of these claims cannot exceed the total dollar amount of assets to be claimed, it always follows that

$$Assets = equities$$

IV. Financial Statements: The Cash Budget

A. **Measurement of Cash Flow.** The income statement and balance sheet are important, but they fall short in one vital respect: They tell little about cash flow, the lifeblood of any venture.

© 1990 Houghton Mifflin Company. All rights reserved.

Many entrepreneurs assume that if their business is earning a profit it must be financially sound. Why isn't this true?

_____

_____

_____

How can entrepreneurs avoid cash-flow problems?

_____

_____

_____

Many entrepreneurs experience cash-flow problems because the sales dollar does not necessarily return when the entrepreneurs need it. In accounting terms, what is this time lag called?

_____

B. **The Heart of the Cash-Flow Problem.** Accounts receivable and inventory are at the heart of the cash-flow problem. To offset them, entrepreneurs use accounts payable. What part do accounts payable play in solving the cash-flow problem?

_____

_____

_____

Depreciation is another item that complicates the cash-flow problem. Many entrepreneurs believe that depreciation is a source of cash. Why are they mistaken?

_____

_____

_____

_____

© 1990 Houghton Mifflin Company. All rights reserved.

Many entrepreneurs run their ventures without a cash budget—a vital managerial tool. According to the SBA, how does cash budgeting help entrepreneurs solve cash-flow problems?

_____

_____

_____

_____

_____

_____

V. **The Limitations of Accounting.** Accounting does not measure what a venture is worth, and it has other limitations as well.

A common belief is that accounting figures are exact. They are not. Why?

_____

_____

_____

_____

_____

_____

Still another limitation is that assets are recorded at the price the entrepreneur paid for them—that is, at cost. This cost stays on the books even though the value of an asset may increase.

Yet another limitation is that the balance sheet reflects dollars of differing purchasing power, unadjusted for price inflation.

© 1990 Houghton Mifflin Company. All rights reserved.

Also accounting is limited to recording only those facts that can be expressed in dollars (for example, a $10,000 purchase of inventory or the receipt of a $1,000 bill from a lawyer). These are objective, verifiable facts. But accounting cannot put a dollar value on intangibles. List two intangibles that accounting cannot measure.

- _____

- _____

Despite its limitations, accounting does enable entrepreneurs to compress many complex events into a handful of financial statements: the income statement, the balance sheet, and the cash budget.

Questions for Mastery

Questions for mastery are found in the textbook at the beginning of every chapter. Answer each question again to reinforce your understanding of the information.

1. What are the uses of accounting?

_____

_____

_____

_____

_____

2. What should a good accounting system do?

_____

_____

_____

_____

_____

3. How do income statements and balance sheets differ?

_____

_____

_____

_____

_____

4. What are the limitations of accounting?

_____

_____

_____

_____

_____

_____

5. What is the importance of cash flow?

_____

_____

_____

_____

Definitions of Key Terms

The following key terms are important in this chapter. In your own words, define each concept.

balance sheet _____

_____

© 1990 Houghton Mifflin Company. All rights reserved.

accounting system _____

_____

income statement _____

_____

profit _____

_____

control _____

_____

accounts receivable _____

_____

accounts payable _____

_____

sales revenues _____

_____

operating expenses _____

_____

cost of goods sold _____

_____

cash system of accounting _____

_____

accrual system of accounting _____

_____

certified public accountant (CPA) _____

_____

© 1990 Houghton Mifflin Company. All rights reserved.

cash budget _____

_____

depreciation _____

_____

True-False Questions

Determine whether the following statements are true or false, then circle T or F. Correct answers are listed at the end of the study guide.

T   F   1.   Entrepreneurs are accountable for the performance and health of their venture.

T   F   2.   A well-designed accounting system helps entrepreneurs spot problems early and head them off.

T   F   3.   A well-designed accounting system should enable the entrepreneur to generate reports, tax returns, and financial statements quickly.

T   F   4.   A well-designed accounting system should collect and process information regardless of the cost involved.

T   F   5.   For most small businesses, there is a standardized accounting system that is available from most CPAs.

T   F   6.   As a general rule, the bigger the venture, the more complex the accounting system.

T   F   7.   If a business is small, there is no need to call in an accountant to design its accounting system.

T   F   8.   Most entrepreneurs view the accountant's role as an active one.

T   F   9.   The best way to choose an accountant is on the recommendation of friends and relatives.

T   F   10.   CPA stands for certified professional accountant.

T   F   11.   Only a CPA can legally guarantee the truth of financial statements.

T   F   12.   Accounting is an end in itself.

T   F   13.   There are two kinds of accounting systems: cash and accrual.

© 1990 Houghton Mifflin Company. All rights reserved.   211

T F 14. An income statement tells entrepreneurs whether they have earned a profit or not.

T F 15. Entrepreneurs should prepare an income statement at least every six months.

T F 16. Profits are what remain after operating expenses have been deducted from sales revenues.

T F 17. For a service business, the income statement should include an item called *cost of goods sold.*

T F 18. Control is a means by which entrepreneurs check their progress against their goals.

T F 19. To control operations in a small business, entrepreneurs should compare actual performance with budgeted performance.

T F 20. The balance sheet summarizes the financial health of a business at one point in time.

T F 21. The balance sheet shows entrepreneurs the sales revenue for a specific time period.

T F 22. The retained earnings account appears on the asset side of the balance sheet.

T F 23. The balance sheet describes the true worth of a business.

T F 24. The right-hand side of the balance sheet tells how entrepreneurs financed their venture.

T F 25. The left-hand side of the balance sheet tells how entrepreneurs have invested the funds entrusted to their care.

T F 26. One definition of a balance sheet would be assets = liabilities + owners' equity.

T F 27. The statement that measures the cash flow of a business is called the *statement of financial condition.*

T F 28. When it comes to paying bills, profits are not the same thing as cash in the bank.

T F 29. One way to avoid cash-flow problems is for entrepreneurs to construct a cash budget.

T F 30. In accounting terms, the lag time between the time a customer buys merchandise on credit and pays for it is called *accounts payable.*

T F 31. For most entrepreneurs, depreciation is a source of cash.

© 1990 Houghton Mifflin Company. All rights reserved.

T   F   32. Assets are recorded at the price the entrepreneur paid for them—that is, at cost.

T   F   33. Because the balance sheet is up to date, all figures in it reflect current purchasing power.

T   F   34. Accounting is limited to those facts that can be expressed in dollars.

T   F   35. Accounting cannot measure the intangible factors in a business.

Multiple-Choice Questions

Write the letter of the correct answer in the blank to the left of the question. Correct answers are listed at the end of the study guide.

_____ 1. Lenders use accounting information to
    a. plan and control.
    b. motivate employees.
    c. evaluate creditworthiness.
    d. approve new stock issues.

_____ 2. Entrepreneurs often blame their failures on
    a. low sales revenues.
    b. wrong mix of inventory.
    c. high operating expenses.
    d. all of the above.

_____ 3. Which of the following statements is _true?_
    a. The only accounting system a small business needs is a checkbook.
    b. An accounting system should collect and process information whatever the cost.
    c. In small businesses, entrepreneurs should develop their own accounting system.
    d. The bigger the venture, the more complex the accounting system.

_____ 4. All of the following are good sources of information for an entrepreneur who is in the process of choosing an accountant _except_
    a. other entrepreneurs who are successful.
    b. a banker.
    c. a lawyer.
    d. friends and relatives.

_____ 5. The _____ answers the question: How profitable is the firm?
    a. income statement
    b. balance sheet
    c. statement of financial position
    d. cash budget

© 1990 Houghton Mifflin Company. All rights reserved.

____ 6. Entrepreneurs should prepare an income statement at least
   a. every two weeks.
   b. every three months, if not once a month.
   c. every six months, if not once every quarter.
   d. once a year.

____ 7. A definition of an income statement for a wholesaling business is
   a. Sales revenues - operating expenses = profit or loss.
   b. Sales revenues - cost of goods sold - operating expenses = profit or loss.
   c. Assets = liabilities + owners' equity.
   d. none of the above.

____ 8. Which of the following statements is *true?*
   a. Profits are the net effect of two opposing flows of money.
   b. In a small business, profits are automatic.
   c. Profits are the difference between assets and liabilities.
   d. Profits are indicated on the cash budget.

____ 9. The balance sheet summarizes the financial health of a business
   a. over a period of six months.
   b. on April 15, when tax reports are due.
   c. at one point in time.
   d. over a year.

____10. The income statement gives the detail behind the changes that have taken place within the _____ category of the balance sheet.
   a. current assets
   b. current liabilities
   c. retained earnings
   d. fixed assets

____11. Which of the following statements is *true?*
   a. Assets + liabilities = owners' equity
   b. Assets = liabilities + owners' equity
   c. Owners' equity + assets = liabilities
   d. Assets + expenses - liabilities = owners' equity

____12. Another term for the balance sheet is
   a. statement of economic return.
   b. statement of profit and assets.
   c. statement of financial condition.
   d. retained earnings.

© 1990 Houghton Mifflin Company. All rights reserved.

13. The financial statement that measures a firm's cash on hand is called a(n)
    a. statement of owners' equity.
    b. income statement.
    c. statement of liabilities.
    d. cash budget.

14. In accounting terms, the amount the entrepreneur owes suppliers but does not have to pay today is called
    a. accounts receivable for the entrepreneur.
    b. accounts payable for the entrepreneur.
    c. profit for the entrepreneur.
    d. an offsetting liability.

15. Which of the following statements is *false?*
    a. A common belief is that accounting figures are precise and exact.
    b. Accounting cannot put a dollar value on teamwork.
    c. Assets are recorded at the price the entrepreneur paid for them.
    d. The balance sheet reports the value of all assets in current purchasing power.

Completion Questions

Write your answer in the blanks provided in each question. Correct answers are listed at the end of the study guide.

1. Although it is the _____ who designs the entrepreneur's accounting system, it is the entrepreneur who needs the _____ supplied by the system in order to plan and control the venture.

2. An accounting system should allow for ready _____ of current financial performance with past performance or budgeted goals. It should generate reports, tax returns, and _____ statements quickly. It also should ensure a high degree of accuracy and completeness. It should collect and process information at _____ cost. And, the system should _____ the incidence of theft and fraud.

3. Entrepreneurs should look for and obtain the right accountant before they plan to launch a venture. In their search for an accountant, entrepreneurs should use these guidelines: (1) Get the names of experienced, reputable accountants from other _____; (2) narrow the list to those who work mostly with _____ businesses; and (3) choose a _____ public accountant.

4. The income statement tells entrepreneurs how well they are doing, whether they have earned a _____ or not. Entrepreneurs should prepare an income statement at least every _____ months, if not every month.

5. Profits are what remain after _____ expenses have been deducted from _____ revenues. Profits are the net effect of _____ opposing flows of money.

6. For those industry groups that sell a product—retailing, wholesaling, and manufacturing—the income statement should include an item called the *cost of* _____ *sold.* For retailers, the cost of goods sold generally represents what they paid wholesalers for the products they sold to _____.

7. In all businesses, _____ is simply a means by which entrepreneurs can check their progress against their _____.

8. The balance sheet summarizes the firm's financial health at _____ point in time. The balance sheet tells entrepreneurs (1) what their venture is worth, at least on paper; (2) what they have invested in such _____ as inventories, land, and equipment; (3) how these assets were _____; and (4) who has what claims against these assets.

9. The _____-hand side of the balance sheet tells how entrepreneurs have financed their venture; the _____-hand side of the balance sheet tells how entrepreneurs invested the funds entrusted to their care.

10. Balance sheets also are called _____ *statements* or *statements of financial* _____.

11. The cash budget measures _____ flow in a business. A cash-flow problem can be traced to accounts _____ and inventory. What really matters in a cash budget is not the volume of _____ at any given time but how soon the entrepreneur gets _____ for products sold.

Essay Questions

1. Often entrepreneurs view the accountant's role as a passive one. Yet accountants can do much more than prepare tax returns. What are some of the more creative activities accountants can help entrepreneurs with?

2. Profits are the net effect of two opposing flows of money. Explain and describe the two flows of money for a typical small business.

3. Explain how entrepreneurs can use an income statement, a balance sheet, and a cash budget to help manage a small business.

The Difference Between Success and Failure

In the typical accounting system, raw data are transformed into financial statements in five steps:

1. Analyzing source documents
2. Journalizing transactions
3. Posting transactions

© 1990 Houghton Mifflin Company. All rights reserved.

4.   Preparing the trial balance
5.   Preparing financial statements

The first three—analyzing, journalizing, and posting—are performed on a continual basis throughout the accounting period. The last two—preparing the trial balance and the financial statements—are performed at the end of the accounting period.

1. *Analyzing source documents.* The basic accounting data are contained in source documents: the receipts, invoices, sales slips, and other documents that show the dollar values of day-to-day business transactions. The accounting cycle begins with the analysis of each of these documents. The purpose of the analysis is to determine which accounts are affected by the documents and how they are affected.

Each transaction results in two or more debits and credits. A *debit* is an increase in an asset account or a decrease in a liability or owners' equity account. A *credit* is a decrease in an asset account or an increase in a liability or owners' equity account. The terms *debit* and *credit* do not mean anything negative or positive. *Debit* simply means "left," and *credit* means "right." The terms tell the bookkeeper which of two columns (left or right) to place entries in when journalizing transactions.

2. *Journalizing transactions.* Every financial transaction is recorded in a journal—a process that is called *journalizing*. The *general journal* is a book of original entry in which all transactions are recorded in order of their occurrence.

An accounting system also can include specialized journals for specific types of transactions that occur frequently. For example, a retail store might have cash receipts, cash disbursements, purchases, and sales journals in addition to its general journal.

3. *Posting transactions.* Next the information entered in the general journal is transferred to the general ledger. The *general ledger* is a book of accounts that contains a separate sheet or section for each account. The process of transferring journal entries to the general ledger is called *posting*. All accounts needed by the firm are combined and stored in a ledger book. Some firms use a loose-leaf notebook to store individual ledger account sheets.

4. *Preparing the trial balance.* A *trial balance* is a summary of the balances of all ledger accounts at the end of the accounting period. To prepare a trial balance, the accountant

(1)   determines and lists the balances for all ledger accounts.
(2)   totals all debit balances.
(3)   totals all credit balances.
(4)   compares the total of the debit balances with the total of the credit balances.

If the totals in the fourth step are equal, the accountant can proceed to the financial statements. If not, there is a mistake somewhere that must be found and corrected before the accountant can proceed.

© 1990 Houghton Mifflin Company. All rights reserved.

5. *Preparing financial statements.* The firm's financial statements are prepared from the information contained in the trial balance. This information is presented in a standardized format in order to make the statements generally accessible to those who have to use them.

Once these statements have been prepared and checked, the firm's books are closed for the accounting period, and a new accounting cycle begins.

© 1990 Houghton Mifflin Company. All rights reserved.

CHAPTER 12

Planning and Control

Learning Objectives

After studying this chapter, you should understand

1. What the problems of growth are

2. Why it is critical to set goals

3. How you set goals

4. How planning and control interact

5. What management by objectives, budgets, and profitgraphs are

Chapter Review

As you read the chapter, complete the following outline with information from the text.

Entrepreneurs are thinkers when they think through the steps of their business plan; they are doers when they carry out those steps. The two processes, thinking and doing, are actually parts of one inseparable process. Why is the process of planning and control a circular one?

_____

_____

_____

I.   **Problems of Growth.** Almost all entrepreneurs want their ventures to grow. Often, though, growth is haphazard because entrepreneurs forget the lessons they learned before launching their ventures—namely that planning and control help keep a venture on track.

Why do entrepreneurs tend to neglect planning and control after a venture is started?

_____

_____

_____

© 1990 Houghton Mifflin Company. All rights reserved.

Chapter 12

A. **Four Stages of Growth.** Many ventures follow the pattern of growth shown in Exhibit 12.1. Generally, however, entrepreneurs fail to handle the later stages of growth as well as they do the earlier stages.

In your own words, define each of the stages of growth.

Prebirth _____

_____

_____

Acceptance _____

_____

_____

Breakthrough _____

_____

_____

Maturity _____

_____

_____

In the breakthrough stage, the rate of growth is so fast that entrepreneurs often cannot keep up with it. Caught unprepared, many blunder. Sales revenues continue to spiral upward as problems begin to surface that cry out for attention. How does each of the items below cause problems for entrepreneurs in the breakthrough stage?

Cash flow _____

_____

Production _____

_____

_____

© 1990 Houghton Mifflin Company. All rights reserved.

Quality _____

_____

_____

Delivery _____

_____

Why does the cycle begin to repeat itself as the venture passes through the maturity stage?

_____

_____

_____

At the same time, competition may become more severe. In the face of all these pressures, entrepreneurs often react rather than respond. They apply inadequate solutions to problems. How did David Allen of Tallgrass Technologies Corporation avoid the problems of growth?

_____

_____

_____

_____

B. **Entrepreneurs as Managers.** Some entrepreneurs tend to be good at creating and nursing a venture through infancy but not so good at carrying its growth through maturity. Why do some businesses succeed while others fail? One answer may be that all the qualities that enable entrepreneurs to succeed during the venture's infancy may not be helpful at the breakthrough stage. This is where managerial skills are important. How can entrepreneurs work at being managers?

    ▪ _____

    _____

    _____

© 1990 Houghton Mifflin Company. All rights reserved.   221

• _____

_____

• _____

_____

Why should entrepreneurs not give up their entrepreneurial bent?

_____

_____

C. **Fast-Growing Ventures.** One study points out that as ventures grow, the number of decisions and activities outstrips the time available for entrepreneurs to handle them. As a result, entrepreneurs must rely increasingly on other people to perform major functions.

II. **Setting Goals.** To help keep their venture alive and well, entrepreneurs should set goals just as they did before launching the venture. Why is the act of setting goals especially important when a venture begins to grow?

_____

_____

Why do you think concentration on organizational goals is so important?

_____

_____

_____

A. **Profit as a Yardstick.** In setting goals, entrepreneurs need to determine what requires immediate attention and what requires long-range planning. What is the difference between immediate and long-range goals?

_____

_____

_____

© 1990 Houghton Mifflin Company. All rights reserved.   222

What role do profits play in the goal-setting process?

_____

_____

_____

_____

B. **Building on Strengths.** To set meaningful goals, entrepreneurs must look first at their own strengths and skills. The process of setting goals based on one's strengths is built on three assumptions. What are they?

- _____

   _____

   _____

   _____

- _____

   _____

- _____

   _____

C. **Management by Objectives.** One method of translating the insights gained from identifying a venture's strengths into concrete goals is management by objectives (MBO). What are the two premises on which MBO is built?

- _____

   _____

   _____

- _____

   _____

© 1990 Houghton Mifflin Company. All rights reserved.

In your own words, describe how an MBO program works.

_____

_____

_____

_____

_____

_____

_____

An MBO program should be built on a hierarchy of goals. Those goals must be clear to the entrepreneur and explicit enough to be shared directly with employees.

Entrepreneurs should set goals with the help of key employees. When managers have a voice in setting goals, commitment is more likely to filter through each layer of the organization.

In what ways are goals really guides to action?

▪ _____

_____

_____

_____

▪ _____

_____

_____

_____

© 1990 Houghton Mifflin Company. All rights reserved.   224

· _____

_____

_____

_____

_____

_____

· _____

_____

_____

_____

D. Action Plans. Setting goals is just the beginning. Next entrepreneurs must decide how best to meet those goals. What are the logical steps they should take to develop an action plan?

· _____

_____

· _____

_____

· _____

Without action plans to breathe life into them, goals are meaningless. These plans can be simple, but they should be in writing.

III. Control and Budgeting. It is not enough just to set goals and draft action plans to meet them. Entrepreneurs also must measure their progress at frequent intervals. This process is called *control*. What role does information play in the control process?

_____

_____

_____

© 1990 Houghton Mifflin Company. All rights reserved.   225

After entrepreneurs get their venture under way, budgets play a vital role as a tool for both planning and control.

Read through the Buick dealership example in Chapter 12 of the text. What role do the following budgets play in the owner's planning process?

New-car sales budget—units _____

_____

_____

_____

New-car sales budget (net of trade-in) _____

_____

_____

_____

New-car selling expense budget _____

_____

_____

_____

Budgets can be used to measure employees' performance, but they should never be the only measure of performance. Why?

_____

_____

_____

A. **Reporting Performance.** To make the best use of budgets, entrepreneurs should compare actual performance to budgeted performance. Discrepancies can signal problems, allowing entrepreneurs to take remedial action.

B. **Return on Sales Versus Return on Investment.** Entrepreneurs measure their own performance using two financial yardsticks: return on sales and return on investment. In your own words, define these yardsticks and what they measure.

© 1990 Houghton Mifflin Company. All rights reserved.

Return on sales _____

_____

_____

_____

_____

Return on investment _____

_____

_____

_____

_____

IV. The Profitgraph

A. **Uses of the Profitgraph.** Another helpful planning and control tool is the profitgraph (Exhibit 12.10). Too few entrepreneurs make use of this remarkably versatile tool.

Profitgraphs give visual answers to three questions. What are those questions?

- _____

_____

- _____

_____

- _____

_____

The profitgraph also answers what-if questions. For example, what would happen to my profits if sales volume goes up 10 percent, but prices, fixed costs, and variable costs rise 5 percent?

B. **Limitations of the Profitgraph.** One word of caution about profitgraphs: The volume-price-cost relationships in them are valid only within relevant ranges of volume. If volume drops too low, undoubtedly the entrepreneur will slice fixed costs.

© 1990 Houghton Mifflin Company. All rights reserved.   227

The following formula also can be used to estimate the breakeven point:

$$\frac{\text{Total fixed costs}}{\text{contribution to fixed costs}} = \text{breakeven point}$$

Although the formula works, it is not as versatile as the profitgraph.

Questions for Mastery

Questions for mastery are found in the textbook at the beginning of every chapter. Answer each question again to reinforce your understanding of the information.

1. What are the problems of growth?

_____

_____

_____

_____

_____

_____

2. Why is it critical to set goals?

_____

_____

_____

_____

© 1990 Houghton Mifflin Company. All rights reserved.

3. How do you set goals?

_____

_____

_____

_____

_____

4. How do planning and control interact?

_____

_____

_____

_____

_____

5. What is management by objectives, budgets, and profitgraphs?

   ▪ _____

   _____

   _____

   ▪ _____

   _____

   _____

   ▪ _____

   _____

   _____

© 1990 Houghton Mifflin Company. All rights reserved.   229

Definitions of Key Terms

The following key terms are important in this chapter. In your own words, define each concept.

immediate goals _____

_____

long-range goals _____

_____

action plans _____

_____

return on sales _____

_____

return on investment _____

_____

efficiency _____

_____

effectiveness _____

_____

prebirth stage _____

_____

acceptance stage _____

_____

breakthrough stage _____

_____

© 1990 Houghton Mifflin Company. All rights reserved.

maturity stage _____

_____

profitgraph _____

_____

management by objectives (MBO) _____

_____

control _____

_____

True-False Questions

Determine whether the following statements are true or false, then circle T or F. Correct answers are listed at the end of the study guide.

T   F   1.   In creating their venture, entrepreneurs are both thinkers and doers.

T   F   2.   Planning and control are parts of a circular process that is vital to the health of a venture.

T   F   3.   For most small businesses, growth is predictable and steady.

T   F   4.   Once a venture gets under way, entrepreneurs tend to spend more time planning and controlling.

T   F   5.   Generally, entrepreneurs fail to handle the early stages of growth as well as they do the later stages.

T   F   6.   The very first stage of growth that a small venture goes through is called the acceptance stage.

T   F   7.   Problems with cash flow, production, quality, and delivery are most common in the breakthrough stage.

T   F   8.   Most entrepreneurs tend to add specialists (accountants, quality-control analysts, customer-service representatives) in the acceptance stage.

T   F   9.   In most successful small businesses, the owners should give up their entrepreneurial bent and become full-time managers.

© 1990 Houghton Mifflin Company. All rights reserved.

T F 10. As the complexity of a business increases, the number of decisions and activities outstrips the time available, so the entrepreneur must rely increasingly on other people to perform major functions.

T F 11. The act of setting goals is especially vital once a venture begins to grow rapidly and adds more workers.

T F 12. The key to the single-minded pursuit of goals is dedication.

T F 13. Once entrepreneurs set goals, it is their responsibility to make sure that every employee understands and pursues them.

T F 14. In setting goals, entrepreneurs must determine what requires immediate attention and what requires long-range planning.

T F 15. A venture must make a profit if it is to survive and grow.

T F 16. Profits are a yardstick that measures the entrepreneur's satisfaction.

T F 17. To set meaningful rather than vague goals, entrepreneurs should look first at their own strengths and skills.

T F 18. In a highly competitive economy, success generally favors the venture that does its job with average skill.

T F 19. A venture's product or service may be outdated quickly, but its profile of special skills will tend to continue for years to come.

T F 20. Management by objectives is effective only in large corporations.

T F 21. True progress can be measured only in relation to the entrepreneur's goals.

T F 22. One of the most important factors in a successful MBO program is the establishment of a hierarchy of goals.

T F 23. Goals that are established as part of an MBO program are for the owner's use; they should not be shared with key employees.

T F 24. When managers and supervisors have a part in setting goals for a small business, the typical result is confusion.

T F 25. After goals have been established, the entrepreneur must develop an action plan to meet those goals.

T F 26. It is a good idea to put action plans in writing.

© 1990 Houghton Mifflin Company. All rights reserved.

T F   27. The control process helps assure entrepreneurs that their own actions, as well as those of employees, are on target.

T F   28. The cash budget is the centerpiece of the business plan because it enables the entrepreneur to discuss the proposed business venture with investors and creditors.

T F   29. To make the best use of budgets, entrepreneurs should establish some means by which actual performance can be compared with budgeted performance.

T F   30. A quarter-by-quarter comparison of budgeted performance with actual performance tells the entrepreneur where problems exist.

T F   31. Return on sales measures the effectiveness of the owners' investment.

T F   32. Return on investment measures the efficiency of a business operation.

T F   33. Another term for profitgraph is *profit and loss statement.*

T F   34. Profitgraphs give entrepreneurs visual answers to what-if questions.

T F   35. The volume-price-cost relationships in a profitgraph are valid only within relevant ranges of volume.

T F   36. The breakeven point also can be found mathematically.

Multiple-Choice Questions

Write the letter of the correct answer in the blank to the left of the question. Correct answers are listed at the end of the study guide.

_____ 1. Which of the following statements is *true?*
   a. Planning and control are two separate processes.
   b. In most small businesses, growth is systematic, a product of planning.
   c. Entrepreneurs do a better job of planning before a venture is started than after the doors are opened.
   d. Entrepreneurs spend more time planning after a venture gets under way.

_____ 2. The four stages in the growth of a venture are
   a. prebirth, acceptance, breakthrough, and collapse.
   b. prebirth, breakthrough, success, and maturity.
   c. acceptance, breakthrough, success, and maturity.
   d. prebirth, acceptance, breakthrough, and maturity.

© 1990 Houghton Mifflin Company. All rights reserved.

_____ 3. Cash flow, production, quality, and delivery problems are most common in the
_____ stage.
   a.   prebirth
   b.   acceptance
   c.   breakthrough
   d.   success

_____ 4. Which of the following statements is *true?*
   a.   Most entrepreneurs have greater control over the breakthrough stage of their venture than the earlier stages.
   b.   Once a venture begins to grow, entrepreneurs should change hats and work at being managers as well as entrepreneurs.
   c.   In the breakthrough stage, growth is so slow that it often passes unnoticed.
   d.   Successful entrepreneurs must give up their entrepreneurial bent and manage the small business as it begins to grow.

_____ 5. The process of setting goals
   a.   is appropriate only when launching a venture.
   b.   is appropriate only after a business gets under way.
   c.   should identify long-range and immediate goals.
   d.   should concentrate on immediate goals because no one knows if the business will survive over a long period of time.

_____ 6. To set meaningful goals, entrepreneurs should look first at their
   a.   product line.
   b.   strengths and weaknesses.
   c.   competition.
   d.   marketing strategy.

_____ 7. Which of the following statements is *true?*
   a.   An MBO program is useless for a small business because it is too complex for most entrepreneurs to use.
   b.   MBO is a powerful took based on two simple premises.
   c.   An MBO program should be used only by entrepreneurs who have had experience in large corporations where the program was used successfully.
   d.   The overriding purpose of an MBO program is to increase sales revenues.

_____ 8. When managers and supervisors have a voice in setting goals,
   a.   commitment is more likely to filter through each layer of the organization.
   b.   the resulting goals are too ambitious for most small businesses.
   c.   decision making becomes more difficult.
   d.   those goals tend to be too broad.

© 1990 Houghton Mifflin Company. All rights reserved.

_____ 9. Goals should
   a.   suggest specific courses of action.
   b.   suggest ways of measuring a venture's performance.
   c.   be challenging enough to excite entrepreneurs and their employees.
   d.   do all of the above.

_____10. Which of the following statements is *true?*
   a.   Setting goals is just the beginning.
   b.   Once established, goals should not be adjusted for changing conditions.
   c.   It's important to prepare an action plan before setting goals.
   d.   All of the above are true.

_____11. Once a venture is under way, budgets play a vital role in
   a.   establishing a business plan.
   b.   planning and control.
   c.   setting the entrepreneur's salary.
   d.   increasing profits.

_____12. Return on sales measures _____; return on investment measures _____.
   a.   profits, expenses
   b.   expenses, profits
   c.   effectiveness, efficiency
   d.   efficiency, effectiveness

_____13. A profitgraph gives entrepreneurs
   a.   visual answers to what-if questions.
   b.   a guaranteed projection of sales revenues.
   c.   a guaranteed projection of total profits.
   d.   all of the above.

_____14. Which of the following statements is *true?*
   a.   The profitgraph is too hard to use to be of practical value.
   b.   A profitgraph is useful only when the volume-price-cost relationships are valid.
   c.   The point at which the revenue and total-cost lines intersect is called the *income point.*
   d.   None of the above is true.

Completion Questions

Write your answer in the blanks provided in each question. Correct answers are listed at the end of the study guide.

1. Planning and control are parts of a _____ process that is vital to the health of a venture. Before the birth of their venture, entrepreneurs tend to plan their moves carefully. Once started, business ventures tend to grow _____.

© 1990 Houghton Mifflin Company. All rights reserved.   235

2. The four stages of growth in a small-business venture are (1) _____, (2) _____, (3) _____, and (4) _____.

3. In the breakthrough stage, the rate of growth is so _____ that entrepreneurs often cannot keep up with it. Entrepreneurs apply _____ solutions to problems. When _____ suddenly begin to level off or slip, they hire _____ to relieve their problems.

4. To help keep their venture alive and well, entrepreneurs should set _____. The act of setting goals is especially vital once a venture begins to grow rapidly and adds more _____. This is when the entrepreneur, acting as a manager, must _____ others toward meeting the venture's goals.

5. In setting goals, entrepreneurs need to determine what requires _____ attention and what requires long-range planning. Once they set goals, entrepreneurs should make sure that every _____ understands and pursues them.

6. Profits are simply a _____ for a job well done—the sale of a product or service that customers need or want. Generally, the _____ the profits, the greater customers' satisfaction. Conversely, the _____ the profits, the poorer customers' satisfaction.

7. To set meaningful goals, entrepreneurs should look first at their own _____ and _____. In a highly competitive economy, success generally favors the venture that does its job with _____ skill.

8. One method of translating into concrete goals the insights gained from identifying a venture's strengths is _____ by objectives. Its power lies in two simple premises: (1) The clearer entrepreneurs' idea of what they want to do, the better the odds that they will succeed—if their intent is to make the most of their venture's _____ and talents; and (2) true progress can be measured only in relation to the _____ goals.

9. Goals must be clear, not only to the entrepreneur, but also to _____. To make sure of their support, the entrepreneur should set goals with the help of such _____ employees as supervisors, managers, and department heads.

10. The process of measurement that helps assure entrepreneurs that their own actions, as well as those of employees, are on target is called _____. The key element of the control process is information that allows entrepreneurs to compare actual performance with _____ performance.

11. A cash budget is the _____ of a business plan because it translates the would-be entrepreneur's operating plans into _____ terms. After entrepreneurs get their venture under way, budgets play an equally vital role as a tool for both _____ and _____.

© 1990 Houghton Mifflin Company. All rights reserved.

12. Budgets enable the manager or entrepreneur to _____ the performance of supervisors and workers. These evaluations, along with other measures of _____, may result in promotions, merit increases in salary, remedial action, or even dismissals.

13. To make the best use of budgets, entrepreneurs should establish some means by which _____ performance can be compared with _____ performance.

14. Return on _____ measures efficiency; return on _____ measures effectiveness.

15. The _____ can give entrepreneurs _____ answers to what-if questions.

Essay Questions

1. The rate of growth in the breakthrough stage is so fast that entrepreneurs often cannot keep up with it. What kinds of problems does the growth experienced in the breakthrough stage cause for the typical small-business owner?

2. One of the most important and at the same time most difficult organizational changes encountered as a venture grows is the evolution of the role played by the entrepreneur. How does the entrepreneur's role change as the business begins to grow?

3. How can budgets and profitgraphs help small-business owners manage a successful venture?

The Difference Between Success and Failure

A *goal* is an end state that the organization is expected to achieve. *Goal setting* is the process of developing—and committing an organization to—a set of goals. Every organization has several types of goals.

Goal Setting

The most fundamental type of goal is the organization's *purpose,* the reason for the organization's existence. A local contractor's purpose is to provide a profit for the owner. Houston Community College's purpose is to provide an education for local citizens. The purpose of the Secret Service is to protect the life of the president. The organization's *mission* is the means by which it tries to fulfill its purpose. Apple Computer Company attempts to fulfill its purpose (making a profit) by manufacturing computers; an automobile repair shop fulfills the same purpose by repairing cars. Finally, *objectives* are specific statements detailing what the organization intends to accomplish as it goes about its mission. For a restaurant, one objective might be that all customers be served within five minutes of their arrival. The owner of a clothing store might adopt the objective that sales increase by 7 percent this year. For a computer store, one objective might be that the delivery time for home computers be reduced by two weeks next year.

© 1990 Houghton Mifflin Company. All rights reserved.   237

Chapter 12

Goals can deal with a variety of factors, among them sales, company growth, costs, customer satisfaction, and employee morale. They also can extend over various periods of time. A small manufacturer may focus primarily on sales objectives for the next six months; Exxon may be more interested in objectives for the year 2000. Finally, goals should be established for every level in the organization, from the owner of the company to operating employees.

Controlling Ongoing Activities

Controlling is the process of evaluating and regulating ongoing activities to ensure that goals are met. To see how controlling works, think about a rocket launched by NASA to place a satellite in orbit. Do NASA personnel simply fire the rocket, then check back in a few days to find out whether the satellite is in place? Of course not. The rocket is monitored constantly, and its course is regulated and adjusted as needed to get the satellite where it should be. In a similar fashion, managerial control involves both close monitoring of the progress of the organization as it works toward its goals and whatever regulating and adjusting are necessary to keep it on course.

For example, suppose that a swimming pool contractor has established a goal of increasing profit by 12 percent next year. To ensure that this goal is reached, the owner might monitor profit on a monthly basis. After three months, if profit has increased by 3 percent, the owner might be able to assume that everything is going according to schedule. Probably no action would be taken. However, if profit has increased by only 1 percent after three months, some corrective action would be needed to get the firm on track. The particular action would depend on the reason for the low increase in profit.

The control function includes three steps. The first is *setting standards,* specific goals to which performance can be compared. (Quantitative goals, like the swimming pool contractor's 3 percent profit increase in three months, are the most useful.) The second step is *measuring actual performance* and comparing it with the standard. The third step is taking *corrective action* as necessary. These steps must be repeated periodically until the primary goal is achieved.

© 1990 Houghton Mifflin Company. All rights reserved.   238

CHAPTER 13

Analysis of Financial Statements, Investments, and Credit

Learning Objectives

After studying this chapter, you should understand

1. How financial analysis fits into the process of planning and control

2. What the methods are of analyzing financial statements and interpreting results

3. What the ways are of evaluating investment opportunities

4. How entrepreneurs can use credit to their advantage

5. What the advantages and disadvantages are of giving credit

Chapter Review

As you read the chapter, complete the following outline with information from the text.

As their growing venture strives toward maturity, entrepreneurs often fail to strike a balance between being entrepreneurial and being managerial. These entrepreneurs generally fail to use their financial statements to spot problems before they occur; or they make unwise investment decisions.

I. **Analysis of Financial Statements.** To plan and control their ventures, entrepreneurs should become skilled at analyzing the numbers in their financial statements.

    A. **The Essence of Financial Analysis.** Comparison lies at the heart of all analyses of financial statements. The comparisons that are most meaningful to entrepreneurs are those that relate to the goals they set for themselves. Entrepreneurs usually have financial goals and nonfinancial goals. What are two examples of financial goals?

    _____

    _____

What are three examples of nonfinancial goals?

_____

_____

_____

Of the goals that can be reduced to numbers, which is the most meaningful?

_____

_____

B.   **Earning a Satisfactory Return.** The best yardstick for assessing return is called *return on investment (ROI).* ROI can be computed three different ways. In your own words, describe each method.

Return on total assets _____

_____

_____

_____

_____

_____

Return on owners' equity _____

_____

_____

_____

_____

© 1990 Houghton Mifflin Company. All rights reserved.   240

Return on permanent capital _____

_____

_____

_____

_____

_____

C. **Maintaining Financial Health.** Besides a satisfactory return on investment, shareholders expect their investment to be protected against excessive risk. To measure their degree of protection against risk, entrepreneurs can use several yardsticks. One relates total debt to total assets; another omits current debt and relates just long-term debt to permanent capital.

D. **Ratio Analysis.** To evaluate financial performance, entrepreneurs should use a technique called *ratio analysis*. In this chapter, we have grouped the ratios into two categories. What are they?

- _____

- _____

II. **Tests of Profitability.** Tests of profitability include calculations for return on investment, return on sales, and inventory turnover.

A. **Return on Investment.** As explained earlier, entrepreneurs can estimate their return on investment using any one of three ratios, depending on whether they define investment as total assets, owners' equity, or permanent capital.

What is the formula for calculating return on assets?

What is the formula for calculating return on owners' equity?

What is the formula for calculating return on permanent capital?

Notice that in estimating the return on assets and on permanent capital, we add the after-tax expense of interest to net profit. Otherwise these returns would be understated. We make the adjustment by multiplying the interest expense by the complement of the tax rate. This is done because interest expense is tax-deductible, and so is offset in part by the effect of taxes.

B. **Return on Sales.** Return on sales, also called *profit margin,* measures how efficiently entrepreneurs are managing their operations.

What does this calculation tell the entrepreneur?

_____

_____

What is the formula for calculating return on sales?

Many entrepreneurs mistakenly believe that return on sales is the best measure of financial performance. Why is return on investment a more significant calculation?

_____

_____

_____

C. **Another Look at Return on Investment.** Intuitively we know that the more we make for each dollar of sales and the more sales we make for each dollar of investment, the greater our return on investment. How do we express this relationship in a formula?

What are two ways in which entrepreneurs can improve their return on investment?

▪ _____

_____

▪ _____

_____

© 1990 Houghton Mifflin Company. All rights reserved.

D. **Inventory Turnover.** Inventory turnover measures how well entrepreneurs are managing their inventories. What is the formula for calculating inventory turnover?

What precautions should entrepreneurs take if the industry in which they operate is seasonal?

_____

_____

_____

_____

_____

III. **Test of Financial Health.** So far we've discussed yardsticks that measure how well entrepreneurs manage their operations and their assets. We now look at yardsticks that measure how well they manage the finances of their ventures.

A. **Solvency.** Solvency is a venture's ability to repay long-term debts, including interest, when due.

What is the formula for calculating the debt ratio?

Notice that this yardstick simply measures the degree to which a venture's assets are financed by creditors. What is an acceptable standard for the debt ratio?

_____

What variation of the debt ratio formula do some entrepreneurs use?

To complete the analysis of solvency, entrepreneurs also should measure times interest earned. What is the formula for calculating times interest earned?

© 1990 Houghton Mifflin Company. All rights reserved.

What does this calculation tell the entrepreneur?

_____

_____

_____

_____

B.   **Liquidity.** Another yardstick that measures exposure to debt is the current ratio.

What is the formula for calculating the current ratio?

The rule of thumb is that a current ratio of 2 to 1 is good.

An even tougher test of liquidity is the quick ratio, which omits inventories. What is the formula for calculating the quick ratio?

Generally a quick ratio of 1 to 1 or better is considered good.

C.   **Customer Credit.** Collection period measures the degree to which a venture finances customers who buy on credit.

What is the formula for calculating receivables turnover?

What is the formula for calculating collection period?

What do these two calculations mean to the entrepreneur?

_____

_____

_____

_____

© 1990 Houghton Mifflin Company. All rights reserved.

IV. **Evaluation of Investment Opportunities.** Entrepreneurs also must be able to evaluate their investment opportunities. For example, should they lease or buy? Should they expand a plant? List four other examples of investment choices.

- _____

- _____

- _____

  _____

- _____

  _____

Each of these choices could make or break a venture. Why?

_____

_____

A. **Cash Payback.** The most popular yardstick of investment worth is simple to understand and easy to apply. Cash payback is the time required for the cash produced by an investment to equal the cash required by the investment.

   What is the drawback to this method of evaluating investment opportunities?

   _____

   _____

   _____

   What should entrepreneurs do to offset this drawback?

   _____

   _____

   _____

   Cash payback has another flaw. It fails to take into account that a dollar received today is worth more to the entrepreneur than a dollar received a year or more from now.

B. **Return on Investment.** Return on investment tells entrepreneurs how much they can earn yearly on each dollar invested. ROI also enables entrepreneurs to compare their estimates of return with their cost of money.

What is the formula for calculating return on original investment?

What is the formula for calculating return on average investment?

C. **Present Value.** We've described three yardsticks for measuring investment worth: cash payback, return on original investment, and return on average investment. These yardsticks give highly different results.

To resolve the confusion, many large corporations use a yardstick called *present value,* which measures the true rate of return offered by an investment opportunity by taking into account the timing of cash returns and outlays over the entire useful life of the investment.

V. **Credit and Collection.** In most industries, entrepreneurs must offer credit or lose customers. Although credit creates customers, it also creates risk. Entrepreneurs must understand how to extend credit without risking failure.

Today the nation's prosperity depends on the widespread use of charge accounts, mortgage loans, bank loans, credit cards, and other means by which customers get products before they can fully afford them. To survive and grow, entrepreneurs should learn how best to give credit and, at the same time, how best to avoid nonpaying customers.

For each of the industries listed below, indicate the percentage of total sales supported by credit.

Manufacturers _____

Wholesalers _____

Retailers and service firms _____

Whenever customers buy on credit, entrepreneurs essentially are advancing them the money to buy. What effect does this have on accounts receivable?

_____ _____

_____

© 1990 Houghton Mifflin Company. All rights reserved.

Entrepreneurs do have the right to charge their customers interest on credit purchases. But products or services should not be used as tools to sell credit. What is the main purpose of credit?

_____

Credit can be costly unless entrepreneurs take pains to control their costs of credit and collection.

A. **Kinds of Credit.** There are two kinds of credit: commercial and consumer. *Commercial credit* is credit that one entrepreneur gives to another. *Consumer credit* is credit that entrepreneurs give to individual customers.

1. **Commercial Credit.** In wholesaling or manufacturing, entrepreneurs often are forced to sell on credit. List three reasons why.

- _____

_____

- _____

_____

- _____

_____

How can entrepreneurs protect themselves from bad credit risks? It is a good idea to turn to credit-rating firms like Dun & Bradstreet for help. What kind of information does Dun & Bradstreet provide?

- _____

_____

- _____

_____

- _____

_____

- _____

_____

© 1990 Houghton Mifflin Company. All rights reserved.

2. **Consumer Credit.** Especially vulnerable to financial loss are entrepreneurs who sell directly to individual customers on credit. To screen these customers, entrepreneurs must settle two questions. What are they?

- _____

_____

- _____

_____

To get the answers, a good place to begin is with a credit application. Next entrepreneurs should get a credit report on each applicant from a local credit bureau. What does this report enable entrepreneurs to do?

- _____

_____

- _____

_____

After comparing the application and the credit report, entrepreneurs can decide whether to give credit. What is the most important factor in this decision?

_____

Credit bureaus have credit information on virtually every person who at one time or another has bought on credit.

B. **Advantages and Disadvantages of Giving Credit.** List seven advantages of selling goods and services on credit.

- _____

_____

- _____

_____

- _____

- _____

_____

- _____

- _____

_____

- _____

_____

What are five disadvantages of selling goods and services on credit?

- _____

_____

- _____

- _____

_____

- _____

_____

- _____

_____

_____

_____

C. **Collection Systems.** At one time or another, most entrepreneurs have trouble
    collecting from credit customers. Slow-paying or nonpaying customers can severely
    strain entrepreneurs' financial resources.

© 1990 Houghton Mifflin Company. All rights reserved.

A sale isn't a sale until the customer pays in full. Otherwise it's a bad debt. Some bad debts can be avoided by close investigation of customers' credit ratings. Another way to avoid bad debts is to design an effective collection system. What should a good collection system do?

- _____
  _____

- _____
  _____

- _____
  _____
  _____

- _____
  _____

- _____
  _____

1. **Aging of Accounts Receivable.** Perhaps the backbone of any collection system is the analysis of accounts receivable—the amounts owed by customers. Why should entrepreneurs prepare an aging schedule?

    _____
    _____
    _____

    How does the aging schedule work as a control device?

    _____
    _____

© 1990 Houghton Mifflin Company. All rights reserved.

2.   **Collection Period.** One yardstick entrepreneurs use to measure their total credit-and-collection performance is the collection period calculation. The collection period tells entrepreneurs how many days' revenues are tied up in accounts receivable. In other words, how long it takes, on average, to collect from credit customers. What is the formula used to determine collection period?

Another way to measure credit-and-collection performance is for entrepreneurs to compare their collection period with that of others in the same industry.

3.   **Credit Cards.** One way to avoid the problems connected with consumer credit is to accept bank or national credit cards. What are two advantages of accepting credit cards?

- _____

_____

- _____

_____

How does the credit card process work?

_____

_____

_____

_____

_____

_____

_____

A fee is charged by the bank or national credit card company involved. What is the fee based on?

_____

© 1990 Houghton Mifflin Company. All rights reserved.   251

Questions for Mastery

Questions for mastery are found in the textbook at the beginning of every chapter. Answer each question again to reinforce your understanding of the information.

1. How does financial analysis fit into the process of planning and control?

   _____

   _____

   _____

   _____

2. What are the methods of analyzing financial statements and interpreting results?

   _____

   _____

   _____

   _____

   _____

   _____

   _____

   _____

3. What are the ways of evaluating investment opportunities?

   _____

   _____

   _____

   _____

   _____

© 1990 Houghton Mifflin Company. All rights reserved.   252

_____

_____

_____

4. How can entrepreneurs use credit to their advantage?

_____

_____

_____

_____

_____

_____

5. What are the advantages and disadvantages of giving credit?

_____

_____

_____

_____

Definitions of Key Terms

The following key terms are important in this chapter. In your own words, define each concept.

ratio analysis _____

_____

permanent capital _____

_____

cash payback _____

_____

Chapter 13

cost of money _____

_____

average investment _____

_____

credit report _____

_____

aging schedule _____

_____

return on investment _____

_____

collection period _____

_____

solvency _____

_____

commercial credit _____

_____

consumer credit _____

_____

True-False Questions

Determine whether the following statements are true or false, then circle T or F. Correct answers are listed at the end of the study guide.

T   F   1.   As their growing ventures strive toward maturity, entrepreneurs often fail to strike a balance between being entrepreneurial and being managerial.

T   F   2.   Financial analysis should be left to accountants.

T F 3. Comparison lies at the heart of all analyses of financial statements.

T F 4. Of the goals that can be reduced to numbers, the most meaningful one is to earn a satisfactory return on the money invested in a venture, consistent with maintaining its financial health.

T F 5. Return on investment tells entrepreneurs how many cents they are earning on each dollar of sales revenue.

T F 6. Investment can be defined in three ways: total assets, owners' equity, and sales revenue.

T F 7. Return on total assets is used to measure how well entrepreneurs have invested all the money entrusted in their care, regardless of where it came from.

T F 8. Return on owners' equity is especially useful to existing and prospective shareholders.

T F 9. Permanent capital is the sum of current debt and long-term debt.

T F 10. To evaluate their financial performance, entrepreneurs should use a technique called *ratio analysis.*

T F 11. Return on sales also is called the *current ratio.*

T F 12. The return on sales calculation tells entrepreneurs how many cents are left over for each dollar of investment.

T F 13. Return on sales measures operating efficiency.

T F 14. Entrepreneurs can improve their return on investment by making better use of their assets.

T F 15. Inventory turnover is calculated by dividing the cost of goods sold by sales revenue.

T F 16. The term *solvency* refers to a venture's ability to repay long-term debt, including interest, when due.

T F 17. Generally a debt ratio of less than 75 percent is considered favorable.

T F 18. The times interest earned ratio measures how low profits can drop without straining a venture's ability to pay interest when due.

T F 19. The current ratio is calculated by dividing current assets by fixed assets.

T F 20. Generally a quick ratio of 1 to 1 or better is considered good.

© 1990 Houghton Mifflin Company. All rights reserved.   255

T F 21. Receivables turnover is calculated by dividing total assets by accounts receivable.

T F 22. The most popular yardstick of investment worth is cash payback.

T F 23. One flaw of the cash payback method is that it fails to take into account savings earned after the payback period.

T F 24. Return on investment enables entrepreneurs to evaluate investment opportunities by comparing their estimate of return with their cost of money.

T F 25. Another widely used method of calculating return on investment relates net profit to average investment.

T F 26. The present value method of evaluating an investment takes into account the timing of cash returns and outlays over the entire useful life of the investment.

T F 27. Almost 70 percent of all sales by wholesalers are credit transactions.

T F 28. About 50 percent of all sales by retailers and service firms are credit transactions.

T F 29. When customers buy on credit, entrepreneurs, in essence, are advancing them the money to buy.

T F 30. In wholesaling and manufacturing, entrepreneurs often can choose whether to sell for cash or credit.

T F 31. Dun & Bradstreet has up-to-date credit ratings on over 9.2 million businesses.

T F 32. Especially vulnerable to financial loss are entrepreneurs who sell directly to individual customers on credit.

T F 33. Credit customers pay less attention to prices.

T F 34. Entrepreneurs who develop good credit investigation procedures do not need to age accounts.

T F 35. The use of bank or national credit cards sharply reduces an entrepreneur's investment in accounts receivable, or even eliminates it completely.

© 1990 Houghton Mifflin Company. All rights reserved.   256

Multiple-Choice Questions

Write the letter of the correct answer in the blank to the left of the question. Correct answers are listed at the end of the study guide.

_____ 1. Which of the following statements is *true?*
    a. It is the accountant's job to analyze financial statements.
    b. To plan and control their venture, entrepreneurs should become skilled at analyzing the numbers in their financial statements.
    c. Analysis of financial statements is not necessary in a small business because the owner is so close to the venture.
    d. None of the above is true.

_____ 2. All of the following are measures of an entrepreneur's return on investment *except* return on
    a. total assets.
    b. owners' equity.
    c. sales revenues.
    d. permanent capital.

_____ 3. All of the following are tests of profitability *except*
    a. return on investment.
    b. return on sales.
    c. the debt ratio.
    d. inventory turnover.

_____ 4. If net profit is $25,000 and sales revenue is $500,000, return on sales revenue is _____ percent.
    a. 5
    b. 10
    c. 20
    d. 50

_____ 5. If cost of goods sold is $1,000,000 and inventory is $200,000, inventory turnover is _____ times a year.
    a. 4
    b. 5
    c. 7.5
    d. 10

_____ 6. All of the following are tests of financial health *except*
    a. the debt ratio.
    b. the current ratio.
    c. the collection period.
    d. inventory turnover.

© 1990 Houghton Mifflin Company. All rights reserved.

_____ 7. The ratio that relates long-term debt to permanent capital is the
   a. current ratio.
   b. quick ratio.
   c. debt ratio.
   d. collection period.

_____ 8. The rule of thumb is that a current ratio of _____ to 1 is good.
   a. 1
   b. 2
   c. 3
   d. 4

_____ 9. The most popular yardstick of investment worth is
   a. cash payback.
   b. return on original investment.
   c. return on average investment.
   d. none of the above.

_____10. Return on investment tells entrepreneurs how much they can earn yearly on each dollar
   a. of sales revenue.
   b. of current assets.
   c. invested.
   d. of fixed assets.

_____11. About _____ percent of all sales by manufacturers involve credit transactions.
   a. 75
   b. 80
   c. 90
   d. 95

_____12. Dun & Bradstreet credit reports
   a. describe what kind of business the buyer is in and how it is managed.
   b. guarantee that the businesses they rate will pay their debts.
   c. list personal information about key employees.
   d. do all of the above.

_____13. To obtain credit information about an individual, the first thing entrepreneurs should do is
   a. contact the individual's employer.
   b. contact the individual's spouse.
   c. have the individual complete a credit application.
   d. obtain a credit report from a credit bureau.

_____14. To analyze accounts receivable, entrepreneurs must prepare a(n)
    a. credit report.
    b. aging schedule.
    c. income statement.
    d. cash budget.

_____15. Which of the following statements is *false?*
    a. Credit card service is available from commercial banks.
    b. The bank assumes all credit risks so long as the entrepreneur follows instructions for approval of credit card purchases.
    c. Receipts from bank credit card purchases are credited to the entrepreneur's checking account within five business days.
    d. The bank charges a percentage of total credit card sales for handling the entrepreneur's credit transactions.

Completion Questions

Write your answer in the blanks provided in each question. Correct answers are listed at the end of the study guide.

1. To plan and _____ their ventures, entrepreneurs should become skilled at _____ the numbers in their financial statements.

2. Although it is the _____ job to design accounting systems and to prepare financial statements, it is not his or her job to analyze the numbers in the financial statements and to interpret them. These are the _____ responsibilities.

3. Comparison lies at the heart of all analyses of financial statements. The comparisons that are most meaningful to entrepreneurs are those that relate to the _____ entrepreneurs set for themselves.

4. The best yardstick to use in assessing return is called *return on* _____. Investment can be defined in three ways: (1) total _____, (2) owners' _____, or (3) _____ capital.

5. The sum of owners' equity and long-term _____ is called permanent _____. It reflects the total amount needed to finance fixed assets and that fraction of current assets not otherwise financed by short-term creditors.

6. To evaluate their financial performance, entrepreneurs should use a technique called ratio _____. In this chapter, we group ratios into two categories: tests of _____ and tests of financial _____.

7. Return on sales is sometimes called *profit* _____. This ratio is calculated by dividing net _____ by sales _____.

8. Inventory turnover is calculated by dividing the cost of _____ sold by _____.

9. The debt ratio is calculated by dividing total _____ by total _____.

10. The current ratio is calculated by dividing current _____ by current _____. The rule of thumb is that a current ratio of _____ to 1 is good.

11. A firm's collection period is calculated by dividing the days in the _____ by the firm's receivables _____. Receivables turnover is calculated by dividing credit _____ by accounts _____.

12. The three methods that entrepreneurs can use to measure their investment opportunities are cash _____, return on _____ investment, and return on _____ investment.

13. Credit is a way of life. To survive and grow, entrepreneurs should learn how best to give credit and, at the same time, how best to avoid _____ customers.

14. There are two kinds of credit. _____ credit is the credit one entrepreneur extends to another. Equally important is _____ credit, which is the credit the entrepreneur gives individual customers.

15. To determine how much credit customers can safely absorb and whether the customers pay _____, entrepreneurs should begin by having them fill out a credit _____. Then entrepreneurs should get a credit _____ on each applicant from the local credit _____.

Essay Questions

1. Entrepreneurs who excel at launching a new venture often do poorly at managing its growth. This is not because they lose the spark of entrepreneurship; it is because they fail to plan and control well. How can the financial analyses—specifically tests of profitability and financial health—that are discussed in this chapter help entrepreneurs plan and control?

2. In the chapter we discuss three yardsticks for measuring investment worth: cash payback, return on original investment, and return on average investment. These three yardsticks give very different results. In fact one may give figures twice those given by another. Which yardstick is the best for evaluating a potential investment? Why?

3. At one time or another, most entrepreneurs have some trouble collecting from credit customers. What type of information should a collection system provide entrepreneurs? What steps would you include in your collection procedures to collect an account that is 90 days past due?

© 1990 Houghton Mifflin Company. All rights reserved.

The Difference Between Success and Failure

The primary purpose of any business is to earn a profit by selling goods and services. When a business extends credit to its customers, it must face the fact that some customers will be unable or unwilling to pay for their credit purchases.

The Five Cs of Credit Management

With this in mind, credit managers must establish policies for determining who receives credit and who does not. Most lenders build their credit policies around the five Cs of credit: character, capacity, capital, collateral, and conditions.

Character. By *character* we mean the borrower's attitude toward his or her credit obligations. Experienced credit managers often see this as the most important factor in predicting whether a borrower will make regular payments and ultimately repay a credit obligation.

Typical questions to consider in judging a borrower's character include the following:

1. Is the borrower prompt in paying bills?
2. Have other lenders had to dun the borrower with overdue notices before receiving payment?
3. Have lenders been forced to take the borrower to court to obtain payment?
4. Has the customer ever filed for bankruptcy? If so, did the customer make an attempt to repay debts voluntarily?

Even personal factors—for example, marital status and drinking or gambling habits—can affect an individual's ability to repay a loan or credit obligation.

Capacity. By *capacity* we mean the borrower's financial ability to meet credit obligations—that is, to make regular loan payments as scheduled in the credit agreement. If the customer is another business, the loan officer or credit manager looks at the firm's income statement. For individuals, the loan officer or credit manager checks salary statements. The borrower's outstanding financial obligations and monthly expenses also are taken into consideration before credit is approved.

Capital. The term *capital* as used here refers to the borrower's assets or net worth. In general, the greater the capital, the greater the borrower's ability to repay a loan of a specific size. The capital position of a business can be determined by examining its financial statements. (Most lenders insist that the business borrower's financial statements be prepared or audited by an independent certified public accountant. This helps ensure that the information contained in the statements is accurate.) For individuals, information on net worth can be obtained by requiring that the borrower complete a credit application. The borrower also must authorize employers and financial institutions to release information to confirm the claims made in the application.

Collateral. For large amounts of credit—and especially for large loans—the lender may require some type of collateral. If the borrower fails to live up to the terms of the credit agreement, the collateral can be sold to satisfy the debt.

Conditions. Here we mean general economic conditions that can affect a borrower's ability to repay a loan or other credit obligation. How well a firm can withstand an economic storm may depend on the particular industry the firm is in, its relative strength within that industry, and its earnings history and potential. For individuals, the basic question of conditions focuses on security—of both the applicant's job and the firm that he or she works for.

Checking Credit Information

The five *C*s are concerned mainly with information that is supplied by the applicant. How can a lender determine whether this information is accurate? That depends on whether the potential borrower is a business or an individual consumer.

Credit information concerning businesses can be obtained from four sources:

1. Dun & Bradstreet, the most widely used credit-reporting agency in the United States. Its Dun & Bradstreet Reports present detailed information about specific firms. It also publishes reference books that include credit ratings for more than 5.3 million businesses.
2. Local credit-reporting agencies. These may require a monthly or yearly fee for providing information on a continual basis.
3. Industry associations, which also may charge a service fee.
4. Other firms that have given the applicant credit.

Various credit bureaus provide credit information on individuals—generally for a fee of from $5 to $20 per request. Here is a list of the three major consumer credit bureaus:

1. TRW Credentials (Orange, California)
2. Trans Union Credit Information Company (Chicago)
3. Credit Bureau, Inc./Equifax (Atlanta)

© 1990 Houghton Mifflin Company. All rights reserved.

CHAPTER 14

Marketing

Learning Objectives

After studying this chapter, you should understand

1. What marketing is

2. Why marketing research is important

3. How marketing research should be carried out

4. How the various marketing activities fit together to form a marketing mix

5. What opportunities are available in export markets

Chapter Review

As you read the chapter, complete the following outline with information from the text.

The entrepreneur's main goal is to create satisfied customers at a profit. Marketing helps do that by moving products or services out of the hands of the entrepreneur and into those of customers.

How would you define the word *market?*

_____

_____

I. **Marketing Research.** Many experts claim that marketing research is the most important marketing activity of all because it helps satisfy the never-ending need for knowledge about markets. What types of marketing information does marketing research provide?

- _____

- _____

- _____

Marketing research falls within the reach of every entrepreneur, no matter how small. Defining, finding, and analyzing the facts about markets are activities any entrepreneur can master.

Most entrepreneurs do marketing research before undertaking a new venture. After startup, however, entrepreneurs often fail to get new facts, mistakenly assuming that their market will not change. Why is this attitude dangerous?

_____

_____

_____

_____

_____

A. **Uses of Marketing Research.** Marketing research replaces opinion with fact. Getting the facts helps offset the risks of doing business in today's fast-changing markets. Entrepreneurs lose sight of the fact that their success begins and ends with the customer; their one key to success is knowing better than competitors do what attracts customers. It is the entrepreneur's unique job to anticipate, adjust to, and capitalize on the sweeping changes that mark our times.

B. **Defining the Need for Facts.** A first step in marketing research is to ask the right questions. What types of questions should marketing research ask in the following areas?

Nature of the product _____

_____

_____

Nature of the market _____

_____

_____

Market size and outlook _____

_____

_____

Pricing _____

_____

_____

Production _____

_____

_____

Competition _____

_____

_____

Marketing _____

_____

_____

The more facts they have, the better entrepreneurs can forge their niche in the marketplace. What do facts enable entrepreneurs to do?

- _____

_____

- _____

- _____

_____

- _____

_____

- _____

Setting realistic market goals is the logical end of marketing research. If they fail to set these goals, entrepreneurs are unlikely to know where they stand or in what direction they are moving.

© 1990 Houghton Mifflin Company. All rights reserved.

C. **Finding Facts.** Few entrepreneurs can justify hiring a marketing researcher. What are three ways in which entrepreneurs get the facts about their markets?

. _____

_____

_____

_____

. _____

. _____

_____

1. **Using Statistical Information.** What can entrepreneurs find out using Census Bureau information?

. _____

_____

_____

_____

. _____

. _____

_____

2. **Using a Marketing Research Firm.** If initial marketing research leads to the decision to do a consumer survey, entrepreneurs should hire the services of a marketing researcher. Why?

_____

_____

_____

_____

_____

© 1990 Houghton Mifflin Company. All rights reserved.

What services should a marketing researcher provide entrepreneurs?

_____

_____

_____

3. **Organizing Part-Time Research.** What can entrepreneurs do for themselves when it comes to marketing research?

_____

_____

_____

D. **Analyzing Facts.** What is the purpose of analyzing facts when conducting marketing research?

_____

_____

_____

1. **Market Segmentation.** Market segmentation is the division of a market into subgroups of customers with similar needs for either a product or a service. A market segment, then, is any group of customers who share one or more traits and therefore similar product needs. In your own words, describe how product-related, geographic, psychographic, and demographic factors can be used to segment a market.

2. **Product-Related Factors** _____

_____

_____

_____

_____

3.   **Geographic Factors** _____

_____

_____

_____

_____

4.   **Psychographic Factors** _____

_____

_____

_____

_____

5.   **Demographic Factors** _____

_____

_____

_____

_____

E.   **Taking Action.** After identifying and researching their market, entrepreneurs are ready to prepare the marketing mix.

II. **Marketing Mix.** The marketing mix is the combination of elements that make up the marketing plan.

A.   **Distribution Channels.** Every manufacturer, wholesaler, retailer, and service firm is part of a distribution network or channel. What is the purpose of a distribution channel?

_____

_____

Who controls distribution channels?

_____

© 1990 Houghton Mifflin Company. All rights reserved.

Exhibit 14.6 shows various channels of distribution. Describe the five channels that can be used to sell consumer products.

- _____
- _____
- _____
- _____
- _____

Describe the four channels that can be used to sell industrial products.

- _____
- _____
- _____
- _____

B. **Price.** Entrepreneurs and other businesspersons are more mysterious about pricing than about any other aspect of their business. In many cases, setting a price poses no problem—especially when a product is identical to those of competitors.

C. **Pricing New Products.** But setting a price can pose a problem for entrepreneurs with new products. In your own words, describe price skimming.

_____

_____

_____

In your own words, describe penetration pricing.

_____

_____

_____

Deciding on a price for a new product is a complex process. For old products, the process is much simpler. The entrepreneur need only decide whether to make and sell the product at its current market price.

© 1990 Houghton Mifflin Company. All rights reserved. 269

1. **Pricing.** The entrepreneur generally needs more than the simple arithmetic of costs and profits to set prices. Yet many entrepreneurs seem to price on a cost-plus basis. Why is cost-plus a natural approach to pricing?

_____

But the Price = costs + fair profit formula doesn't always guarantee a profit. Why?

_____

_____

_____

What noncost questions should entrepreneurs ask before setting a price?

- _____

_____

- _____

_____

_____

_____

- _____

_____

- _____

_____

_____

_____

_____

- _____

_____

2. **Pricing for Wholesalers and Retailers.** On many products, wholesalers and retailers are free to set their own prices. They generally use a markup approach. Markup is the difference between selling price and purchase cost. There are two different methods of using markup. In your own words, explain markup as a percentage of the selling price.

_____

_____

_____

In your own words, explain markup as a percentage of the purchase cost.

_____

_____

_____

3. **Pricing for Services.** How are services usually priced?

_____

_____

D. **Advertising.** Entrepreneurs use advertising to communicate to customers about their product or service. Naturally they focus on benefits to buyers. Entrepreneurs also may try to convince customers that their product is better than those of competitors.

Entrepreneurs should make every advertising dollar count through careful planning. Well-planned advertising meets four goals. What are they?

- _____

- _____

- _____

- _____

Although many entrepreneurs do not plan, astute entrepreneurs plan their advertising expenditures, prepare their message, and select media. Briefly explain what these processes involve.

© 1990 Houghton Mifflin Company. All rights reserved.

1. **Planning Advertising Expenditures** _____

   _____

   _____

   _____

2. **Preparing the Advertising Message** _____

   _____

   _____

   _____

3. **Selecting Media** _____

   _____

   _____

   _____

What role do advertising agencies play in preparing advertising for small businesses?

_____

_____

_____

_____

E. **Personal Selling.** Personal selling takes over where advertising leaves off. Advertising coaxes the customer to buy; it stimulates interest. But advertising rarely closes the sale. Entrepreneurs also must rely on personal selling—meeting customers face to face to help them make up their minds.

© 1990 Houghton Mifflin Company. All rights reserved.

1. **Interaction Between Advertising and Personal Selling.** Because their goal is to create loyal customers, entrepreneurs should strike the right balance between advertising and personal selling. In your own words, define pull strategy.

   _____

   _____

   _____

   In your own words, define push strategy.

   _____

   _____

   _____

2. **The Selling Process.** Although no two selling situations are exactly alike, salespersons generally follow a seven-step process to sell a product. Describe those steps.

   Prospecting _____

   _____

   _____

   Approaching customers _____

   _____

   _____

   Presenting the product _____

   _____

   _____

   Demonstrating the product _____

   _____

   _____

© 1990 Houghton Mifflin Company. All rights reserved.   273

Overcoming objections _____

_____

_____

Closing the sale _____

_____

_____

Following through _____

_____

_____

3. **Finding the Right Salespersons.** Personal selling varies in importance by industry. In retailing, for example, personal selling is indispensable. To build a nucleus of loyal customers, entrepreneurs must find the right salespersons. The first step in the process is answering three questions. What are they?

- _____

- _____

- _____

F. **Sales Promotion.** Sales promotion makes both advertising and personal selling more effective. It can take many forms. List five of them.

- _____

- _____

_____

- _____

- _____

- _____

G. **Service.** Why is service important?

_____

_____

_____

_____

H. **Publicity.** What is publicity?

_____

_____

What are three common forms of publicity?

- _____

- _____

- _____

III. **Preparing a Marketing Mix.** After learning what it takes to create customers, entrepreneurs are ready to prepare their marketing mix. It is up to them to mix the ingredients of distribution, price, advertising, personal selling, sales promotion, service, and publicity in amounts that will give the most for each marketing dollar.

The marketing mix varies widely from industry to industry. Even within an industry the marketing mix may vary among competitors. It also will vary over the life of a business.

The goal of marketing is to find a mix that creates satisfied customers at a profit.

Why is it important to keep records of marketing costs?

_____

_____

Why must entrepreneurs make sure their venture is market oriented?

_____

_____

_____

_____

IV. **Export Marketing.** The U.S. share of world export sales has dropped sharply since 1955. Despite the opportunities foreign markets represent, many entrepreneurs avoid them. The reasons are threefold. Explain each of the fears listed below.

Fear of the unknown _____

_____

_____

Fear of long-distance relationships _____

_____

_____

Fear of the complex _____

_____

_____

A. **Using Professional Help.** The above fears are real, even healthy. No entrepreneur should ignore the risks involved in exporting. But these fears may dissolve once entrepreneurs avail themselves of the professional help, much of it free, that is available from the federal government and Chambers of Commerce.

The U.S. Bureau of International Commerce (BIC) has information on file on foreign import organizations in all countries. This information allows entrepreneurs to locate agents and distributors, get current sales leads, and obtain profiles on individual foreign companies.

Besides its computerized services, BIC also offers entrepreneurs a host of personal services. Describe each of these services.

© 1990 Houghton Mifflin Company. All rights reserved.

Free counseling _____

_____

_____

_____

Publications _____

_____

_____

_____

Promotional events _____

_____

_____

_____

Workshops _____

_____

_____

_____

B. **Preparing a Marketing Plan.** To best serve a foreign market, entrepreneurs should prepare a separate marketing plan. This plan should rely heavily on marketing research already done by others.

Only after collecting and analyzing all available information should entrepreneurs prepare their marketing plan, with the help of a lawyer versed in drafting international sales contracts.

© 1990 Houghton Mifflin Company. All rights reserved.

Questions for Mastery

Questions for mastery are found in the textbook at the beginning of every chapter. Answer each question again to reinforce your understanding of the information.

1. What is marketing?

    _____

    _____

    _____

2. Why is marketing research important?

    _____

    _____

    _____

    _____

3. How should marketing research be carried out?

    _____

    _____

    _____

    _____

4. How do the various marketing activities fit together to form a marketing mix?

    _____

    _____

    _____

    _____

© 1990 Houghton Mifflin Company. All rights reserved.

5. What opportunities are available in export markets?

_____

_____

_____

_____

Definitions of Key Terms

The following key terms are important in this chapter. In your own words, define each concept.

marketing _____

_____

random sampling _____

_____

advertising _____

_____

market _____

_____

markup _____

_____

market segmentation _____

_____

U.S. Bureau of International Commerce (BIC) _____

_____

marketing mix _____

_____

© 1990 Houghton Mifflin Company. All rights reserved.

penetration price policy _____

_____

skimming price policy _____

_____

distribution channel _____

_____

push strategy _____

_____

pull strategy _____

_____

True-False Questions

Determine whether the following statements are true or false, then circle T or F. Correct answers are listed at the end of the study guide.

T   F   1.   The entrepreneur's primary goal is to create satisfied customers at a profit.

T   F   2.   In the text, we use the term *market* to refer to a large geographic area.

T   F   3.   Marketing research is an activity that only large corporations can afford.

T   F   4.   Entrepreneurs are more likely to do marketing research after a venture has started than before it is launched.

T   F   5.   Today, buying habits change so fast that success belongs largely to those entrepreneurs who keep a close watch on their markets and, if necessary, quickly change their line of products or services to keep pace.

T   F   6.   The key to an entrepreneur's success is knowing better than competitors what attracts customers.

T   F   7.   Because entrepreneurs need a lot of customers, they should ignore market niches and concentrate on the market as a whole.

T   F   8.   Setting realistic market goals is the logical end product of marketing research.

© 1990 Houghton Mifflin Company. All rights reserved.

T F 9. For most small firms, the only practical way to conduct marketing research is to hire a marketing researcher.

T F 10. Entrepreneurs can gather a lot of useful information from public libraries and trade associations.

T F 11. To reduce the cost of marketing research, entrepreneurs should design consumer survey questionnaires themselves.

T F 12. The only practical way to get accurate research information is to survey everyone in a geographic area.

T F 13. Trade associations are an inside source of information.

T F 14. Market segmentation is the process of dividing a market into subgroups of customers with similar needs for either a product or a service.

T F 15. When entrepreneurs divide a market according to the benefits that customers expect from the product, they are using product-related factors to segment the market.

T F 16. Geographic factors—climate, terrain, and natural resources—can influence customers' product needs.

T F 17. When entrepreneurs divide a market on the basis of customers' ages, they are using psychographic factors to segment the market.

T F 18. The purpose of a distribution channel is to move products from producers to users.

T F 19. The only viable channel of distribution is the manufacturer-to-user channel.

T F 20. A skimming price policy is used when the cost of developing the new product is high and the product may become obsolete in a short time.

T F 21. When entrepreneurs set a low initial price in an effort to capture customers quickly, they are using a penetration price policy.

T F 22. Even psychology can enter into the pricing decision.

T F 23. The easiest formula for entrepreneurs to use in setting prices is Price = costs + fair profit.

T F 24. Markup is simply the difference between selling price and purchase cost.

T F 25. In practice, markup is expressed not in dollars but as a percentage of either selling or overhead costs.

© 1990 Houghton Mifflin Company. All rights reserved.

T   F   26.   During a recession, some entrepreneurs drop advertising in the mistaken belief that it is an unnecessary expense.

T   F   27.   Media account for almost 70 percent of advertising costs.

T   F   28.   Newspapers account for approximately 27 percent of all advertising expenditures.

T   F   29.   The first step in the personal selling process is approaching the customer.

T   F   30.   The most important step in the personal selling process is following through.

T   F   31.   Personal selling varies in importance by industry.

T   F   32.   Free samples to introduce a new product are a form of sales promotion.

T   F   33.   Giving customers flowers attached to a box of detergent if they buy the detergent is using a piggyback premium.

T   F   34.   Publicity is an unpaid message about a venture or its products sent through a mass medium.

T   F   35.   The marketing mix is about the same for all small-business owners in all industries.

T   F   36.   The goal of marketing is to find a mix that creates satisfied customers at a profit.

T   F   37.   After preparing their marketing mix, entrepreneurs should take pains to keep accurate records of marketing costs.

T   F   38.   Since 1955, the U.S. share of world export sales gradually has increased.

T   F   39.   The U.S. Department of Commerce conducts workshops on export marketing throughout the country.

T   F   40.   To serve a foreign market best, entrepreneurs should prepare a separate marketing plan that relies heavily on marketing research already done by others.

© 1990 Houghton Mifflin Company. All rights reserved.

Multiple-Choice Questions

Write the letter of the correct answer in the blank to the left of the question. Correct answers are listed at the end of the study guide.

_____ 1. All of the following are marketing tools *except*
   a.   marketing research.
   b.   advertising.
   c.   cost-benefit analysis.
   d.   pricing.

_____ 2. Which of the following statements is *true?*
   a.   A venture's survival and growth depend largely on the quality of its marketing research.
   b.   Only large corporations can afford to conduct marketing research.
   c.   Marketing research is more likely to be performed by an entrepreneur after a venture is launched than before it is started.
   d.   All of the above are true.

_____ 3. To find their market niche, entrepreneurs should
   a.   pay a market researcher to do all their marketing research.
   b.   look ahead.
   c.   concentrate on advertising geared to the general population.
   d.   do all of the above.

_____ 4. Entrepreneurs can use Census Bureau data to determine
   a.   the average yearly income per family.
   b.   the percentage of families who own their home.
   c.   the percentage of families who own automobiles.
   d.   all of the above.

_____ 5. To conduct a consumer survey, entrepreneurs should
   a.   create their own questionnaires.
   b.   ask a lot of questions to avoid built-in bias.
   c.   hire a marketing researcher.
   d.   talk with everyone in their market area.

_____ 6. All of the following are outside sources of data *except*
   a.   accounting records.
   b.   marketing research firms.
   c.   suppliers.
   d.   trade associations and newspapers.

_____ 7. Market segmentation is
   a.   the process of adding up individual market segments to determine the total market for a product.
   b.   the process of dividing a market into subgroups of customers who have similar needs for a product or a service.
   c.   always done on the basis of age.
   d.   always done on the basis of product-related factors.

_____ 8. Which of the following statements about distribution channels is *false?*
   a.   Manufacturers control most distribution channels.
   b.   Entrepreneurs must decide whether to sell directly to users or through middlemen.
   c.   Entrepreneurs often begin selling through manufacturers' agents, then hire their own salespersons.
   d.   Only manufacturers, wholesalers, and retailers are part of distribution networks.

_____ 9. When entrepreneurs charge customers what the market will bear, they are using a(n) _____ pricing policy.
   a.   markup
   b.   penetration
   c.   illegal
   d.   skimming

_____10. Which of the following statements is *false?*
   a.   Deciding on a price for a new product is a complex process.
   b.   The process of pricing an old product is relatively simple.
   c.   Even psychology can enter into a pricing decision.
   d.   Pricing decisions affect only the manufacturer, not the retailers and wholesalers who handle the product.

_____11. Entrepreneurs use advertising
   a.   to communicate to customers about their product or service.
   b.   only rarely because it is so expensive.
   c.   because its effectiveness is easy to measure.
   d.   as a form of sales promotion.

_____12. When entrepreneurs advertise in a local newspaper, they are using a _____ strategy.
   a.   pull
   b.   push
   c.   markup
   d.   penetration

© 1990 Houghton Mifflin Company. All rights reserved.

____13. When salespeople underline a product's benefits to customers as well as the ways in which it is better than competitors' products, they are
   a.   approaching the customers.
   b.   presenting the product.
   c.   demonstrating the product.
   d.   overcoming objections.

____14. Which of the following statements about the marketing mix is *true?*
   a.   The marketing mix is the same for all industries.
   b.   Entrepreneurs must mix the ingredients in amounts that will give the most for each marketing dollar.
   c.   Entrepreneurs should concentrate on distribution channels and pricing, and ignore the other ingredients.
   d.   The marketing mix stays the same throughout the life of a venture.

____15. One of the reasons entrepreneurs avoid export markets is
   a.   their fear of the unknown.
   b.   low demand for U.S. products overseas.
   c.   excessive regulation.
   d.   lack of government support.

Completion Questions

Write your answer in the blanks provided in each question. Correct answers are listed at the end of the study guide.

1. Many experts claim that marketing _____ is the most important marketing activity of all. Why? Because it helps _____ the never-ending need for knowledge about markets.

2. Most entrepreneurs do market research before _____ a new venture. After startup, entrepreneurs _____ to get new facts, mistakenly assuming that their _____ will not change. This attitude is _____. Unless they remain in tune with their markets, entrepreneurs may soon find themselves without customers.

3. Market research replaces opinion with _____. The more facts they have, the better entrepreneurs can forge _____ in the marketplace that are suited to their skills.

4. Consumer research is not for _____. It takes the skills of a _____ to work up a questionnaire free of bias—the basic requirement for a _____.

5. The word _____ refers to groups of individuals or organizations seeking products or services in the entrepreneur's industry. Market _____ is the process of dividing a total market into _____ of customers who have similar needs for either a product or a service.

© 1990 Houghton Mifflin Company. All rights reserved.   285

6. Markets can be segmented using four groups of factors: (1) product-_____ factors, (2) _____ factors, (3) _____ factors, and (4) _____ factors.

7. Every manufacturer, wholesaler, retailer, and service firm is part of a _____ network. The network's purpose is to move products from producers to _____.

8. When entrepreneurs charge what the market will bear, they are using a _____ price policy. When they set a low initial price in an effort to capture customers quickly, they are using a _____ price policy.

9. Entrepreneurs use advertising to _____ to customers about their product or service.

10. Personal _____ takes over where advertising leaves off. Because their goal is to create loyal _____, entrepreneurs should strike the right balance between advertising and personal selling.

11. Although no two selling situations are exactly alike, _____ generally follow a _____-step process.

12. Sales _____ makes both advertising and personal selling more effective. It can take many forms, among them (1) _____ to spur salespersons to sell more, (2) free _____ to introduce a new product, and (3) _____ to build up a product's image.

13. Marketing mix _____ widely from industry to industry. Even within an industry, marketing mix may vary among _____. And it also will vary during the life of a venture. The goal of marketing is to find a mix that creates satisfied customers at a _____.

14. Foreign markets are a fertile source of sales opportunities. In fact, billions of dollars worth of products and services are exported yearly to virtually all countries in the world. Of that total volume, less than _____ percent is accounted for by small business.

15. The reasons entrepreneurs tend to avoid export markets are threefold: (1) their fear of the _____, (2) their fear of long-_____ relationships, and (3) their fear of the _____.

16. To best serve a foreign market, entrepreneurs should prepare a separate _____ plan. this plan should rely heavily on marketing research already done by others, mostly by the Department of _____, local Chambers of _____, and (3) _____ countries themselves.

Essay Questions

1. Many experts claim that marketing research is the most important marketing activity of all. What types of questions should marketing research answer for the small-business owner?

© 1990 Houghton Mifflin Company. All rights reserved.

2. In giant corporations, the president can draw on in-house resources for marketing research. These corporations have marketing research departments staffed with high-powered professionals, many holding a master's degree in business administration. Yet few entrepreneurs can justify hiring a marketing researcher, let alone establishing a marketing research department. So how do entrepreneurs get the facts about their markets?

3. Describe the ways to segment a market.

4. Although no two selling situations are exactly alike, salespersons generally follow a seven-step process to sell a product. Describe the process a salesperson would use to sell a personal computer.

5. Foreign markets are a fertile source of sales opportunities. In fact, billions of dollars worth of products and services are exported yearly to virtually all countries of the world. Of that total volume, less than 5 percent is accounted for by small business. What are the reasons small-business owners avoid export markets?

The Difference Between Success and Failure

The market for consumer products is extremely important to all marketers for two reasons. American consumers have tremendous purchasing power. And perhaps more important, consumer buying patterns affect the markets for all goods—industrial goods as well as consumer goods.

To see this, we need only realize that the markets for industrial goods are derived from the markets for consumer goods. Without consumer goods, there would be no need for industrial goods. For example, suppose consumers stopped buying cars. The markets for sheet steel, fenders, assembly plants, spark plug gauges, and a host of other industrial products would either shrink or disappear entirely.

A market consists of people with needs, money to spend, and the desire and authority to spend it. Let us look first at consumer income, then at consumer buying behavior.

Consumer Income

Purchasing power is created by income. However, as every taxpayer knows, not all income is available for spending. For this reason, marketers define income in three different ways. *Personal income* is the income an individual receives from all sources less the Social Security taxes the individual must pay. *Disposable income* is personal income less all additional personal taxes. These taxes include income, estate, gift, and property taxes levied by local, state, and federal governments. About 5 percent of all disposable income is saved. On average, about 50 percent is spent on necessities (food, clothing, shelter). *Discretionary income* is disposable income less savings and expenditures on necessities. Discretionary income is of particular interest to marketers because consumers have the most choice in spending it. Consumers use their discretionary income to purchase items ranging from automobiles and vacations to movies and pet food.

© 1990 Houghton Mifflin Company. All rights reserved.

Americans are willing to spend not only present income but also income they have not yet earned. Credit cards are one means of "buying now and paying later." About 70 percent of American households have at least one credit card.

Consumer Buying Behavior

There has been a great deal of research regarding consumers' buying habits and behavior. Psychologists, for example, have found that Abraham Maslow's hierarchy of needs (see Chapter 16) has some application to buying behavior. People buy to meet unsatisfied lower-level needs first. Social scientists have found that there are also social, economic, and cultural influences on the way people buy. We limit our discussion of buying behavior to the more obvious buying patterns.

Why Do Consumers Buy? If we eliminate deep psychological and social motivations for buying, we come up with a very simple answer to this question. Consumers buy because they would rather have a particular good or service than the money they have to spend to buy it. More specifically, consumers may choose to buy a product for the following reasons:
1. They have a use for the product.
2. They like the convenience the product offers.
3. They believe the purchase will enhance their wealth.
4. They take pride in ownership.
5. They buy for safety.

What Do Consumers Buy? The table below shows how consumer spending is divided among various categories of products. As we have noted, the greatest proportion of disposable income is spent on food, clothing, and shelter. After these necessities have been provided, consumers tend to spend mostly on transportation, insurance, medical care, recreation, and contributions. (A mere 1 percent of total disposable income amounts to around $30 billion, so none of the categories in the table is really small in terms of total dollars spent.)

© 1990 Houghton Mifflin Company. All rights reserved.

PRODUCT	PERCENT OF DISPOSABLE INCOME
Reading	0.6
Tobacco	1.0
Personal care	1.0
Alcoholic beverages	1.4
Education	1.6
Other	1.8
Contributions	3.5
Medical care	4.6
Recreation	4.9
Clothing	5.9
Insurance	8.9
Food	15.0
Transportation	18.8
Housing	31.0

Source: Department of Labor, Bureau of Labor Statistics, "Survey of Consumer Expenditures," 1989.

Where Do Consumers Buy? Probably the most important factor that influences a consumer's decision on where to buy a particular product is his or her perception of the store. Consumers' general impressions of a store's products, prices, and sales personnel can mean the difference between repeat sales and lost business. Consumers distinguish among various types of retail outlets (specialty shops, department stores, discount outlets), and they choose particular types of stores for specific purchases. Many retail outlets go to a great deal of trouble to build and maintain a particular image, an image that is reflected in the products they carry.

Consumers also select the businesses they patronize on the basis of location, product assortment, and services (credit terms, return privileges, free delivery).

When Do Consumers Buy? In general, consumers buy when buying is most convenient. Certain business hours have long been standard for stores that sell consumer products. However, many of these establishments have stretched their hours to include evenings and Sundays (where local laws permit Sunday business). Ultimately, within each area, consumers themselves control when they do their buying.

© 1990 Houghton Mifflin Company. All rights reserved.

CHAPTER 15

Computers

Learning Objectives

After studying this chapter, you should understand

1. What the different types of computers are

2. How a small business can benefit from using a computer

3. How to find the right computer consultant

4. What some business applications of software are

5. What the entrepreneur should consider in selecting computer software and hardware

Chapter Review

As you read the chapter, complete the following outline with information from the text.

Collecting, analyzing, and reporting information are vital to the venture's survival and growth. In this chapter we examine computers—tools that help small-business owners manage information.

I. **Computer Basics.** The computer revolution has all but engulfed small business. Experts predict that computers will soon be as common as typewriters.

   A. **Types of Computers.** There are three basic types of computers. In your own words, describe them.

   Mainframes _____

   _____

   _____

   _____

Minicomputers _____

_____

_____

_____

Microcomputers _____

_____

_____

_____

B. **Computer Hardware.** Every computer consists of a basic set of physical components called *hardware* (Exhibit 15.2). Explain the function of each of these components.

Central processing unit _____

_____

Input unit _____

_____

Primary (short-term) memory _____

_____

_____

External storage (secondary or long-term memory) _____

_____

_____

Output unit _____

_____

C. **Computer Software.** *Software* is the term used for computer programs. These programs give the computer its instructions.

© 1990 Houghton Mifflin Company. All rights reserved.

How can small-business owners avoid hiring a full-time computer programmer?

_____

_____

II. **Computers and Small Business.** To make effective use of computers, entrepreneurs must become computer literate.

    A. **Benefits of Computer Use.** A computer makes good business sense. How can a computer affect a small firm's productivity?

_____

_____

_____

_____

_____

A computer streamlines the flow of work, reducing labor costs. Describe how a computer can reduce the number of hours an entrepreneur spends processing orders.

_____

_____

_____

Exhibit 15.3 lists the most important benefits of using a computer. What are they?

_____   _____

_____   _____

_____   _____

_____   _____

Entrepreneurs have too much at stake to ignore the computer's potential. Yet only 40 percent of the nation's small businesses used a computer in 1988 (Exhibit 15.4).

    B. **Software Applications for Small Businesses.** Computers can help streamline almost limitless office functions. Exhibit 15.5 lists some applications of software in small businesses.

© 1990 Houghton Mifflin Company. All rights reserved.

1. **Spreadsheets.** How can spreadsheet software help a small-business owner?

    _____

    _____

    _____

    _____

    What type of questions can spreadsheet programs answer?

    _____

2. **Word Processing.** How can word-processing software help a small-business owner?

    _____

    _____

    _____

    _____

3. **Database Management.** What does database management software do?

    _____

    _____

    _____

    _____

© 1990 Houghton Mifflin Company. All rights reserved.

How would it be used to facilitate a marketing program?

_____

_____

_____

_____

_____

4. **Project Management.** How can project management software help small-business owners?

_____

_____

_____

5. **Graphics Presentation.** What does graphics presentation software do?

_____

_____

_____

6. **Electronic Publishing.** What types of jobs can entrepreneurs carry out with electronic publishing software?

_____

_____

_____

© 1990 Houghton Mifflin Company. All rights reserved.

III. Installing a Computer System. Before installing a computer system, entrepreneurs should take time to explore what the system can do for them.

Entrepreneurs must carefully identify and define why they need to computerize. List two reasons why a computer consultant may be a necessary part of the decision-making process.

- _____

  _____

- _____

  _____

A. Hiring a Computer Consultant. In selecting a computer consultant, entrepreneurs should make sure the consultant understands their product. One way to do this is to ask the consultant to write a statement summarizing how the product is produced and marketed. What else should the statement do?

_____

_____

One clue that can help entrepreneurs evaluate a consultant is the consultant's working knowledge of the business's procedures and terminology.

Next entrepreneurs should commission a proposal for action. What should this contract specify?

_____

_____

Communication here is critical. Entrepreneurs must be able to understand exactly what the consultant is proposing.

B. Selecting Software. Although it might seem more logical to choose a computer system and then choose software, it is actually wiser to select the software first. Why?

_____

_____

_____

A computer is only as good as its software. What does this statement mean?

_____

_____

_____

With so many software packages available, it often is difficult to choose the one that best meets entrepreneurs' needs. Where can entrepreneurs turn for help choosing the right software?

_____

_____

C. **Selecting Hardware.** Having decided what software best fits their needs, entrepreneurs are ready to select the right hardware. What does the Bank of America recommend in the following areas?

Software requirements _____

_____

_____

_____

_____

Reputation and reliability _____

_____

_____

_____

_____

_____

© 1990 Houghton Mifflin Company. All rights reserved.

Expandability _____

_____

_____

_____

Cost _____

_____

_____

_____

_____

Maintenance _____

_____

_____

_____

_____

_____

_____

Compatibility _____

_____

_____

_____

D. **Selecting a Vendor.** Once a computer satisfies most, if not all, of the entrepreneurs' requirements, they can narrow the field of vendors, select one, negotiate terms, and purchase the software and hardware.

© 1990 Houghton Mifflin Company. All rights reserved.

What four factors affect the choice of a vendor?

_____   _____

_____   _____

What are two good sources of recommendations about a computer vendor?

- _____

- _____

Questions for Mastery

Questions for mastery are found in the textbook at the beginning of every chapter. Answer each question again to reinforce your understanding of the information.

1. What are the different types of computers?

_____

_____

_____

2. How can a small business benefit from using a computer?

_____

_____

_____

_____

_____

_____

3. How do you find the right computer consultant?

_____

_____

_____

© 1990 Houghton Mifflin Company. All rights reserved.

4. What are some business applications of software?

    _____

    _____

    _____

    _____

5. What should the entrepreneur consider in selecting computer software and hardware?

    _____

    _____

    _____

    _____

    _____

    _____

Definition of Key Terms

The following key terms are important in this chapter. In your own words, define each concept.

mainframe _____

    _____

minicomputer _____

    _____

microcomputer _____

    _____

hardware _____

    _____

© 1990 Houghton Mifflin Company. All rights reserved.   300

software _____

_____

central processing unit _____

_____

input unit _____

_____

output unit _____

_____

floppy disk _____

_____

programmer _____

_____

True-False Questions

Determine whether the following statements are true or false, then circle T or F. Correct answers are listed at the end of the study guide.

T   F   1. Collecting, analyzing, and reporting information are vital activities for today's small-business owners.

T   F   2. Although the computer revolution has engulfed big business, it has not affected small business.

T   F   3. With the invention of the transistor and the integrated circuit, computers have become smaller, more powerful, and less expensive.

T   F   4. There are three basic types of computers: mainframes, minicomputers, and microcomputers.

T   F   5. Mainframe computers are the largest and slowest computers available today.

T   F   6. Minicomputers often are called *desktop* or *laptop computers.*

T   F   7. Microcomputers are commonly known as personal computers.

© 1990 Houghton Mifflin Company. All rights reserved.   301

T   F   8.   Microcomputers are the least powerful of the three types of computers.

T   F   9.   Mainframe computers are popular with small businesses because they are relatively inexpensive.

T   F   10.   External storage is an unnecessary feature for microcomputers.

T   F   11.   *Software* means "computer programs."

T   F   12.   Pascal, BASIC, and FORTRAN are computer languages.

T   F   13.   In order to use a computer, a small-business owner must hire a full-time computer programmer.

T   F   14.   Ready-made software is too expensive for most small-business owners.

T   F   15.   To make effective use of computers, entrepreneurs must become computer literate.

T   F   16.   Computer literacy means knowing about electronics.

T   F   17.   The best reason for a small business to install a computer system is that it means good business.

T   F   18.   According to the National Federation of Independent Business, productivity means getting more output with less input.

T   F   19.   According to the National Federation of Independent Business, the most important benefit of using a computer is improved business information.

T   F   20.   In 1988, over 70 percent of the nation's small businesses used a computer.

T   F   21.   Spreadsheet software is used to process standardized letters.

T   F   22.   Database management software records, stores, organizes, manipulates, retrieves, and summarizes data.

T   F   23.   Database management software manipulates the data that used to be stored on file cards.

T   F   24.   Project management software helps entrepreneurs create graphic images and displays.

T   F   25.   Electronic publishing software can help entrepreneurs create brochures and newsletters.

© 1990 Houghton Mifflin Company. All rights reserved.

T F 26. Before installing a computer system, entrepreneurs should take time to explore what a system can do for their business.

T F 27. Most entrepreneurs have the expertise to identify their needs themselves.

T F 28. A contract with a computer consultant should specify what the proposed system will do for the small business.

T F 29. A small-business owner should select the computer hardware first, then the software.

T F 30. Today all software runs on all computer systems.

T F 31. A computer is only as good as its software.

T F 32. Before deciding on software, the entrepreneur should talk with other entrepreneurs who already have chosen software.

T F 33. Because the price of replacement equipment is so low, small-business owners do not have to worry about the maintenance costs of their computers.

T F 34. Compatibility—the ability to "talk" with other computers—should not be a factor in choosing a computer system for a small business.

T F 35. Perhaps the best way to find a computer vendor is to ask other entrepreneurs if they are satisfied with a vendor's performance.

Multiple-Choice Questions

Write the letter of the correct answer in the blank to the left of the question. Correct answers are listed at the end of the study guide.

_____ 1. Which of the following statements is *false?*
   a. Collecting, analyzing, and reporting information are vital activities that small-business owners cannot afford to dismiss.
   b. The computer revolution has all but engulfed small business.
   c. Thanks to the invention of the transistor, computers are much larger now than they were when they were first invented.
   d. Computers were invented in 1946.

_____ 2. The largest and fastest computer is the
   a. mainframe.
   b. minicomputer.
   c. microcomputer.
   d. desktop computer.

© 1990 Houghton Mifflin Company. All rights reserved.

_____ 3. The most popular computer among small-business owners is the
    a. mainframe.
    b. minicomputer.
    c. microcomputer.
    d. multicomputer.

_____ 4. The least expensive computer is the
    a. mainframe.
    b. minicomputer.
    c. microcomputer.
    d. multicomputer.

_____ 5. The physical components of a computer system are called the
    a. software.
    b. hardware.
    c. processor.
    d. program.

_____ 6. The heart of a computer system is the
    a. output unit.
    b. primary memory.
    c. input unit.
    d. central processing unit.

_____ 7. The keyboard on which users enter the data to be processed is called the _____ unit.
    a. output
    b. primary
    c. input
    d. central processing

_____ 8. The programs that give the computer its instructions are also called
    a. software.
    b. hardware.
    c. memory.
    d. processors.

_____ 9. Which of the following statements is *true?*
    a. A small-business owner must hire a computer programmer in order to use a computer effectively.
    b. To make effective use of computers, entrepreneurs must become computer literate.
    c. An understanding of electronics is essential to computer literacy.
    d. None of the above is true.

© 1990 Houghton Mifflin Company. All rights reserved.

____10. Productivity means getting
     a.   a computer.
     b.   a computer and a computer programmer.
     c.   more input with less output.
     d.   more output with less input.

____11. In 1988, only _____ percent of the nation's small businesses used a computer.
     a.   20
     b.   30
     c.   40
     d.   50

____12. _____ software organizes numerical data into rows and columns, and automatically calculates them.
     a.   Spreadsheet
     b.   Project management
     c.   Word-processing
     d.   Graphics presentation

____13. _____ software allows entrepreneurs to plan, track, and analyze complex projects.
     a.   Spreadsheet
     b.   Project management
     c.   Word-processing
     d.   Graphics presentation

____14. When purchasing a computer system, a small-business owner may find it advantageous to
     a.   hire a computer consultant.
     b.   buy the model at the top of the line.
     c.   buy the hardware first, then the software.
     d.   buy the hardware and not worry about the software.

____15. When purchasing a computer system, the best way to find a reliable vendor is to
     a.   look in the Yellow Pages.
     b.   go to an office equipment store.
     c.   go to a shopping mall.
     d.   talk to an entrepreneur who has purchased a system.

Completion Questions

Write your answer in the blanks provided in each question. Correct answers are listed at the end of the study guide.

1. There are three basic types of computers: _____, _____, and microcomputers.

© 1990 Houghton Mifflin Company. All rights reserved.

2. Microcomputers are commonly known as _____ computers. They also are called _____ or *laptop computers.*

3. Every computer consists of a basic set of physical components, known as _____.

4. A computer system consists of a _____ processing unit, an input unit, _____ (short-term) memory, external storage, and an _____ unit.

5. _____ is a term used for computer programs. These programs give the computer its _____.

6. Installing a computer system makes good business sense for a small business. Among the benefits are improved _____. Productivity means getting more output with less _____.

7. Many businesses use _____ software for writing standardized letters. With the use of a high-quality _____, each letter looks as if it was typed individually.

8. _____ management software records, stores, organizes, manipulates, retrieves, and summarizes _____.

9. Electronic, or _____, publishing software prepares and _____ a wide variety of _____-quality documents.

10. A _____ with a computer consultant should specify what the _____ system will be able to do for the business. It should be written in language that is easy to _____.

11. Although it may seem more logical to choose a computer system and then choose the _____ to use on it, it actually is wiser to select the software _____.

12. Perhaps the best way to find a computer vendor is to talk to other _____ who have purchased a computer system from the vendor and are satisfied with their purchase.

Essay Questions

1. Experts predict that computers will soon become as common as typewriters. Today there are three basic types of computers. In your own words describe each of them. Which type of computer is best for a small business? Why?

2. *Software* is the term used for computer programs, which give the computer its instructions. In the text a number of software packages are described. Pick two of them and describe what each can do for the small-business owner.

3. When purchasing a computer system, an entrepreneur must narrow the field of vendors, select one, negotiate terms, then purchase the software and hardware. What factors should be considered in choosing a vendor for a computer system?

© 1990 Houghton Mifflin Company. All rights reserved.

The Difference Between Success and Failure

A computer is a machine that can accept, store, manipulate, and transmit data following a specific set of instructions. It is not our purpose here to teach you how to use computers. (In fact you already may be proficient in computer use. More and more people are becoming computer literate each day.) Instead we identify the main components of the computer and define basic computer terms.

Computer Components

Most computers and computer systems consist of five basic components:

1. Input unit
2. Memory (storage) unit
3. Central processing unit
4. Arithmetic-logic unit
5. Output unit

The *input unit* is the device by which you enter data into the computer. In the past, data were fed to computers on punched cards, which were read by the input unit. Few systems use this method now. Instead data are entered through a keyboard (much like a typewriter keyboard) or on magnetic tapes or disks that the input unit can read.

The *memory unit* (or *storage unit*) stores all data entered into the computer and processed by it. One measure of a computer's power is the amount of data it can store at one time. This memory capacity is given in bytes. One byte is the capacity to store one character; K bytes is the capacity to store 1,024 characters. A personal computer with 256 K memory is capable of storing almost 60 pages of this book.

The *central processing unit* guides the entire operation of the computer. It transfers data and sends processing directions to the various other units in the proper sequence to carry out the user's instructions. The arithmetic-logic unit is the part of a computer that performs mathematical operations, comparisons of data, and other types of data transformations.

The *output unit* is the mechanism by which a computer transmits processed data to the user. Most computer output is printed on paper or displayed on a televisionlike screen called a *monitor.*

Hardware and Software

Computer *hardware* is the electronic equipment or machinery that makes up a computer system. The keyboard, the memory, the central processing unit, the arithmetic-logic unit, and the monitor or printer are all hardware. *Software,* on the other hand, is the set of instructions that tells a computer what to do. These instructions are called a *computer program.* The program controls the way the computer processes data.

© 1990 Houghton Mifflin Company. All rights reserved.   307

CHAPTER 16

Human Relations

Learning Objectives

After studying this chapter, you should understand

1. What human relations is

2. What participatory management is

3. What the needs of employees are and how they can be satisfied

4. What distinguishes the entrepreneur as a leader

5. What the most important aspects of wage and salary policies are

Chapter Review

As you read the chapter, complete the following outline with information from the text.

Far from being a mysterious science, human relations often is nothing more than good will and applied common sense. Much of an entrepreneur's success in human relations depends on simple things. But many entrepreneurs ignore these simple things, especially when their venture begins to grow.

I.   **The Importance of Human Relations.** So massive are many businesses today that workers lose all sense of human contact with their employers. What robs workers of their sense of personal pride?

_____

Often entrepreneurs lose sight of the importance of meaningful work in their rush to boost revenues. The result is unhappy workers.

Entrepreneurs can buy workers' time. But they cannot buy their enthusiasm, initiative, or loyalty. These they must earn.

© 1990 Houghton Mifflin Company. All rights reserved.

In return for their loyalty and enthusiasm, workers expect three things from entrepreneurs. What are they?

- _____

_____

- _____

_____

- _____

_____

All workers, whatever their abilities, have the right to be treated with respect and dignity.

Exhibit 16.1 shows four different styles of leadership. In your own words, describe them.

Oppressive autocratic _____

_____

_____

_____

Benevolent autocratic _____

_____

_____

_____

Consultative _____

_____

_____

_____

© 1990 Houghton Mifflin Company. All rights reserved.

Participatory _____

_____

_____

_____

One way for managers to instill a strong sense of purpose in workers is to share decision making with them. What is the basic premise of participatory management?

_____

_____

_____

Participatory management encourages managers to share decision making with workers. What else does it encourage managers to do?

- _____

- _____

- _____

- _____

Participatory management may not work well with all employees. It may not be for every venture. And it may not be for every entrepreneur. But studies suggest that participatory management can work well, especially in ventures that are struggling to keep pace with shifting markets or are growing at a fast pace. Why?

_____

_____

_____

The Japanese use participatory management almost exclusively. Their objective—group unity—helps them achieve two things. What are they?

_____

_____

© 1990 Houghton Mifflin Company. All rights reserved.   311

II. **Human Needs and Employee Motivation.** According to psychologists, needs are what motivate us. The process of motivation is circular—a person feels a need, makes an effort to satisfy the need, and receives feedback that leads to a new need. Workers are motivated to behave in certain ways because of their needs for money, security, and status.

Work helps satisfy these needs. It gives them money with which to buy security (food, clothing, shelter). How does work satisfy employees' status needs?

_____

_____

_____

_____

A. **Maslow's Hierarchy of Needs.** Dr. Abraham Maslow classified all human needs in order of their importance to the individual, and presented them in five levels (Exhibit 16.2). In your own words, describe each level.

Physiological needs _____

_____

_____

Safety _____

_____

_____

Belongingness and love _____

_____

_____

Esteem _____

_____

_____

© 1990 Houghton Mifflin Company. All rights reserved.   312

Self-actualization _____

_____

_____

B. **Theory X and Theory Y.** Douglas McGregor proposed two theories of human behavior—Theory X and Theory Y—that focus on the assumptions entrepreneurs and managers make about employee motivation.

Exhibit 16.3 compares the two theories. What are the assumptions associated with Theory X?

- _____

- _____

- _____

- _____

What are the assumptions associated with Theory Y?

- _____

- _____

- _____

- _____

_____

How do McGregor's theories relate to Maslow's hierarchy of needs?

_____

_____

_____

C. **The Hawthorne Experiment.** Workers want entrepreneurs to treat them as individuals; they crave recognition for a job well done. What happens when workers are treated as individuals was demonstrated by the now-famous Hawthorne Experiment. Describe the experiment.

_____

_____

_____

_____

_____

_____

_____

What were the findings of the Hawthorne Experiment?

_____

_____

_____

_____

III. **The Entrepreneur as Leader.** Today, managing often is looked on as the job of getting work done through others. But managing means much more. It means making it possible for others to work easily and productively, and bringing out the best in them.

First, entrepreneurs must want to help employees become achievers. What many entrepreneurs lack is an understanding of just how much managerial style can affect the survival and growth of their venture. They need to analyze their managerial style. Take a few minutes and answer the questions on the Likert scale in Exhibit 16.4. What do your answers tell you about your managerial style?

_____

_____

_____

© 1990 Houghton Mifflin Company. All rights reserved.

A. **Self-Image.** Entrepreneurs cannot begin to know their workers without first knowing themselves. Why is the entrepreneur's self-image so important?

_____

_____

_____

_____

_____

What advice does Robert Townsend offer the small-business owner?

_____

_____

_____

B. **The Entrepreneur as Coach.** Entrepreneurs can learn the art of bringing out the best in their workers by using the methods athletic coaches do. How do coaches help their players perform better?

• _____

_____

• _____

_____

_____

• _____

_____

_____

© 1990 Houghton Mifflin Company. All rights reserved.

Creating this kind of work atmosphere is difficult. No two workers are exactly alike. What appeals to one may repel another. To help workers achieve their best, then, entrepreneurs must understand their individual needs.

C. **Giving Recognition to Workers.** Entrepreneurs should help workers earn status, to improve their opinions of themselves and their jobs. In what ways can entrepreneurs help workers earn status?

- _____

- _____

_____

- _____

_____

- _____

- _____

_____

Growing ventures attract talented men and women. To keep their ventures growing entrepreneurs must share them with their workers. In what ways can entrepreneurs share a venture with their workers?

- _____

- _____

_____

- _____

- _____

- _____

_____

© 1990 Houghton Mifflin Company. All rights reserved.

Entrepreneurs must earn their workers' respect and loyalty. Of course, there is no one best way to manage a venture. Each entrepreneur has a unique style of managing. But successful entrepreneurs tend to do many of the same things. What are they?

- _____

- _____

- _____

_____

- _____

- _____

- _____

- _____

Of these, the pursuit of excellence day in and day out is the most critical. Generally, excellence is a product of expectations. Entrepreneurs who expect excellence from their workers often get it.

Entrepreneurs crave workers' loyalty. Some entrepreneurs, however, expect workers to stick by them through good times and bad; and regardless of how they are treated.

True loyalty means working up to one's capabilities, doing the best one knows how. True loyalty is to the job, not the entrepreneur.

D. **The McKinsey Study on Excellence.** In the early 1980s, few business subjects sparked more interest than excellence or, more accurately, the pursuit of excellence. One study was done by a large management-consulting firm, McKinsey & Company. List the traits it found in successful smaller businesses.

- _____

- _____

- _____

- _____

- _____

- _____

© 1990 Houghton Mifflin Company. All rights reserved.

- _____
- _____
- _____
- _____

IV. Wage and Salary Policies. A human relations policy must be supported by attractive wage and salary incentives. Motivation and pay go hand in hand. Generally, highly motivated workers produce at a higher rate and hence merit more pay. In turn they expect their pay to reflect the skills and energy they put into their jobs.

To attract and keep good workers, entrepreneurs should make sure their pay scale compares favorably with those of competitors, or they may find themselves stripped of talent.

A. Legal Obligations. No matter how wages and salaries are set, entrepreneurs must meet certain legal obligations. For example, entrepreneurs who pay more than $50 in quarterly wages must pay Social Security taxes. What does the payment of these taxes require entrepreneurs to do?

- _____
  _____
- _____
- _____
  _____

Besides Social Security taxes, entrepreneurs must meet other legal obligations. How do the items listed below affect employers?

Federal income taxes _____

_____

_____

Workers' compensation insurance _____

_____

_____

State unemployment insurance _____

_____

_____

_____

Federal unemployment taxes _____

_____

_____

_____

Federal wage and hour laws _____

_____

_____

_____

Civil Rights Act, Title VII _____

_____

_____

_____

_____

B. **Fringe Benefits.** Fringe benefits, a form of pay, have given the average worker a standard of living higher than ever before. What benefits does the average worker now receive?

- _____

- _____

- _____

- _____

© 1990 Houghton Mifflin Company. All rights reserved.

In 1985 these benefits cost the average employer about 33 percent of the yearly payroll—and the percentage keeps rising almost every year.

Why do entrepreneurs have to offer attractive fringe benefits?

- _____

- _____

- _____

- _____

_____

Questions for Mastery

Questions for mastery are found in the textbook at the beginning of every chapter. Answer each question again to reinforce your understanding of the information.

1. What is human relations?

_____

_____

_____

2. What is participatory management?

_____

_____

_____

_____

© 1990 Houghton Mifflin Company. All rights reserved.

3. What are the needs of employees and how can they be satisfied?

    _____

    _____

    _____

    _____

    _____

    _____

4. What distinguishes the entrepreneur as a leader?

    _____

    _____

    _____

    _____

5. What are the most important aspects of wage and salary policies?

    _____

    _____

    _____

    _____

    _____

Definitions of Key Terms

The following key terms are important in this chapter. In your own words, define each concept.

physiological needs _____

_____

safety needs _____

_____

belongingness and love needs _____

_____

esteem needs _____

_____

self-actualization needs _____

_____

Theory X _____

_____

Theory Y _____

_____

workers' compensation _____

_____

participatory management _____

_____

managing _____

_____

needs _____

_____

fringe benefits _____

_____

© 1990 Houghton Mifflin Company. All rights reserved.

True-False Questions

Determine whether the following statements are true or false, then circle T or F. Correct answers are listed at the end of the study guide.

T   F   1.   So massive are many businesses today that workers lose all sense of human contact with their employers.

T   F   2.   In many industries, a high degree of mechanization gives workers a real sense of pride.

T   F   3.   One of the tenets of human relations is that life can be made more enjoyable by making work more routine.

T   F   4.   Employers can buy their workers' enthusiasm.

T   F   5.   Workers generally do better when they are singled out for personal attention.

T   F   6.   Workers expect employers to give them a chance to advance as a venture grows.

T   F   7.   The oppressive autocrat may ask employees for recommendations before making decisions.

T   F   8.   Most employees respond well to the oppressive autocratic style of leadership.

T   F   9.   The benevolent autocrat's attitude toward employees is warm, friendly, courteous, and respectful.

T   F   10. In the consultative style of leadership, entrepreneurs make the final decisions.

T   F   11. The process of shared decision making is called *perpetual management.*

T   F   12. Studies show that happy workers sometimes are simply happy—not necessarily productive.

T   F   13. A manager with an autocratic leadership style usually finds it easy to adapt to participatory management.

T   F   14. For a small business, the autocratic style of leadership is always the best way to manage.

T   F   15. Perhaps the best known practitioners of participatory management are the Americans.

T   F   16. The process of motivation is circular.

© 1990 Houghton Mifflin Company. All rights reserved.   323

T   F   17. Workers are motivated to behave in certain ways because they need certain things.

T   F   18. Work helps satisfy workers' physical and emotional needs.

T   F   19. According to Maslow, the first or lowest level of needs is associated with the need to belong.

T   F   20. According to Maslow, the highest or fifth level of needs is self-actualization.

T   F   21. A Theory Y worker must be forced to do work under threat of punishment.

T   F   22. According to Theory X, work is as natural as rest.

T   F   23. The overriding reason for using Theory Y rather than Theory X is that entrepreneurs are much more likely to succeed by satisfying the human needs of their employees than by ignoring them.

T   F   24. A classic example of what happens when workers are treated as individuals was demonstrated in the 1920s by the Halo Experiment.

T   F   25. Entrepreneurs can determine whether their managerial style is authoritarian or participative by using the Likert scale.

T   F   26. There is no similarity between the role of a coach and the role of an entrepreneur.

T   F   27. Entrepreneurs can help employees earn status and gain a better opinion of themselves and their jobs by taking workers' ideas and suggestions to heart.

T   F   28. True worker loyalty is to the entrepreneur, not the job.

T   F   29. Successful small businesses create and develop small market niches.

T   F   30. According to McKinsey & Company, successful small businesses compete on price, not value.

T   F   31. Successful small businesses motivate with money.

T   F   32. Good human relations must be supported by attractive wage and salary incentives.

T   F   33. Employees who work for a small firm know the entrepreneur cannot pay salaries that compare with larger firms so they don't worry about money.

T   F   34. For every employee who earns more than $50 in quarterly wages, the firm must pay Social Security taxes.

© 1990 Houghton Mifflin Company. All rights reserved.

T   F   35. Entrepreneurs are responsible for matching the dollar amount the employee contributes to federal income tax.

T   F   36. If entrepreneurs sell across state lines, hold federal government contracts, or have revenues in excess of $500,000, they must abide by federal wage and hour laws.

T   F   37. In 1985, fringe benefits cost an average of 27 percent of the employer's payroll.

T   F   38. Fringe benefits are so common today that workers look on them as a right, not a privilege.

Multiple-Choice Questions

Write the letter of the correct answer in the blank to the left of the question. Correct answers are listed at the end of the study guide.

_____ 1. An entrepreneur can buy all of the following *except* a
     a. worker's time.
     b. worker's loyalty.
     c. worker's physical presence at a given place.
     d. measured number of skilled muscular motions per hour.

_____ 2. Entrepreneurs who adopt the _____ leadership style are absolute dictators.
     a. benevolent autocratic
     b. consultative
     c. oppressive autocratic
     d. participatory

_____ 3. A leadership style that is both task oriented and employee oriented at the same time is
     a. benevolent autocratic.
     b. consultative.
     c. oppressive autocratic.
     d. participatory.

_____ 4. The practice of shared decision making is called _____ management.
     a. participatory
     b. perpetual
     c. innovative
     d. benevolent

© 1990 Houghton Mifflin Company. All rights reserved.

_____ 5. The best-known practitioners of participatory management are the
- a. Americans.
- b. British.
- c. Germans.
- d. Japanese.

_____ 6. Workers seek status through
- a. promotions.
- b. merit salary increases.
- c. the acquisition of new skills.
- d. all of the above.

_____ 7. According to Maslow, all of the following are needs *except*
- a. love.
- b. safety.
- c. money.
- d. esteem.

_____ 8. According to _____, entrepreneurs assume that employees hate work and so must be forced to do it under threat of punishment.
- a. Theory X
- b. Theory Y
- c. the McKinsey study
- d. Hawthorne Experiment

_____ 9. To foster sharing, entrepreneurs should
- a. set broad goals.
- b. create opportunities for personal growth.
- c. adopt the benevolent autocratic leadership style.
- d. try to routinize employees' work as much as possible.

_____10. The McKinsey study found that successful smaller businesses
- a. innovate as a way of life.
- b. concentrate on large market segments.
- c. compete on price, not value.
- d. are reluctant to experiment.

_____11. Which of the following statements is *false*?
- a. A human relations policy must be supported by attractive wage and salary incentives.
- b. To attract and keep good workers, entrepreneurs should make sure their pay scale compares favorably with those of competitors.
- c. One sound policy is to pay workers on merit, gearing their pay to performance.
- d. To avoid the problem of employee turnover, entrepreneurs should pay the highest salaries of their geographical region.

© 1990 Houghton Mifflin Company. All rights reserved.

_____12. Entrepreneurs who pay more than $50 in _____ wages must pay Social Security taxes.
    a.   monthly
    b.   quarterly
    c.   semiannual
    d.   yearly

_____13. If they pay salaries and wages or have workers who report tips, entrepreneurs must withhold a certain amount from each worker's paycheck for
    a.   federal income taxes.
    b.   workers' compensation insurance.
    c.   federal unemployment taxes.
    d.   all of the above.

_____14. All of the following are considered fringe benefits today *except*
    a.   paid vacations.
    b.   life insurance.
    c.   paid leave for illness.
    d.   workers' compensation insurance.

_____15. In 1985, fringe benefits accounted for _____ percent of the employer's yearly payroll.
    a.   22
    b.   27
    c.   30
    d.   33

Completion Questions

Write your answer in the blanks provided in each question. Correct answers are listed at the end of the study guide.

1. The _____ autocrat is an absolute dictator. The _____ autocrat is task oriented and employee oriented at the same time.

2. _____ management is the practice of shared decision making. It assumes that if entrepreneurs recognize the _____ needs of workers as well as their economic needs, workers will respond with _____ performance and will help shape the venture's changing goals.

3. The process of motivation is _____. Workers are motivated to behave in certain ways because of their _____ for certain things, among them money, security, and status.

4. Maslow classified all human needs in order of importance to the _____ and presented them as a pyramid of _____ levels.

© 1990 Houghton Mifflin Company. All rights reserved.

5. Set forth by _____, Theory X and Theory Y are two of the most widely quoted theories about human behavior. Theory _____ assumes that employees hate work and must be forced to do it under threat of punishment. According to Theory _____, work is as natural as rest.

6. In the 1920s, Professor Elton _____ of Harvard University asked 2,000 workers at the _____ plant of the Western Electric Company how they felt about their jobs, their bosses, and the company.

7. One way to determine if a manager's leadership style is _____ or participative is to use the _____ scale.

8. Entrepreneurs crave workers' _____. Some entrepreneurs, however, believe that their workers should be _____ loyal to them. This kind of false loyalty weakens a venture. True loyalty is to the _____, not the entrepreneur.

9. According to the McKinsey study, successful smaller businesses _____ as a way of life, create and develop small market _____, and compete on _____, not price.

10. To attract and keep good workers, entrepreneurs should make sure their pay scale compares favorably with those of _____.

11. For employees who earn more than _____ in quarterly wages, the firm must pay _____ Security taxes. Employers also must withhold a certain amount from each worker's paycheck to pay the worker's federal _____ taxes.

12. In 1985, fringe benefits accounted for _____ percent of the average employer's payroll.

Essay Questions

1. One way for entrepreneurs to instill a strong sense of purpose in workers is to share decision making with them. In the real world, what are some ways that a small-business owner can let workers share in the decision-making process?

2. What are the advantages and disadvantages of each of the four major leadership styles discussed in the text?

3. How can entrepreneurs help workers earn status, to gain a better opinion of themselves and their jobs, and give recognition where recognition is due?

4. In the 1980s, few business subjects sparked more interest than excellence or, more accurately, the pursuit of excellence. Although most authors focused on successful big businesses and what made them tick, others looked at successful small businesses. One such study was done by McKinsey & Company. According to the results of that study, what traits do successful small businesses have in common?

© 1990 Houghton Mifflin Company. All rights reserved.

The Difference Between Success and Failure

Compensation Decisions

Compensation is the payment employees receive in return for their labor. Its importance to employees is obvious. And because compensation can account for up to 80 percent of a firm's operating costs, it is equally important to employers. For most firms, designing an effective compensation system requires three separate management decisions.

The Wage-Level Decision. Employers first must position the firm's general pay level relative to pay levels of comparable firms. In other words, should the firm pay its employees less than, more than, or about the same as similar organizations? Most firms choose a pay level near the industry average. A firm that is not in good financial shape may pay less than the going rate. Large prosperous organizations, by contrast, may pay a little more than average to attract and retain the most capable employees.

The Wage-Structure Decision. Next employers must decide on relative pay levels for all the positions within the firm. Should managers be paid more than secretaries? Should secretaries be paid more than custodians? The product of this decision (actually, it is a set of decisions) often is called the firm's *wage structure.*

The wage structure almost always is developed on the basis of a job evaluation. *Job evaluation* is the process of determining the relative worth of the various jobs in a firm. Most observers probably would agree that a secretary should make more money than a custodian, but how much more? Twice as much? One and a half times as much? Job evaluation should provide the answers to these kinds of questions.

A number of techniques can be used to evaluate jobs. The simplest is to rank all the jobs in the firm according to their value to the firm. A more common method is based on job analysis. Points are allocated to each job for each of its elements and requirements. The more points a job is allocated, the more important it is presumed to be and the higher its level in the firm's wage structure.

The Individual-Wage Decision. Finally the specific payments that individual jobholders will receive must be determined. Consider the case of two secretaries working side by side. Job evaluation has been used to determine the relative level of their pay within the firm's wage structure. However, suppose one secretary has 15 years of experience and can type 80 words a minute. The other has 2 years of experience and can type only 55 words a minute. In most firms, these people would not receive the same pay. Instead a wage range would be established for the secretarial position. Suppose this range was $6.00 to $10.00 an hour. The more experienced and proficient secretary would be paid an amount near the top of the range (say, $9.80 an hour). The less experienced secretary would receive a lower amount within the range (say, $6.75 an hour).

© 1990 Houghton Mifflin Company. All rights reserved.   329

Types of Compensation

Hourly Wage. An *hourly wage* is a specific amount of money paid for each hour of work. People who earn wages are paid their hourly wage for the first 40 hours worked in any week. Then they are paid one and a half times their hourly wage for time worked in excess of 40 hours. (That is, they are paid time and a half for overtime.) Workers in retailing and fast-food chains, on assembly lines, and in clerical positions usually are paid an hourly wage.

Weekly or Monthly Salary. A *salary* is a specific amount of money paid for an employee's work during a set calendar period, regardless of the actual number of hours worked. Salaried employees receive no overtime pay, but they do not lose pay when they are absent from work (within reasonable limits). Most professional and managerial positions are salaried.

Commissions. A *commission* is a payment that is some percentage of sales revenue. Sales representatives and sales managers often are paid entirely through commissions or through a combination of commissions and salary.

Bonuses. A *bonus* is a payment in addition to wages, salary, or commission. Bonuses are really rewards for outstanding job performance. They may be distributed to all employees or only to certain employees within the organization. Some firms distribute bonuses to all employees every Christmas. The size of the bonus depends on the firm's earnings and the particular employee's length of service with the firm. Other firms offer bonuses to employees who exceed specific sales or production goals.

Profit Sharing. *Profit sharing* is the distribution of a percentage of the firm's profit among its employees. The idea is to motivate employees to work effectively by giving them a stake in the company's financial success. Some firms link their profit-sharing plans to employee retirement programs; that is, employees receive their profit-sharing distributions, with interest, when they retire.

© 1990 Houghton Mifflin Company. All rights reserved.

CHAPTER 17

Purchasing and Inventories

Learning Objectives

After studying this chapter, you should understand

1. What purchasing is

2. Why efficient purchasing is important

3. What inventories are

4. How inventories can be controlled

5. What the relationship is between purchasing and inventories

Chapter Review

As you read the chapter, complete the following outline with information from the text.

How well entrepreneurs do their buying may spell the difference between profit and loss.

I. **The Importance of Purchasing.** The goal of purchasing should be to improve a venture's profit. This is why entrepreneurs should make every effort to choose materials, services, and sources of supply that best meet their needs at the lowest possible cost, without sacrificing quality for price.

   To some entrepreneurs, the idea that purchasing can make or break a venture seems far-fetched. It is not. How much do businesses in the following industries spend on purchasing materials from suppliers?

   Wholesalers _____

   Retailers _____

   Manufacturers _____

© 1990 Houghton Mifflin Company. All rights reserved.

II. Purchasing Management. Purchasing covers much more ground than just buying. What else does purchasing require entrepreneurs to do?

- _____

- _____

- _____

  _____

- _____

  _____

- _____

  _____

The classic rule of thumb is to buy materials and services of the right *quality* of the right *quantity* at the right *time* from the right *supplier* at the right *price*.

A. Purchasing Guidelines. How do each of these guidelines affect the purchasing process?

1. Buying the Right Quality _____

  _____

  _____

  _____

  _____

2. Buying the Right Quantity _____

  _____

  _____

  _____

  _____

© 1990 Houghton Mifflin Company. All rights reserved.

3.   Buying at the Right Time _____

_____

_____

_____

_____

4.   Buying from the Right Suppliers _____

_____

_____

_____

_____

5.   Buying at the Right Price _____

_____

_____

_____

_____

B.   The Purchasing Cycle. By following these guidelines, entrepreneurs are likely to make wise purchases. The SBA recommends a four-step purchasing cycle. Describe each of the steps in that cycle.

Estimating needs _____

_____

_____

_____

_____

_____

© 1990 Houghton Mifflin Company. All rights reserved.   333

Selecting a supplier _____

_____

_____

_____

_____

_____

_____

Negotiating the purchase _____

_____

_____

_____

_____

Following through _____

_____

_____

_____

C. **Keeping Records.** Entrepreneurs must keep records as their venture begins to grow. What should a good recordkeeping system enable entrepreneurs to keep track of?

- _____

- _____

- _____

- _____

- _____

- _____

D. **Measuring Purchasing Performance.** Entrepreneurs should measure their purchasing performance at least once a year. What two questions should they ask?

- _____

_____

- _____

A common way to measure purchasing performance is to compare the cost of goods sold with the industry average.

III. **Inventory Management.** In manufacturing, *inventory* means the raw materials that are stored in warehouses to make a product. In retailing, it means the products for sale that are stored in stock rooms and on display shelves.

Why have inventory at all?

- _____

_____

- _____

_____

- _____

_____

- _____

- _____

- _____

- _____

Every entrepreneur should think through the reasons for inventory before planning and controlling inventory levels.

© 1990 Houghton Mifflin Company. All rights reserved.   335

A. Forecasting and Control. To plan their inventory, entrepreneurs always should begin by forecasting their sales revenues. At best, forecasts are intelligent guesswork. For most entrepreneurs, two central questions defy precise answers. What are they?

- _____

- _____

To decide on the right amount of merchandise to order, entrepreneurs should rely on a tool called *inventory control*. Inventory control strikes a balance among conflicting pressures. What are the goals of inventory control (Exhibit 17.4)?

- _____

_____

- _____

_____

- _____

_____

B. Turnover Analysis. Together with the revenue forecast, turnover analysis enables entrepreneurs to estimate how many months' supply to keep on hand. Turnover is generally the best measure of how well entrepreneurs are managing their purchases.

What does a low turnover mean?

_____

_____

What does a high turnover mean?

_____

_____

What is a stockout?

_____

_____

© 1990 Houghton Mifflin Company. All rights reserved.

Why do inventory turnovers differ in different industries?

_____

_____

_____

As a way to judge inventories, turnover is by no means flawless. What is the relationship between the rate of turnover and profit?

_____

_____

_____

There is no one best way to control inventories. In fact technique is less important here than the method of analysis. Why?

_____

_____

_____

C. **Physical Inventory.** A physical inventory compares actual materials on hand to those shown in the inventory records. If book inventory and physical inventory differ, the records should be adjusted immediately. List four reasons for an inventory shortage.

_____   _____

_____   _____

How can receiving and billing procedures create an inventory shortage?

_____

_____

_____

_____

© 1990 Houghton Mifflin Company. All rights reserved.

• _____

_____

_____

_____

• _____

_____

_____

_____

D. **Inventory Costs.** Buying and holding inventories are costly. Many entrepreneurs count only the purchase price of materials, ignoring the costs incurred after their purchase. What are those costs?

• _____

• _____

• _____

• _____

One estimate puts the average carrying cost at 21 percent of the purchase cost of inventory. However, carrying costs vary sharply from industry to industry.

Carrying costs are extremely hard to measure, particularly the cost of money and the cost of shortages. How do each of these factors affect entrepreneurs?

Cost of money _____

_____

_____

_____

_____

_____

Cost of shortages _____

_____

_____

_____

_____

What does the cost of shortages include?

- _____

_____

- _____

_____

_____

- _____

Questions for Mastery

Questions for mastery are found in the textbook at the beginning of every chapter. Answer each question again to reinforce your understanding of the information.

1. What is purchasing?

_____

_____

_____

2. Why is efficient purchasing important?

_____

_____

_____

© 1990 Houghton Mifflin Company. All rights reserved.

3. What are inventories?

_____

_____

_____

4. How can inventories be controlled?

_____

_____

_____

_____

_____

5. What is the relationship between purchasing and inventories?

_____

_____

_____

_____

Definitions of Key Terms

The following key terms are important in this chapter. In your own words, define each concept.

turnover _____

_____

inventory _____

_____

© 1990 Houghton Mifflin Company. All rights reserved.

inventory control _____

_____

purchase requisition _____

_____

carrying costs _____

_____

cost of money _____

_____

cost of shortages _____

_____

stockout _____

_____

physical inventory _____

_____

book inventory _____

_____

purchasing cycle _____

_____

True-False Questions

Determine whether the following statements are true or false, then circle T or F. Correct answers are listed at the end of the study guide.

T   F   1. How well entrepreneurs do their buying may spell the difference between profit and loss.

T   F   2. The goal of purchasing should be to improve a venture's profits.

T   F   3.   Wholesalers spend 60 to 65 cents of every sales dollar to purchase materials for resale.

T   F   4.   Retailers spend between 80 and 90 cents of every sales dollar to purchase materials for resale.

T   F   5.   Manufacturers spend 20 to 50 cents of every sales dollar to purchase raw materials.

T   F   6.   Entrepreneurs should try to buy materials of the right quality, of the right quantity, at the right time, from the right supplier, at the right price.

T   F   7.   In retailing, too little inventory can result in a loss of customers.

T   F   8.   Picking the right supplier is one of the entrepreneur's most challenging decisions.

T   F   9.   When purchasing raw materials or other supplies, the right price is always the lowest price.

T   F   10. For most merchandise, there are several potential suppliers.

T   F   11. A good recordkeeping system enables entrepreneurs to keep track of order cycles.

T   F   12. As defined in the text, inventory relates to both material goods and services.

T   F   13. To plan their inventory, entrepreneurs should begin by forecasting their sales revenues.

T   F   14. To decide on the right amount of merchandise to order, entrepreneurs should rely on a tool called *inventory control.*

T   F   15. Inventory turnover is the average number of times that inventory is sold out during the year.

T   F   16. If the average yearly turnover for wholesale grocers is 100, an inventory turnover of 90 would indicate that the grocer is doing an exceptional job of managing inventory.

T   F   17. In general, the less money tied up in inventory, the better, so long as stockouts are held to an acceptable level.

T   F   18. Manufacturers have a very narrow range of inventory turnovers.

T   F   19. As a way to judge inventories, turnover is flawless.

© 1990 Houghton Mifflin Company. All rights reserved.

T   F   20. Inventory control consists of one mathematical formula that tells entrepreneurs when it is time to reorder merchandise.

T   F   21. Simple mathematical formulas are the most effective tool small-business owners have to determine when to reorder merchandise.

T   F   22. To make sure that the actual amount of material on hand equals that shown in inventory records, entrepreneurs should take a perpetual inventory.

T   F   23. If entrepreneurs find that book inventory and physical inventory differ, they should adjust the records on a monthly basis.

T   F   24. Of all the reasons for inventory shortage, pilferage is the most easily understood.

T   F   25. If the amount of merchandise a firm receives is less than the amount invoiced, the entrepreneur is paying the difference.

T   F   26. According to the SBA, most entrepreneurs adopt procedures to protect against inventory shortages caused by poor receiving procedures, poor billing procedures, and merchandise damage.

T   F   27. The average carrying cost of inventory is 45 percent of the purchase cost of the inventory.

T   F   28. The main reason entrepreneurs ignore carrying costs may be that they rarely appear as such in accounting records.

T   F   29. The cost of shortages includes loss of good will and future orders.

T   F   30. The dollar cost of shortages defies computation.

Multiple-Choice Questions

Write the letter of the correct answer in the blank to the left of the question. Correct answers are listed at the end of the study guide.

_____ 1. Manufacturers spend _____ cents of every dollar to purchase raw materials from suppliers for conversion into finished products.
   a. 20 to 50
   b. 30 to 60
   c. 40 to 60
   d. 50 to 70

© 1990 Houghton Mifflin Company. All rights reserved.   343

_____ 2. If the entrepreneur's profit-to-sales ratio is 2 percent, purchase savings of $1,000 would be equivalent to the profit earned on a sales increase of
   a. $5,000.
   b. $10,000.
   c. $20,000.
   d. $50,000.

_____ 3. The first step in the purchasing cycle is
   a. estimating needs.
   b. selecting a supplier.
   c. negotiating the purchase.
   d. following through.

_____ 4. A good recordkeeping system should enable entrepreneurs to keep track of
   a. all orders received and all shipments made to customers.
   b. the rates at which purchased materials are used.
   c. the names of suppliers and their price lists.
   d. all of the above.

_____ 5. Which of the following statements is _false?_
   a. To plan their inventory, entrepreneurs should begin by forecasting their sales revenues.
   b. To decide on the right amount of merchandise, entrepreneurs should rely on a tool called _inventory control._
   c. In forecasting sales revenues, the two central questions are When should I order? and How much should I pay?
   d. As a way to judge inventories, turnover is by no means flawless.

_____ 6. If the average yearly turnover for wholesale grocers is 100, an inventory turnover of 110 would indicate
   a. that the entrepreneur is carrying slow-moving merchandise.
   b. that the entrepreneur is carrying fast-moving merchandise.
   c. that the entrepreneur should change suppliers.
   d. none of the above.

_____ 7. The inventory turnover for wholesaler grocers
   a. is the same as that for all other wholesalers or retailers.
   b. differs from that of most other wholesalers or retailers.
   c. is unimportant if the grocery store is a small business.
   d. is the same as the inventory turnover for restaurants.

_____ 8. To make sure that the actual amount of material on hand equals that shown in the inventory records, entrepreneurs should take a(n)
   a. immediate inventory.
   b. perpetual inventory.
   c. physical inventory.
   d. book inventory.

© 1990 Houghton Mifflin Company. All rights reserved.

_____ 9. Which of the following statements is *false?*
   a. Pilferage is the most easily understood reason for a difference between book inventory and physical inventory.
   b. Entrepreneurs may ignore opportunities to return merchandise to suppliers when it arrives in a condition unfit for resale.
   c. Entrepreneurs may have poor receiving procedures that result in their paying for merchandise that is never received.
   d. According to the SBA, most entrepreneurs don't take steps to guard against theft.

_____10. Inventory carrying costs include all of the following *except*
   a. storage and handling.
   b. paperwork.
   c. interest, insurance, and property taxes.
   d. postage.

_____11. One estimate puts the average carrying cost at _____ percent of the purchase cost of inventory.
   a. 15
   b. 21
   c. 33
   d. 35

_____12. The most crucial of all inventory carrying costs is the cost of
   a. money.
   b. shortages.
   c. storage and handling.
   d. paperwork.

_____13. The cost of shortages can include
   a. revenues lost because orders could not be filled.
   b. excess costs incurred to speed up production.
   c. loss of good will and future orders.
   d. all of the above.

Completion Questions

Write your answer in the blanks provided in each question. Correct answers are listed at the end of the study guide.

1. The goal of purchasing should be to improve a venture's _____. To some entrepreneurs, the idea that _____ can make or break a venture seems farfetched. It is not.

2. Notice how widely purchasing varies in its impact. It is vital in _____ and _____; it is less so in manufacturing.

© 1990 Houghton Mifflin Company. All rights reserved.

3. It is the entrepreneur's responsibility to buy materials and services of the right _____, of the right _____, at the right _____, from the right _____, at the right _____.

4. The SBA suggests that entrepreneurs follow a purchasing cycle that includes four steps: (1) _____ needs, (2) selecting a _____, (3) _____ the purchase, and (4) _____ through.

5. In manufacturing, _____ means the raw materials that are stored in warehouses. In retailing, it means the products for sale to _____ that are stored in stock rooms and on display shelves.

6. To plan their inventory, entrepreneurs should begin by _____ their sales revenues. At best, _____ are intelligent guesswork.

7. Inventory turnover is defined as the _____ number of times inventory is sold out during the year. Inventory turnover is generally the best measure of how well entrepreneurs manage their _____.

8. In general, the _____ money tied up in inventory, the better, so long as _____ are held to an acceptable level.

9. To make sure that the actual amount of material on hand equals that shown in inventory records, entrepreneurs should take a _____ inventory. If they find that the _____ inventory and physical inventory differ, they should adjust their records _____.

10. There are many reasons for an inventory shortage. For example, materials may have been _____, lost, thrown away, or overlooked when the _____ inventory was taken. Or entrepreneurs may have poor _____ and billing procedures.

11. To buy and hold inventories is costly. One estimate puts the average _____ costs at _____ percent. Carrying costs are hard to measure, particularly the cost of _____ and the cost of _____.

Essay Questions

1. Purchasing covers much more ground than the simple act of buying. In its broader sense, what does purchasing require entrepreneurs to do?

2. Describe the five purchasing guidelines presented in the text. How are these guidelines related to the purchasing cycle?

3. Information is a critical part of inventory control. What kind of information should a good recordkeeping system include?

© 1990 Houghton Mifflin Company. All rights reserved.

4. To make sure that the actual amount of material on hand equals that shown in the inventory records, entrepreneurs should take a physical inventory. What are some of the reasons book inventory and physical inventory might differ?

The Difference Between Success and Failure

Purchasing. The purchasing process consists of all the activities involved in obtaining needed materials, supplies, and parts from other firms. The purchasing function is far from routine and is very important. The objective of purchasing is to ensure that materials are available when they are needed, in the proper amounts, and at minimum cost.

Supplier Selection. Purchasing personnel constantly should be on the lookout for new or backup suppliers, even when their needs are being met by their present suppliers. It may become necessary to change suppliers for any of a number of reasons. Or such problems as strikes and equipment breakdowns may cut off the flow of purchased materials from a primary supplier.

Purchase Planning. An important factor in purchase planning is lead time. *Lead time* is the time that elapses between the placement of an order and the receipt of that order. If a production facility runs out of a part or material, it probably will have to shut down. And because rent, wages, and insurance expenses still must be paid, a shutdown can be expensive. However, large stockpiles of materials also are costly because the money invested in stored materials does not contribute to the firm or its operations. The objective of purchase planning is to balance these two opposing factors—to be sure that sufficient purchased materials are on hand without paying excessive storage costs.

Inventory Control. Small-business owners are concerned with three types of inventories. *Raw-materials inventories* are stockpiles of materials that will become part of the product during the manufacturing process. These include purchased materials, parts, and subassemblies. The *work-in-process inventory* consists of products that have been partially completed but require further processing. *Finished-goods inventories* consist of completed goods that are waiting shipment to customers.

Associated with each type of inventory are a *holding cost,* or storage cost, and a *stockout cost,* the cost of running out of inventory. *Inventory control* is the process of managing inventories in a way that minimizes inventory costs, including holding costs and potential stockout costs.

Because firms can incur huge inventory costs, much attention has been devoted to inventory control. The "just-in-time" system being used by Japanese (and now American) automakers is one product of this attention. Another is computer-controlled inventory systems. In smaller firms, microcomputer-based systems are being used to keep track of inventories, provide periodic inventory reports, and alert managers to impending stockouts.

What is most important, however, is not how inventories are controlled but the fact that they are controlled. Small-business owners are responsible for making sure that sufficient inventories are on hand and that they are acquired at the lowest possible cost.

© 1990 Houghton Mifflin Company. All rights reserved. 347

CHAPTER 18

Taxation

Learning Objectives

After studying this chapter, you should understand

1. Why taxes are necessary

2. What the difference is between tax avoidance and tax evasion

3. Why tax planning is important

4. What some ways of saving or postponing taxes are

5. Why it is vital to keep good tax records

Chapter Review

As you read the chapter, complete the following outline with information from the text.

Few subjects spark more controversy than taxes. Most taxpayers grumble about them, and entrepreneurs are no exception.

I. **The Need for Taxes.** Although no one wants to pay taxes, few entrepreneurs would quarrel with the need for at least some taxes. As Oliver Wendell Holmes put it, "Taxes are what we pay for a civilized society."

Taxes flow in a circular direction. Money paid out in taxes has a way of coming back to entrepreneurs and other taxpayers in the form of benefits.

No business, big or small, has a duty to pay more taxes than the law demands. But the public perception is that businesses evade rather than avoid taxes.

II. Tax Avoidance Versus Tax Evasion. There is a distinction between tax avoidance and tax evasion. How would you define *tax avoidance?*

_____

_____

_____

_____

How would you define *tax evasion?*

_____

_____

Tax laws change yearly, often in ways that directly affect profits. To keep up with these changes, entrepreneurs should rely on their lawyers or accountants for the latest tax information. These professionals also can help entrepreneurs save taxes.

In addition to federal income taxes, what other taxes do entrepreneurs pay?

_____   _____

_____   _____

_____

III. Legal Forms of Organization and Tax Planning. How much a venture pays in federal taxes depends heavily on its legal form of organization. The choice of form can spell the difference between profit and loss.

   A. Regular Corporations. Perhaps the first step in understanding corporate federal income taxes is to define what taxable income means. On average, over a period of years, taxable income roughly equals the amount that corporations report as book profit before federal income taxes.

   In any given year, taxable income can differ sharply from book profit. This seeming contradiction comes about because the goal of tax accounting differs from that of financial accounting. What is the goal of tax accounting?

_____

_____

_____

© 1990 Houghton Mifflin Company. All rights reserved.   350

What is the goal of financial accounting?

_____

_____

_____

The Internal Revenue Code recognizes both goals. For example, it permits entrepreneurs to use one depreciation method for tax purposes and another for financial-reporting purposes.

As an incentive to invest in new fixed assets, the Tax Reform Act of 1986 allows entrepreneurs to depreciate the cost of most fixed assets over just a few years for tax purposes. The act also dropped the term *depreciation,* substituting the term *accelerated cost recovery system (ACRS).*

The ACRS allows entrepreneurs to depreciate most equipment over 3, 5, or 10 years. List three items that are covered in the 3-year asset class.

- _____

- _____

- _____

List three types of items that are covered in the 5-year asset class.

- _____

- _____

- _____

List three types of items that are covered in the 10-year asset class.

- _____

- _____

- _____

Exhibit 18.5 shows the yearly rates at which entrepreneurs can depreciate their cost of fixed assets for each of these classes. Work through the example in the text (page 554) that illustrates the ACRS method. This example also compares the ACRS method with the straight-line method of depreciation.

© 1990 Houghton Mifflin Company. All rights reserved.

The corporation is the only legal form of organization that the Internal Revenue Code recognizes as a legal "person." As a result, income tax rates for corporations differ from those applicable to either sole proprietorships or partnerships. The only exception is the S corporation.

Corporations get tax breaks of up to $75,000 of their taxable income. What is the corporate tax rate at the following income levels?

Up to $50,000 _____

$50,000-$75,000 _____

Over $75,000 _____

B. **S Corporations.** The S corporation is a hybrid form of organization, a cross between a regular corporation and a general partnership (see Chapter 7). How is an S corporation similar to a corporation?

_____

How is an S corporation similar to a partnership?

_____

_____

C. **Partnerships and Sole Proprietorships.** Partnerships and sole proprietorships fall under almost precisely the same tax laws as the S corporation. In a partnership, the partners themselves are taxed, not the partnership. The partnership serves only as a kind of pipeline through which profits or losses flow straight to the partners. On what basis does each partner compute his or her federal income tax?

_____

_____

How is this different from the way shareholders compute their taxes?

_____

_____

© 1990 Houghton Mifflin Company. All rights reserved.

Similarly the tax laws do not recognize the sole proprietorship as a separate legal entity, so sole proprietors also are taxed as individuals. Sole proprietors cannot take advantage of such corporate tax-sheltered benefits as life and health insurance, nor can they pay themselves tax deductible salaries. But they do have two tax advantages. What are they?

- _____
_____

- _____
_____

How can general partners engineer their tax consequences?

- _____
_____
_____
_____

- _____
_____
_____
_____

D. **Limited Partnerships.** The traditional tax-shelter vehicle is the limited partnership. The partners are "limited" because the tax law limits their personal liability to their investment. (It also denies them the right to take part in management.)

IV. Other Aspects of Tax Planning

A. **Inventory Values and Taxes.** Inventory values can strongly affect entrepreneurs' tax bills, especially in times of fast-rising prices. The basic problem is how best to value ending inventory. There are two common approaches. In your own words, describe them.

© 1990 Houghton Mifflin Company. All rights reserved.

FIFO (first-in, first-out) _____

_____

_____

_____

_____

LIFO (last-in, first-out) _____

_____

_____

_____

Of the two methods, LIFO saves more taxes. It keeps book profits down by matching present selling prices with present costs. The example in the text (page 557) shows the effect of inventory values on taxes.

The Internal Revenue Code allows entrepreneurs to use LIFO for income tax purposes, but only if they also use LIFO in their published financial statements.

B. **Targeted Jobs Credit.** Entrepreneurs can avail themselves of targeted jobs credits by employing certain disadvantaged people. How much is the tax credit for targeted jobs?

_____

Which employees are eligible?

- _____

_____

- _____

- _____

- _____

C. Estate and Gift Taxes. Under the Economic Recovery Tax Act of 1981, entrepreneurs can leave everything to their spouse tax-free. The law also exempts all taxable estates of $600,000 or less. And if an estate is subject to tax, the maximum rate is 55 percent, the lowest rate is 37 percent.

Tax laws also allow an unlimited number of $10,000 gifts—$20,000 if the donor is married—to be given away tax-free each year.

Today, an entrepreneur's family can have a net worth of more than $1 million and still avoid paying estate taxes as property passes from one generation to the next. The key here is sound estate planning. What should this planning cover?

- _____

_____

- _____

- _____

_____

D. Other Federal Taxes. A variety of other taxes complete the federal tax structure. How do these taxes affect entrepreneurs?

Employment taxes _____

_____

_____

_____

_____

Excise taxes _____

_____

_____

V. Keeping Tax Records. Compliance with federal, state, and local tax laws requires a staggering amount of paperwork. Recording and withholding taxes, as well as reporting and paying taxes, must be done accurately and promptly.

© 1990 Houghton Mifflin Company. All rights reserved.

In dealing with taxes, entrepreneurs play a double role. As debtors, they pay federal income taxes on profits. As agents, they withhold federal income taxes and Social Security taxes from their own salaries as well as from the wages of employees, then pass them on to the proper government agency.

The best way to meet the government's recordkeeping requirements is to design an accounting system that also generates tax information. What do tax laws require entrepreneurs to keep permanent records on?

- _____
  _____
- _____
- _____
- _____
  _____

A. **Filing Tax Returns.** To make sure they meet their tax obligations, entrepreneurs should keep a tax calendar. What happens if an entrepreneur fails to file returns or to pay taxes on time?

_____

_____

Can the Internal Revenue Service hold the entrepreneur personally responsible for taxes owed by a venture, even if it is incorporated?

_____

B. **Auditing.** Entrepreneurs can count on having their tax returns audited from time to time by the IRS. What do computers help the IRS to do?

- _____
- _____
- _____
- _____

- _____

_____

There are two primary reasons why a tax return may be selected for an audit. What are they?

- _____

- _____

When the IRS selects a return for auditing, what does it look for?

- _____

- _____

- _____

- _____

- _____

Often there is honest disagreement between the IRS and the entrepreneur on how certain items should be handled. But the IRS can demand proof of questionable deductions. Clearly it is vital to be painstakingly thorough in all tax matters.

Questions for Mastery

Questions for mastery are found in the textbook at the beginning of every chapter. Answer each question again to reinforce your understanding of the information.

1. Why are taxes necessary?

_____

_____

2. What is the difference between tax avoidance and tax evasion?

_____

_____

_____

_____

3. Why is tax planning important?

_____

_____

_____

_____

4. What are some ways of saving or postponing taxes?

_____

_____

_____

_____

5. Why is it vital to keep good tax records?

_____

_____

_____

_____

© 1990 Houghton Mifflin Company. All rights reserved.

Definitions of Key Terms

The following key terms are important in this chapter. In your own words, define each concept.

taxable income _____

_____

accelerated cost recovery system (ACRS) _____

_____

straight-line depreciation _____

_____

targeted jobs credit _____

_____

employment taxes _____

_____

tax evasion _____

_____

tax avoidance _____

_____

S corporation _____

_____

tax accounting _____

_____

financial accounting _____

_____

FIFO _____

_____

© 1990 Houghton Mifflin Company. All rights reserved.

Chapter 18

LIFO _____

_____

excise taxes _____

_____

True-False Questions

Determine whether the following statements are true or false, then circle T or F. Correct answers are listed at the end of the study guide.

T   F   1.   Entrepreneurs must know precisely what taxes they must pay and, equally important, how taxes can affect the survival and growth of their venture.

T   F   2.   President John Kennedy said that "taxes are what we pay for a civilized society."

T   F   3.   Taxes flow in a circular direction.

T   F   4.   There often is vast disagreement about who should bear the burden of taxation.

T   F   5.   No business, big or small, has a duty to pay more taxes than the law demands.

T   F   6.   Tax evasion has the blessings of the Supreme Court, Congress, and state legislatures.

T   F   7.   Tax avoidance is the willful failure to live up to the spirit and letter of the tax law.

T   F   8.   Tax laws change yearly, often in ways that directly affect profits.

T   F   9.   To keep abreast of changes in the tax laws, entrepreneurs should review the Internal Revenue Code at least once every calendar quarter.

T   F   10.   How much a venture pays in federal income taxes depends in part on its legal form of organization.

T   F   11.   On the average and over a period of years, taxable income is very different from the book profit reported by most corporations.

T   F   12.   The goals of tax accounting and financial accounting are basically the same.

T   F   13.   The Internal Revenue Code allows entrepreneurs to use one depreciation method for tax purposes and another for financial-reporting purposes.

© 1990 Houghton Mifflin Company. All rights reserved.

T   F   14. The accelerated cost recovery system (ACRS) allows entrepreneurs to depreciate the cost of most fixed assets over just a few years.

T   F   15. Automobiles are included in the five-year asset class for depreciation purposes.

T   F   16. According to the ACRS, some buildings are included in the five-year asset class.

T   F   17. For a three-year asset, the entrepreneur is entitled to use a 33 percent depreciation rate during the first year.

T   F   18. For a five-year asset, the entrepreneur is entitled to use a 20 percent depreciation rate during the first year.

T   F   19. Limited partnerships are the only legal form of organization that the Internal Revenue Code recognizes as a so-called legal person, separate and distinct from its owners.

T   F   20. Income tax rates for corporations differ from those applicable to either sole proprietorships or to partnerships.

T   F   21. Investors in an S corporation enjoy limited liability.

T   F   22. In an S corporation, personal losses are limited to an amount equal to one-half of the individual's personal investment.

T   F   23. There must be fewer than 35 shareholders in an S corporation.

T   F   24. The partnership serves as a pipeline through which profits or losses flow straight to the partners.

T   F   25. Sole proprietors can deduct the cost of life and health insurance as legitimate business deductions.

T   F   26. Tax law allows partners to engineer their tax consequences.

T   F   27. A partnership can lease or buy property or borrow money from its partners, all with predictable tax consequences.

T   F   28. In the LIFO inventory method, entrepreneurs assume that the oldest materials are sold first.

T   F   29. With FIFO, if prices go up, taxes are lower because this method keeps book profits down.

T   F   30. The Internal Revenue Code allows entrepreneurs to use LIFO for income tax purposes, but only if they also use LIFO in their published financial statements.

T F   31. The targeted jobs credit is equal to 25 percent of the first $12,000 of wages per eligible employee for the first year of employment, and 25 percent of such wages for the second year.

T F   32. Under current tax law, entrepreneurs can leave everything to their spouse tax-free.

T F   33. Current tax law exempts all taxable estates of $600,000 or less from federal taxes.

T F   34. Today, with sound planning, an entrepreneur's family can have a net worth of more than $1 million and still avoid paying estate taxes as the property passes from generation to generation.

T F   35. Entrepreneurs must pay unemployment taxes if they employ one or more people for 10 weeks each during the year.

T F   36. The IRS cannot hold the entrepreneur personally responsible for taxes owed by a venture that is incorporated.

T F   37. An entrepreneur's tax return may be audited because it was selected at random or because it was prepared inaccurately.

Multiple-Choice Questions

Write the letter of the correct answer in the blank to the left of the question. Correct answers are listed at the end of the study guide.

_____ 1. According to Exhibit 18.2, the federal government collects _____ percent of every tax dollar paid to federal, state, or local governments.
   a. 19
   b. 25
   c. 40
   d. 56

_____ 2. Tax avoidance
   a. has the blessings of the Supreme Court and Congress.
   b. is the willful failure to live up to the spirit and the letter of the tax law.
   c. is practiced only by large profitable corporations.
   d. is none of the above.

_____ 3. To keep abreast of changes in the tax law, entrepreneurs should
   a. review the Internal Revenue Code at least once every calendar quarter.
   b. rely on their lawyer or accountant for the latest tax information.
   c. subscribe to a monthly tax newsletter.
   d. contact the SBA.

_____ 4. Taxable income means
    a.   profit that is left over after all taxes have been paid.
    b.   the total of all sales revenues received from all sources.
    c.   on average and over a period of years, the same amount that is reported as book profit for most corporations.
    d.   none of the above.

_____ 5. According to Exhibit 18.4, regular corporations contribute _____ percent of all federal tax revenues.
    a.   2
    b.   10
    c.   14
    d.   74

_____ 6. According to the ACRS, a truck would be included in the _____ asset class.
    a.   3-year
    b.   5-year
    c.   10-year
    d.   18-year

_____ 7. According to the ACRS, computers would be included in the _____ asset class.
    a.   3-year
    b.   5-year
    c.   10-year
    d.   18-year

_____ 8. The Internal Revenue Code recognizes the _____ as a so-called legal person, separate and distinct from its owners.
    a.   sole proprietorship
    b.   general partnership
    c.   limited partnership
    d.   corporation

_____ 9. For a corporation that has taxable income under $50,000, the corporate tax rate is _____ percent.
    a.   15
    b.   18
    c.   25
    d.   34

_____ 10. S corporations are
    a.   subject to the corporate tax rates discussed in the chapter.
    b.   a form of organization in which investors have limited liability.
    c.   subject to double taxation.
    d.   a cross between a regular corporation and a sole proprietorship.

© 1990 Houghton Mifflin Company. All rights reserved.

_____11. In the _____ inventory method, entrepreneurs assume that the youngest materials are sold first.
    a.   FIFO
    b.   LIFO
    c.   unit-cost
    d.   turnover

_____12. The targeted jobs credit is equal to _____ percent of the first $6,000 of wages per eligible employee for the first year of employment.
    a.   25
    b.   35
    c.   40
    d.   60

_____13. Under current estate and gift tax laws, estates valued at _____ or less are entirely exempt from federal taxes.
    a. $300,000
    b. $400,000
    c. $500,000
    d. $600,000

_____14. An example of an excise tax would be a tax on
    a.   unearned income.
    b.   real estate.
    c.   the manufacture of tobacco products.
    d.   interest and dividends.

_____15. Which of the following statements is *false?*
    a.   In dealing with taxes, entrepreneurs must play a double role.
    b.   The IRS can hold an entrepreneur personally responsible for taxes owed by a venture even if it is incorporated.
    c.   Government computers handle 20 million tax returns a year.
    d.   To be sure they meet their tax obligations, entrepreneurs should keep a tax calendar.

Completion Questions

Write your answers in the blanks provided in each question. Correct answers are listed at the end of the study guide.

1. No business, big or small, has a duty to pay more taxes than the law demands. Tax _____ has the blessings of the Supreme Court, Congress, and state legislatures. Tax _____, on the other hand, is the willful failure to live up to the spirit and letter of the tax law.

© 1990 Houghton Mifflin Company. All rights reserved.

2. To keep abreast of tax changes, entrepreneurs should rely on their _____ or _____ for the latest tax information.

3. How much a venture pays in federal income taxes depends on which _____ form of organization the entrepreneur chooses. So critical is this choice that its consequences can spell the difference between _____ and _____.

4. The goal of _____ accounting is to minimize taxes. The goal of _____ accounting is to report fairly the revenues, expenses, and profits earned in a given period.

5. The accelerated _____ recovery system (ACRS) allows entrepreneurs to _____ most equipment over just a few years.

6. The Internal Revenue Code recognizes the _____ as a legal person, separate and distinct from its owners.

7. Investors in an S corporation enjoy _____ liability but are taxed like a _____.

8. The partnership serves as a kind of _____ through which profits or _____ flow straight to the partners.

9. The traditional tax-shelter vehicle is the _____ partnership. In this type of organization, the partners are called _____ because the tax law limits their personal liability to their _____, and also denies them the right to take part in management.

10. In the _____ inventory method, entrepreneurs assume that the oldest materials are sold first. In the _____ inventory method, entrepreneurs assume that the youngest materials are sold first. Of the two methods, _____ saves more in taxes.

11. Today, an entrepreneur's family can have a net worth of more than $_____ million and still avoid paying any estate taxes as property passes from one generation to the next. But to achieve that result, the entrepreneur must do a sound job of _____ with the help of an accountant, a lawyer, and an insurance agent.

12. In dealing with taxes, entrepreneurs play a _____ role. As _____, they pay federal income taxes on profits. As _____, they withhold federal income and Social Security taxes from their own salaries as well as from the wages of employees, then pass them on to the proper government agency.

13. There are two main reasons why an entrepreneur's tax return may be audited. First, it may be selected at _____. Second, and more serious, a return may be audited because it was prepared _____ or was _____.

© 1990 Houghton Mifflin Company. All rights reserved.

Essay Questions

1. No business, big or small, has a duty to pay more taxes than the law demands. What is the difference between tax avoidance and tax evasion?

2. Tax laws change yearly, often in ways that directly affect profits. How can an entrepreneur keep up with changing tax laws?

3. In 1986 a dramatic change took place in the tax law with passage of the Tax Reform Act. This act replaced a complex and slow depreciation system with the accelerated cost recovery system (ACRS). In your own words, describe the ACRS.

4. Compliance with federal, state, and local tax laws requires a staggering amount of paperwork. The best way to relieve the workload is to design an accounting system that also generates tax information. What types of information must an entrepreneur keep to satisfy IRS requirements?

The Difference Between Success and Failure*

A well-managed business should never have a problem meeting its tax obligations. Its owner will have developed a systematic approach to handling federal, state, and local taxes. Just as good management keeps its accounts payable under control, so it keeps taxes from getting out of hand.

Agent and Debtor. The owner-manager of a small business plays two roles in managing taxes: debtor and agent. In the role of debtor, the owner-manager is liable for various taxes and pays them as part of business obligations. For example, each year the owner-manager owes federal income taxes, which are paid out of the earnings of the business. Another example of the debtor's role is the local real estate tax owed on property owned by the businessperson.

In the role of agent, the owner-manager of a small business collects various taxes and passes the funds on to the appropriate government agency. For example, each payday federal income and Social Security taxes are deducted from employees' wages. In some states, state income taxes also are deducted. In some localities, the owner-manager also may be involved in collecting a local income tax. In the role of agent, the owner-manager passes the taxes on to the appropriate government agency.

Types of Taxes. The two best-known federal taxes are income taxes and Social Security taxes. Other taxes set by the federal government are unemployment taxes and excise taxes. Although state taxes vary from state to state, the three major types of state taxes are unemployment taxes, income taxes, and sales taxes. It is essential to know what taxes your state requires you to pay as a debtor and what taxes it requires you to collect as an agent. In some states, a businessperson who fails to remit state-withheld taxes can be charged with embezzlement.

---

*Adapted from Stephen P. Radics, Jr., *Steps in Meeting Your Tax Obligations* (Small Marketer's Aids no. 142) Washington, D.C.: Small Business Administration, revised January 1975).

© 1990 Houghton Mifflin Company. All rights reserved.

Counties, towns, and cities impose various kinds of taxes. Among them are real estate taxes, personal property taxes, taxes on gross receipts of businesses, and unincorporated business taxes. A license to do business is also a tax, even though some owner-managers don't think of it as such.

A Final Comment. Make sure that you file tax reports when they are due and pay taxes on time. Failure to file or pay taxes when due can lead to penalties (fines and/or jail sentences) and interest on the tax money that is involved. In many cases, the officers of a company can be held personally responsible for taxes owed by their corporation. In addition, criminal charges can be imposed when monies—such as income tax withholdings—that are held in escrow for others are not available on the date due.

Good recordkeeping is essential in determining liability. For this reason, your records should be reviewed by an accountant for acceptability for audit by the various taxing authorities. It is good management to coordinate your overall accounting with tax due dates so that tax liabilities can be ascertained without too much extra work. Moreover, an accountant can relieve you of time-consuming paperwork and can research tax problems that arise with a view toward saving money for your firm.

© 1990 Houghton Mifflin Company. All rights reserved.

CHAPTER 19

Risk Management and Insurance

Learning Objectives

After studying this chapter, you should understand

1. What types of risk there are

2. Why it is important to develop a program of risk management

3. What the different ways of dealing with risk are

4. What different types of insurance coverage are available

5. How important a pension program is

Chapter Review

As you read the chapter, complete the following outline with information from the text.

Entrepreneurs soon find that risk is their constant companion; their ability to manage it depends largely on their attitude. If entrepreneurs ignore risk, they are likely to blunder. But if they face up to it, they can enhance their chances of survival and growth.

I. **The Idea of Risk.** Risk defies easy definition. To the layperson, risk generally means the possibility of losing one's health, reputation, or self-image. But to the entrepreneur, risk means the chance of financial loss. When we talk about risk in this chapter, we mean financial risk, the kind that can result in dollar losses. In your own words, explain how each of these losses could affect an entrepreneur's financial statements.

Reduced sales revenues _____

_____

Increased operating expenses _____

_____

Reduced assets _____

_____

© 1990 Houghton Mifflin Company. All rights reserved.

Increased liabilities _____

_____

Notice that all of these potential losses have one thing in common: Their occurrence cannot be foreseen. When these kinds of losses occur, the entrepreneur is caught by surprise.

Risks can be classified into three main types: pure, speculative, and fundamental (Exhibit 19.1). Define and give an example of each type.

Pure risk _____

_____

_____

_____

Speculative risk _____

_____

_____

_____

Fundamental risk _____

_____

_____

_____

II. **Risk Management Programs.** Obviously it may seem that entrepreneurs are aware of all risks, especially those that may affect the survival and growth of their venture. Yet entrepreneurs often ignore risk, especially risk that is not always apparent.

Entrepreneurs should fully analyze their exposure to loss. Only through this kind of analysis can they protect their venture against loss from pure risk.

© 1990 Houghton Mifflin Company. All rights reserved.   370

Why is risk management more art than science?

_____

_____

_____

What should a risk-management program do?

• _____

• _____

• _____

A. **Pinpointing Risks.** Because losses affect a venture monetarily, financial statements are a good place to start pinpointing where losses can occur. Entrepreneurs should use a checklist to make sure they have overlooked nothing.

The job of pinpointing risks never ends. Entrepreneurs must constantly be aware of risks and their possible effect on the venture.

B. **Estimating the Effects of Losses.** Entrepreneurs should get professional help in estimating how losses may affect their venture. After estimating the dollar cost of each possible loss, entrepreneurs must make two other estimates. What are they?

• _____

• _____

C. **Selecting Ways to Deal with Risk.** With the help of an insurance agent, entrepreneurs should select the best combination of ways to deal with a given risk. They have four choices. Explain how each choice can be used to deal with risk.

Avoid risk entirely _____

_____

_____

_____

Absorb risk through self-insurance _____

_____

_____

_____

Prevent the occurrence of loss, cut the chances of its occurrence, or reduce its
severity _____

_____

_____

_____

_____

Shift the risk to others, through insurance _____

_____

_____

III. Insurance and the Transfer of Risk. One way of dealing with risk is through insurance.
Insurance is simply a means of letting an outside party absorb risk.

What is a premium?

_____

_____

What is an insurance policy?

_____

_____

By buying insurance, entrepreneurs trade the uncertainty of a major loss for the certainty
or a minor one (the premium).

© 1990 Houghton Mifflin Company. All rights reserved.

To be insurable, a risk must meet four criteria. What are they?

- _____
- _____
  _____
- _____
- _____
  _____

A. **Risk in Large Numbers.** Risks must exist in large numbers. What is the law of averages?

_____

_____

_____

B. **Chance Happenings Beyond Control.** Give an example of a chance happening that is beyond the control of the entrepreneur.

_____

_____

Why are theft and shoplifting generally uninsurable?

_____

_____

_____

C. **Readily Measurable.** Losses must be measurable in dollars and hard to falsify, so that insurers can verify them.

© 1990 Houghton Mifflin Company. All rights reserved.   373

D. **Severe Losses.** Entrepreneurs generally purchase insurance to protect their ventures from financial loss. To protect their venture against fire, windstorms, and other natural disasters, entrepreneurs may buy property insurance. What types of assets does property insurance cover?

_____

_____

_____

What do insurance companies do to discourage the deliberate destruction of these kinds of assets?

_____

_____

Why do entrepreneurs need liability insurance coverage?

_____

_____

_____

What is key-person life insurance?

_____

_____

_____

Why is key-person life insurance useful in a partnership?

_____

_____

What kinds of losses does business-interruption insurance cover?

_____

_____

_____

© 1990 Houghton Mifflin Company. All rights reserved.

What is a fidelity bond?

_____

_____

_____

V. **Selecting an Insurance Agent.** Perhaps no other industry is more carefully tailored to the needs of individual customers than the insurance industry. Insurers have something for virtually every entrepreneur. Entrepreneurs can readily buy the insurance program that best suits their own needs as well as those of their venture.

In order to buy the "right" insurance, entrepreneurs need the help of an insurance agent. Insurance agents are qualified by training and experience to design insurance programs geared to each entrepreneur's needs.

How do entrepreneurs find a competent insurance agent?

_____

_____

What is the advantage of choosing an insurance agent who offers one-stop service?

_____

_____

What is the alternative to one-stop service?

_____

_____

Why is it to the entrepreneur's advantage to select an independent insurance agent?

_____

_____

How can an entrepreneur check out an insurance company?

_____

_____

© 1990 Houghton Mifflin Company. All rights reserved.   375

VI. Fringe Benefits. We've discussed the types of insurance that protect a venture from extraordinary financial loss. Other types of insurance protect not the venture, but its employees.

    A. Life Insurance. Life insurance protects a family from loss of income on the untimely death of its breadwinners.

What is term life insurance?

_____

_____

_____

_____

What is whole life insurance?

_____

_____

_____

What are two other names for whole life insurance?

_____

_____

Entrepreneurs can buy group life insurance if they have four or more employees. What are the advantages of a group life insurance policy?

▪ _____

▪ _____

What is a contributory plan?

_____

_____

B. **Social Security.** Run by the federal government, Social Security is a compulsory minimum kind of insurance. It provides families with income to live on when a breadwinner dies, retires, or is unable to work. Today Social Security covers almost all of the nation's employees.

Why do some economists refer to Social Security payments as taxes rather than premiums?

_____

_____

What is the current rate and wage base for Social Security?

Rate _____

Wage base _____

The law also requires that entrepreneurs pay a sum equal to that withheld from the earnings of each employee.

C. **Health and Accident Insurance.** Health and accident insurance is another vital form of protection. It protects employees against the high cost of hospitalization and physicians' services.

VII. Pension Plans. Pension plans protect entrepreneurs against the risk of financial hardship when they retire. They are part of the retirement system, a system economists call a *three-legged stool.* What are the three "legs" of the stool?

- _____

- _____

- _____

Unlike large corporations, many entrepreneurs cannot justify the cost of a private pension plan for themselves or their employees. List three reasons why.

- _____

_____

- _____

_____

© 1990 Houghton Mifflin Company. All rights reserved.

▪ _____

_____

_____

A. Keogh Plans. In 1974 Congress passed into law the Employment Retirement Income Security Act (ERISA). This act enables many entrepreneurs and their employees to shelter money from taxes while accumulating a nest egg on which to retire.

What is ERISA commonly called?

_____

How much can entrepreneurs and their employees set aside in a Keogh plan each year?

_____

What are the plan's features?

▪ _____

_____

▪ _____

▪ _____

_____

_____

▪ _____

_____

_____

To set up a Keogh plan, entrepreneurs should approach a commercial bank, a savings and loan association or an insurance company.

B. Individual Retirement Accounts. The Individual Retirement Account (IRA) is another tax shelter available to entrepreneurs and their employees. How much can entrepreneurs and their employees invest in an IRA?

_____

© 1990 Houghton Mifflin Company. All rights reserved.

Questions for Mastery

Questions for mastery are found in the textbook at the beginning of every chapter. Answer each question again to reinforce your understanding of the information.

1. What types of risk are there?

_____

_____

_____

2. Why is it important to develop a program of risk management?

_____

_____

_____

3. What are the different ways of dealing with risk?

_____

_____

_____

_____

_____

4. What different types of insurance coverage are available?

_____

_____

_____

_____

_____

© 1990 Houghton Mifflin Company. All rights reserved.

5. How important is a pension program?

_____

_____

_____

Definitions of Key Terms

The following key terms are important in this chapter. In your own words, define each concept.

avoidance of risk _____

_____

self insurance _____

_____

transfer of risk _____

_____

pure risk _____

_____

speculative risk _____

_____

fundamental risk _____

_____

property insurance _____

_____

liability insurance _____

_____

© 1990 Houghton Mifflin Company. All rights reserved.

fidelity bond _____

_____

term insurance _____

_____

whole life insurance _____

_____

group life insurance _____

_____

premium _____

_____

ERISA _____

_____

Individual Retirement Account (IRA) _____

_____

True-False Questions

Determine whether the following statements are true or false, then circle T or F. Correct answers are listed at the end of the study guide.

T   F   1.   Entrepreneurs' ability to manage risk depends largely on their attitude.

T   F   2.   As used in this chapter, *risk* means financial risk, the kind that can result in dollar losses.

T   F   3.   Risk (dollar losses) has no effect on a small-business venture's financial statements.

T   F   4.   With pure risk, the entrepreneur can either gain or lose.

T   F   5.   Fundamental risk differs from both pure and speculative risk in its impersonality.

T   F   6. Some specific sources of fundamental risk are floods, earthquakes, inflation, and war.

T   F   7. Risk management is more science than art.

T   F   8. Entrepreneurs should seek the help of an insurance agent to design a risk-management program.

T   F   9. Because losses affect a venture monetarily, financial statements are a good starting point for pinpointing where losses can occur.

T   F   10. It is the entrepreneur's job to pinpoint risks and gauge their possible effect on the venture.

T   F   11. Self-insurance is common among small-business owners.

T   F   12. Holding safety education programs for workers is an example of risk avoidance.

T   F   13. Most entrepreneurs deal with risk by transferring it.

T   F   14. Insurance is simply a means of letting an outside party absorb risk.

T   F   15. A risk is insurable if the risk exists in small numbers.

T   F   16. To be insurable, insured losses must be under the control of the entrepreneur.

T   F   17. To be insurable, losses must be readily measurable.

T   F   18. To be insurable, probable losses must be so severe that the entrepreneur is incapable of absorbing them.

T   F   19. With insurance, the odds are fixed so that the insurer runs only the slightest risk of losing financially.

T   F   20. Property insurance protects against losses caused by negligence on the part of the business owner or the owner's employees.

T   F   21. Liability coverage insures the entrepreneur's buildings, equipment, and inventories.

T   F   22. To protect heirs from being forced to sell a venture in order to pay estate taxes, entrepreneurs may buy key-person life insurance.

T   F   23. To protect their venture against theft and fraud committed by their employees, entrepreneurs may buy liability insurance.

© 1990 Houghton Mifflin Company. All rights reserved.   382

T F 24. It generally is best to select an independent insurance agent, one who represents a number of insurers.

T F 25. One source of information about individual insurance agents is *Best's Insurance Reports*.

T F 26. The most basic form of life insurance is whole life insurance.

T F 27. Entrepreneurs can purchase group life insurance if they employ four or more people.

T F 28. Most group life insurance plans are contributory.

T F 29. Because Social Security is compulsory by law, economists often refer to Social Security payments as taxes rather than premiums.

T F 30. The cost of administering a pension plan for a small business is quite low.

T F 31. Another name for the Employment Retirement Income Security Act (ERISA) is the Keogh plan.

T F 32. The Keogh plan allows entrepreneurs and their employees to shelter as much as 30 percent of their taxable income—to a limit of $20,000—a year.

T F 33. All the entrepreneur's employees with three years or more of service must be included in the Keogh plan.

T F 34. To set up a Keogh plan, entrepreneurs should approach commercial banks, savings and loan associations, or insurance companies.

T F 35. The Individual Retirement Account (IRA) gives every worker in the country the opportunity to set aside up to $6,000 a year for retirement.

Multiple-Choice Questions

Write the letter of the correct answer in the blank to the left of the question. Correct answers are listed at the end of the study guide.

_____ 1. With _____ risk, the entrepreneur can only lose or break even.
   a. pure
   b. speculative
   c. fundamental
   d. impersonal

____ 2. With _____ risk, the entrepreneur can either gain or lose.
    a.   pure
    b.   speculative
    c.   fundamental
    d.   impersonal

____ 3. Which of the following statements is *false?*
    a.   Entrepreneurs often ignore risk, especially risk that is not always apparent.
    b.   Entrepreneurs should fully analyze their exposure to loss.
    c.   Entrepreneurs should seek the expert help of an insurance agent when designing a risk-management program.
    d.   If the entrepreneur is careful, risk management is more science than art.

____ 4. All of the following are acceptable ways of dealing with risk *except*
    a.   avoidance.
    b.   preventing
    c.   refusal.
    d.   transfer.

____ 5. Which of the following statements about insurable risk is *true?*
    a.   The risk must exist in large numbers.
    b.   Insured losses must be chance happenings that are beyond the entrepreneur's control.
    c.   Probable losses must be so severe that the entrepreneur is incapable of absorbing them.
    d.   All of the above statements are true.

____ 6. _____ insurance generally covers such assets as buildings, equipment and inventories.
    a.   Key-person life
    b.   Property
    c.   Liability
    d.   Business-interruption

____ 7. _____ insurance protects against losses caused by negligence.
    a.   Key-person life
    b.   Property
    c.   Liability
    d.   Business-interruption

____ 8. _____ insurance may be useful in partnerships to buy out the heirs of a deceased partner.
    a.   Key-person life
    b.   Property
    c.   Liability
    d.   Business-interruption

© 1990 Houghton Mifflin Company. All rights reserved.

_____ 9. The best source of information about insurance companies is
    a.   Dun & Bradstreet.
    b.   a local banker.
    c.   *The Wall Street Journal.*
    d.   *Best's Insurance Reports.*

_____10. A form of life insurance that gives pure protection with no provision for savings is called
    a.   term insurance.
    b.   whole life insurance.
    c.   a fidelity bond.
    d.   health and accident insurance.

_____11. All of the following are characteristic of group life insurance policies *except*
    a.   low premiums.
    b.   waived medical examinations.
    c.   medical coverage.
    d.   contributory plans.

_____12. Which of the following statements is *false?*
    a.   Social Security is a minimum kind of insurance.
    b.   Because Social Security is compulsory, economists often refer to Social Security payments as taxes rather than premiums.
    c.   The entrepreneur has the option of matching the contributions made by employees.
    d.   The Social Security Act was originally passed by Congress in 1935.

_____13. Under the Keogh plan, entrepreneurs and their employees can set aside, tax-free, as much as _____ percent of their taxable income—with a limit of $30,000 a year—in a retirement plan.
    a.   10
    b.   20
    c.   30
    d.   40

_____14. Under current Keogh plan legislation,
    a.   all the entrepreneur's employees with two or more years of service must be included in the plan.
    b.   all funds contributed are fully tax-deductible.
    c.   most of the funds contributed are protected by law.
    d.   capital gains are taxed in the year the capital gain occurs.

_____15. An entrepreneur can contribute up to _____ a year to an IRA.
    a. $1,000
    b. $2,000
    c. $3,000
    d. $4,000

© 1990 Houghton Mifflin Company. All rights reserved.

Completion Questions

Write your answer in the blanks provided in each question. Correct answers are listed at the end of the study guide.

1. When we mention risk in this chapter, we mean the chance of _____ loss. This loss may show up in the balance sheet or in the income statement as reduced _____ revenues, increased _____ expenses, reduced _____, or increased _____.

2. With _____ risk, the entrepreneur can only lose or break even. With _____ risk, the entrepreneur can either gain or lose. Fundamental risk differs from the other two types of risk in its _____.

3. An effective risk management program is one that _____ risks that can cause dollar losses, _____ how severe these losses may be, and _____ the best way to treat each risk.

4. With the help of an _____ agent, entrepreneurs should select the best combination of ways to deal with risk. They may choose to _____ risk entirely, _____ risk through self-insurance, _____ the occurrence of loss, or _____ risk to others through insurance.

5. _____ is simply a means of letting an outside party absorb risk. For a _____, the outside party agrees to pay the entrepreneur a specified sum of money to cover losses suffered under conditions spelled out in a written _____.

6. Basically a risk is insurable if it meets four tests:
   (1) The risk must exist in _____ numbers, (2) insured losses must be _____ happenings that are beyond the entrepreneur's control, (3) losses must be readily _____, and (4) probable losses must be so _____ that the entrepreneur is incapable of absorbing them.

7. _____ insurance covers such assets as buildings, equipment, and inventories.

8. _____ insurance protects against losses caused by negligence.

9. To protect heirs from being forced to sell their venture in order to pay estate taxes, entrepreneurs may buy _____ life insurance. This type of insurance also can be useful in _____ to buy out the heirs of a deceased partner.

10. Agents who offer _____ service are more likely to do a painstaking job of analyzing all the entrepreneur's insurance needs because they earn a commission on not just one but many lines of insurance. It is generally best to select an _____ agent, one who represents a number of insurers.

© 1990 Houghton Mifflin Company. All rights reserved.

11. Life insurance protects a family from loss of income on the untimely death of its _____. The basic form of life insurance is _____ insurance. It gives pure _____, meaning there is no savings plan connected with the policy.

12. Another basic type of life insurance is _____ life insurance, sometimes called *straight life* or *ordinary life*. It differs from term insurance in that premiums are paid throughout the _____ lifetime with the whole amount of the policy payable on the insured's death.

13. Entrepreneurs can buy _____ life insurance if they employ _____ or more people. This plan offers advantages that are denied to individuals. For one, _____ examinations usually are waived. Another advantage is that group premiums are _____ than individual premiums.

14. In 1974 Congress passed the Employment Retirement _____ Security Act (ERISA). Popularly called the *Keogh plan,* the law allows entrepreneurs and their employees to set aside, tax-free, as much as _____ percent of their taxable income—with a limit of _____ a year—in a retirement plan.

Essay Questions

1. Risks can be classified into three types: pure, speculative, and fundamental. In your own words, describe each type of risk as it applies to a small business, and give an example of each type.

2. With the help of an insurance agent, entrepreneurs should select the best combination of ways to deal with risk. There are four choices open to them. Explain each choice and give an example of how entrepreneurs can use each method to deal with risk.

3. Next month Joe and Mary Garner will open their own retail clothing store. Like most people starting a business, they want to protect their investment. Their store space is leased and occupies 2,000 square feet in the middle of a strip shopping center. Their beginning inventory is valued at $45,000, and the store's fixtures and remodeling cost $22,000. Once they open, the owners plan to hire two full-time employees and one part-time employee. If you were the Garners, what type of insurance coverage would you purchase?

4. Many entrepreneurs face financial hardship when they retire. How can they protect themselves against this type of risk?

Chapter 19

The Difference Between Success and Failure

Insurance is available to cover most pure risks, but specialized or customized policies can be expensive.   A part of effective risk management is to ensure that when insurance is purchased, the coverage is proper for the individual situation. Three questions can be used as guidelines: What hazards must be insured against? Is the cost of insurance coverage reasonable in this situation? What other risk-management techniques can be used to reduce insurance costs?

Fire Insurance. *Fire insurance* is insurance that covers losses due to fire. The standard fire insurance policy provides protection against partial or complete loss of a building and/or its contents when that loss is caused by fire or lightning. Premiums depend on the construction of the building, its use and contents, whether risk reduction devices (like smoke and fire alarms) have been installed in the building, and other factors. If a fire does occur, the insurance company reimburses the policyholder for either the actual dollar loss or the maximum amount stated in the policy, whichever is lower. *Extended coverage* is insurance protection against damage caused by windstorm, hail, explosion, riots or civil commotion, aircraft, vehicles, and smoke. Extended coverage is available as an endorsement (addition) to some other insurance policy—usually a fire insurance policy. Normally losses caused by war, nuclear radiation or contamination, and water (other than in storms) are excluded from extended-coverage endorsements.

Burglary, Robbery, and Theft Insurance. *Burglary* is the illegal taking of property through forcible entry. A kicked-in door, a broken window pane or pry marks on a window sill are evidence of a burglary or attempted burglary. *Robbery* is the unlawful taking of property from an individual by force or threat of violence. A thief who uses a gun to rob a gas station is committing robbery. *Theft* (or *larceny*) is a general term that means the wrongful taking of property that belongs to another. Insurance policies are available to cover burglary only, robbery only, theft only, or all three. Premiums vary with the type and value of the property covered by the policy.

Motor Vehicle Insurance. Individuals and businesses purchase automobile insurance because it is required by state law, because it is required by the firm financing purchase of the vehicle, or because they want to protect their investment. *Automobile liability insurance* is insurance that covers financial losses resulting from injuries or damages caused by the insured vehicle. Liability insurance does not pay for the repair of the insured vehicle. *Automobile physical damage insurance* is insurance that covers damage to the insured vehicle. *Collision* insurance pays for the repair of damage resulting from an accident. Most collision coverage includes a deductible amount—anywhere from $50 up—that the policyholder must pay. *Comprehensive insurance* covers damage to the insured vehicle that is caused by fire, theft, hail, dust storm, vandalism, and almost anything else that could damage a car except collision and normal wear and tear.

© 1990 Houghton Mifflin Company. All rights reserved.   388

Marine (Transportation) Insurance. Marine or transportation coverage provides protection against the loss of goods that are being shipped from one place to another. It is the oldest type of insurance. The term *marine insurance* was coined at a time when only goods transported by ship were insured. Today marine insurance is available for goods shipped over water or land. *Ocean marine insurance* protects the policyholder against loss or damage to a ship or its cargo on the high seas. *Inland marine insurance* protects against loss or damage to goods shipped by rail, truck, air, or inland barge. Both types cover losses resulting from fire, theft, and most other hazards.

Business Liability Insurance. Business liability coverage protects the policyholder from financial losses resulting from an injury to another person or damage to another person's property. During the past ten years or so, both the number of liability claims and the size of settlements have increased dramatically. The result has been heightened awareness of the need for liability coverage—along with rising premiums for this coverage.

Public liability insurance is insurance that protects the policyholder from financial losses due to injuries suffered by others as a result of negligence on the part of a business owner or employee. It covers injury or death due to hazards at the place of business or resulting from the actions of employees. *Product liability insurance* is insurance that protects the policyholder from financial losses due to injuries suffered by others as a result of using the policyholder's products.

Workers' Compensation. Workers' compensation insurance covers medical expenses and provides salary continuation for employees who are injured while they are at work. This insurance also pays benefits to the dependents of workers who are killed on the job. Today every state requires that employers provide some form of workers' compensation insurance, with benefits established by the state.

© 1990 Houghton Mifflin Company. All rights reserved.

CHAPTER 20

The Social Responsibilities of Entrepreneurs

Learning Objectives

After studying this chapter, you should understand

1. What the social responsibilities of entrepreneurs are

2. How property rights may conflict with social rights

3. What the public's perception of business is

4. What special problems minorities, women, and the handicapped face

5. What consumerism is

Chapter Review

As you read the chapter, complete the following outline with information from the text.

If this is the age of computers, it is also the age of nervousness. A vague feeling of helplessness plagues many people, including entrepreneurs. In this chapter we discuss the entrepreneur's responsibility for solving the problems that society faces.

I. **The Meaning of Social Responsibility.** Many entrepreneurs believe that what is good for their venture is likely to be good for the community in which they invest their energies and money. They see their investments sparking new products, new services, new jobs. And as their ventures prosper, they see themselves as benefactors of the community.

At one time the public seemed to accept this view. Today, it does not. There has been a steady erosion of the ideas basic to free enterprise. What are those ideas?

_____   _____

_____   _____

© 1990 Houghton Mifflin Company. All rights reserved.

Today, property rights are being challenged by social rights. List six of those social rights.

_____   _____

_____   _____

_____   _____

It is not that social rights have eliminated property rights. It is that property rights are subject to the needs of the community.

A.   **Negative and Distorted Views of Business.** Few entrepreneurs are willing to concede that the good of the community should come before property rights. As a result, the public tends to have a low opinion of business.

Students in particular seem to have a negative view of business. What are the results of studies that measure what students think about business?

·   _____

·   _____

     _____

Actually profits average only 3 cents of every sales dollar. And they play a vital role in keeping the economy healthy. Still the public believes that business is greedy, and that taxes and regulations should be used to keep profits down.

As members of the business world, entrepreneurs must share the blame for the public's distorted image of business. In their rush to sell products, they often create the impression that their goals are purely materialistic, that they care little about social problems.

American business people are respected all over the world for their knowledge and salesmanship. But when it comes to selling themselves to society, they do a poor job.

B.   **Entrepreneurs' Feelings of Helplessness.** Few entrepreneurs know how to overcome their sense of futility about economic and environmental problems. But this feeling of helplessness can be overcome if entrepreneurs make their ideas known to those around them and take an active role in resolving social problems. What kinds of things can entrepreneurs do?

·   _____

·   _____

·   _____

© 1990 Houghton Mifflin Company. All rights reserved.

- _____

_____

- _____

C. **Positive Action.** Many entrepreneurs and other businesspeople are responding to today's social challenges with positive action. For example, many industries have drafted codes of behavior. What do these codes do?

_____

_____

Often entrepreneurs cannot choose to ignore social responsibility. Exhibit 20.3 lists some of the federal agencies that force entrepreneurs and other businesspersons to act in socially responsible ways. What are the primary activities of these agencies?

Consumer Product Safety Commission _____

_____

Environmental Protection Agency _____

_____

_____

Equal Employment Opportunity Commission _____

_____

_____

Food and Drug Administration _____

_____

_____

Occupational Safety and Health Administration _____

_____

Office of Federal Contract Compliance Programs _____

_____

_____

II. Civil Rights and Employment Discrimination

A. **Minorities.** Today most businesses claim to be equal opportunity employers. Many are indeed working to erase bigotry and provide full equality of opportunity.

Good intentions, however, do not guarantee good results. It is true that some progress has been made. But to many entrepreneurs, being an "equal opportunity employer" simply means being willing to consider minorities for employment. Few minority members move into managerial jobs. And few minority members find themselves in line jobs that count.

Entrepreneurs who just pay lip service to the principles of equal opportunity are not living up to their social responsibilities. All the talk about equal opportunity cannot hide the fact that business still discriminates—openly or unconsciously—against blacks, Native Americans, Hispanics, and other minority groups.

B. **The Handicapped.** In the rush for equal opportunity, those with handicaps have been largely overlooked. Yet discrimination against them in the workplace is a serious problem. What do studies tell us about handicapped workers?

- _____

_____

- _____

III. The Impact of Consumerism.
The coming of consumerism may be traced to 1966, when Ralph Nader began making headlines with his exposés of unsafe automobiles. Since then, he has helped launch a consumer movement. Thanks largely to Nader's efforts, consumers are no longer alone in the fight against dishonest businesspersons.

The primary goal of the consumer movement is to help erase private abuses of the public interest. What does the consumer movement try to do?

- _____

- _____

_____

© 1990 Houghton Mifflin Company. All rights reserved.

- _____

_____

- _____

_____

Today almost every community in the country has a consumer group. These groups already have made their mark on business and the federal government. For example, in response to consumerism, the Federal Trade Commission (FTC) has hired hundreds of consumer specialists. What do these specialists do?

- _____

- _____

_____

- _____

_____

A. **Opposing Views of Consumerism.** Traditionally the FTC has investigated mergers and other practices that could hamper free trade. Now that the FTC has joined the consumer movement, one official stated that "every business is involved in some sort of misrepresentation."

Though exaggerated, the statement echoes the attitude of Nader and other consumer advocates. In response, some businesses are going to great lengths to please consumers. But others believe that government—at all levels—has overreacted to consumerism. And often the price of consumer protection is higher costs.

B. **Benefits of Consumerism.** Despite its critics, the consumer movement has left its mark in many areas. What are three of those areas?

- _____

_____

_____

- _____

_____

© 1990 Houghton Mifflin Company. All rights reserved.

■ _____

_____

_____

_____

Although consumerism has struck fear in the hearts of many entrepreneurs, it also has encouraged tens of thousands of consumers. Remember, the only true test of a satisfactory product or service is a satisfied customer. With this test as their guide, entrepreneurs need never worry about doing the right thing.

Questions for Mastery

Questions for mastery are found in the textbook at the beginning of every chapter. Answer each question again to reinforce your understanding of the information.

1. What are the social responsibilities of entrepreneurs?

_____

_____

_____

_____

2. How may property rights conflict with social rights?

_____

_____

_____

3. What is the public's perception of business?

_____

_____

_____

_____

© 1990 Houghton Mifflin Company. All rights reserved.

4. What special problems do minorities, women, and the handicapped face?

_____

_____

_____

_____

5. What is consumerism?

_____

_____

_____

Definitions of Key Terms

The following key terms are important in this chapter. In your own words, define each concept.

property rights _____

_____

social rights _____

_____

Consumer Bill of Rights _____

_____

Equal Employment Opportunity Commission _____

_____

Food and Drug Administration _____

_____

Occupational Safety and Health Commission _____

_____

© 1990 Houghton Mifflin Company. All rights reserved.

equal opportunity employer _____

_____

institutional racism _____

_____

consumerism _____

_____

Federal Trade Commission (FTC) _____

_____

Congress Watch _____

_____

True-False Questions

Determine whether the following statements are true or false, then circle T or F. Correct answers are listed at the end of this chapter in the study guide.

T   F   1. The view that "what's good for General Motors is good for the country" is no longer accepted by the public.

T   F   2. Today property rights are being challenged by social rights.

T   F   3. The right of individualism and the right to unhindered competition are examples of social rights.

T   F   4. Your right to enjoy your property is no longer subject simply to paying your taxes and obeying the laws.

T   F   5. According to George Cabot Lodge, the good of the community should come before property rights.

T   F   6. Few entrepreneurs agree with Lodge's thinking.

T   F   7. Studies indicate that students believe that businesses have high moral standards.

T   F   8. Most students believe that businesses make 35 percent profit.

T   F   9. Profits actually average only 3 cents of every sales dollar.

© 1990 Houghton Mifflin Company. All rights reserved.

T F 10. In their rush to sell products, entrepreneurs often create the impression that their goals are purely materialistic.

T F 11. For the individual entrepreneur, the very size of social problems creates a feeling of helplessness.

T F 12. Today most businesses claim to be equal opportunity employers.

T F 13. Many entrepreneurs believe that being an equal opportunity employer simply means being willing to consider minorities for employment.

T F 14. Many minority members move into managerial jobs.

T F 15. Although discrimination against Native Americans and Hispanics is still a problem, discrimination against blacks is no longer a problem.

T F 16. Discrimination against those with handicaps is often more severe than discrimination against minorities.

T F 17. Among those who are handicapped, absenteeism is a major problem.

T F 18. The coming of consumerism can be traced to 1966, when Ralph Nader began making headlines with his exposés of unsafe automobiles.

T F 19. The main goal of the consumer movement is to help erase private abuses of the public interest.

T F 20. The nation's Better Business Bureaus processed about 500,000 consumer complaints in 1988.

T F 21. Some entrepreneurs believe that the government—at all levels—has overreacted to consumerism.

T F 22. Dr. Erika Wilson found that 32 percent of the 180 small businesspersons she interviewed in Los Angeles felt no social responsibility at all.

Multiple-Choice Questions

Write the letter of the correct answer in the blank to the left of the question. Correct answers are listed at the end of this chapter in the study guide.

_____ 1. All of the following are property rights *except*
   a. individualism.
   b. unhindered competition.
   c. equal opportunity.
   d. the limited role of government.

© 1990 Houghton Mifflin Company. All rights reserved.

_____ 2. All of the following are social rights *except*
   a. equal opportunity.
   b. justice.
   c. good health.
   d. individualism.

_____ 3. Profits actually average only _____ cents of every sales dollar.
   a. 2
   b. 3
   c. 4
   d. 5

_____ 4. Which of the following statements about profits is *false?*
   a. Most students believe that businesses make profits of 75 percent.
   b. Profits attract investors to small businesses.
   c. Profits help finance new products.
   d. Profits play a vital role in keeping the economy healthy.

_____ 5. Which of the following statements is *false?*
   a. In their rush to sell products, entrepreneurs often create the impression that their goals are purely materialistic.
   b. Many businesspersons, including entrepreneurs, are trying to do something about social problems.
   c. When it comes to explaining their role in society, American businesspeople do a poor job.
   d. In a recent study, a majority of students rated businesses very high in moral and ethical standards.

_____ 6. The federal agency that investigates and resolves complaints of discrimination in employment based on race or sex is the
   a. Consumer Product Safety Commission.
   b. Environmental Employment Agency.
   c. Equal Employment Opportunity Commission.
   d. Federal Trade Commission.

_____ 7. The federal agency that sets and enforces safety and health standards in the workplace is the
   a. Office of Federal Contract Compliance Programs.
   b. Occupational Safety and Health Administration.
   c. Food and Drug Administration.
   d. Product Safety Commission.

____ 8. Which of the following statements is *false?*
   a.   A new and subtle deterrent to black mobility is institutional racism.
   b.   It is unlawful for an employer to discriminate against any individual because of that individual's race, color, religion, sex, or national origin.
   c.   Native Americans and Hispanics do not face discrimination in the workplace.
   d.   Today most businesses claim to be equal opportunity employers.

____ 9. Research studies show that
   a.   absenteeism among those with handicaps often approaches zero.
   b.   handicapped workers are not as dedicated as nonhandicapped workers.
   c.   discrimination against handicapped workers is not as severe as discrimination against other minority groups.
   d.   handicapped workers are unable to compensate for their disabilities.

____ 10. The main goal of the consumer movement is to
   a.   help erase private abuses of the public interest.
   b.   teach consumers to care.
   c.   educate consumers on their opportunities and their responsibilities to make changes.
   d.   make institutions more open, accessible, and accountable to consumers.

____ 11. In response to consumerism, the FTC has hired hundreds of consumer specialists to
   a.   spot-check businesses for violations of FTC rules.
   b.   investigate complaints about faulty products or slipshod service.
   c.   educate consumers on how not to be taken in by dishonest businesspersons.
   d.   do all of the above.

____ 12. In 1988, the nation's Better Business Bureaus processed more than _____ million consumer complaints.
   a.   1.2
   b.   1.4
   c.   3.4
   d.   4.8

____ 13. According to the Better Business Bureaus, the industry that ranked first in the number of consumer complaints was
   a.   insurance.
   b.   retail sales.
   c.   service firms.
   d.   financial services.

____ 14. Dr. Erika Wilson found that _____ percent of the 180 small businesspersons she interviewed mentioned responsibilities to their customers, employees, or community
   a.   85
   b.   88
   c.   90
   d.   95

© 1990 Houghton Mifflin Company. All rights reserved.   401

Completion Questions

Write your answer in the blanks provided in each question. Correct answers are listed at the end of this chapter in the study guide.

1. The changing attitudes among Americans has steadily eroded the ideas basic to _____ enterprise, ideas such as _____, personal _____ rights, unhindered _____, and the limited role of _____.

2. Today property rights are being challenged by such _____ rights as _____ opportunity, _____, good _____, clean _____, _____, and a decent _____.

3. The American people tend to have a distorted or _____ view of business. According to one study, _____ believe that businesses have _____ moral and ethical standards. Most think that businesses make _____ percent profits. Profits actually average only _____ cents of every sales dollar.

4. As members of the business world, _____ must share the blame for the public's distorted image of business. In their rush to sell products, they often create the impression that their goals are purely _____.

5. Today most businesses claim to be _____ opportunity employers. Many are indeed working to erase _____ and to provide full equality of opportunity.

6. To many entrepreneurs, being an equal opportunity employer simply means being willing to consider _____ for employment. Few minority members move into _____ jobs, for example.

7. Blacks are not the only minority group that faces discrimination. Native _____, Hispanics and other minorities face similar problems. All the talk about equal opportunity cannot hide the fact that business still _____ against minorities either openly or unconsciously.

8. In the rush for equal opportunity, the _____ have been largely overlooked. Yet discrimination against them often is more _____ than that against minorities.

9. The coming of _____ can be traced to _____ when Ralph Nader began making headlines with his exposés of unsafe automobiles. Since then, he has helped launch a consumer movement that now spans the _____.

10. The main goal of the consumer movement is to help erase _____ abuses of the public interest. In essence, the consumer movement tries to teach consumers to _____, to make _____ more open, to _____ consumers on their opportunities and their responsibilities, and to teach consumers how to learn what is going on.

© 1990 Houghton Mifflin Company. All rights reserved.

11. Dr. Erika Wilson found that only _____ percent of the 180 small businesspersons she interviewed felt no social responsibility at all. The remaining 88 percent mentioned responsibilities to their _____, employees, or _____.

Essay Questions

1. Social rights are not eliminating property rights, but they are reducing their significance. According to George Cabot Lodge, the good of the community should come before property rights. Do you agree? Justify your answer.

2. Few entrepreneurs know how to overcome their sense of futility about economic and environmental problems. They know that the giant pieces of a new order are falling into place, and they feel helpless. How can entrepreneurs make their ideas known to those around them? How can entrepreneurs help do things like make the streets safer, clean the air, and make their plants safer places to work?

3. To many entrepreneurs, being an equal opportunity employer simply means being willing to consider minorities for employment. Is this attitude justifiable? How can entrepreneurs help eliminate discrimination?

4. Some entrepreneurs believe that government—at all levels—has overreacted to consumerism. Is the cost of consumerism worth it from the entrepreneur's standpoint? From the consumer's standpoint?

The Difference Between Success and Failure

Social responsibility is as important for small businesses as it is for large corporations. Often the success of a small business is tied to the owner's efforts to be socially responsible. The Small Business Administration has published a pamphlet called "Six Methods for Success in a Small Store."* It stresses the importance of a small business acting as a responsible "citizen." Among the suggestions:

1. *Cater to the customer.* Your number one job should be to please customers. Learn their likes and dislikes. Tell the truth about your products even if it means a lost sale.

2. *Build an image.* Many a small-store owner fumbles this role. Use your personality to encourage people to think favorably of your store. Don't do things that will make your customers doubt your honesty or sincerity.

3. *Encourage teamwork.* The satisfaction customers get from trading with you will be only as good as your employees. Teach your employees to know what to do, how to do it, and when to do it.

*Adapted from "Six Methods for Success in a Small Store," (Washington, D.C.: U.S. Small Business Administration, 1978).

© 1990 Houghton Mifflin Company. All rights reserved.

4. *Pay your civic rent.* A store's opportunities for expansion are tied up with the growth of the community in which it is located. You pay your civic rent when you take part in local clubs and other organizations that work to build the community. Use caution: Take on only what you can handle.

© 1990 Houghton Mifflin Company. All rights reserved.

Answer Key

Chapter 1

True-False Questions

1.	T	11.	F	21.	T
2.	F	12.	T	22.	T
3.	T	13.	T	23.	F
4.	T	14.	F	24.	T
5.	F	15.	F	25.	T
6.	T	16.	T	26.	T
7.	T	17.	T	27.	F
8.	F	18.	T	28.	T
9.	T	19.	F	29.	T
10.	T	20.	F	30.	F

Multiple-Choice Questions

1.	b	6.	d	11.	b
2.	a	7.	a	12.	d
3.	d	8.	d	13.	c
4.	c	9.	d	14.	c
5.	a	10.	b	15.	d

Completion Questions

1. Hammurabi, 300, 2100
2. low, sinners, interest
3. 1,683, 40
4. assets, equity, revenues, employees
5. 500, owned, managed
6. American Motors, dominate
7. 99, 19, half
8. higher, owners' equity
9. 600,000, half, 18, 10
10. bad, expenses, customers, poor
11. increased
12. failures, unqualified, rise

© 1990 Houghton Mifflin Company. All rights reserved.

Chapter 2

True-False Questions

1.	T	11.	T	21.	F
2.	T	12.	T	22.	T
3.	F	13.	F	23.	T
4.	T	14.	F	24.	T
5.	F	15.	F	25.	T
6.	T	16.	T	26.	T
7.	T	17.	F	27.	F
8.	T	18.	T	28.	T
9.	F	19.	T		
10.	F	20.	T		

Multiple-Choice Questions

1.	b	5.	d	9.	b
2.	d	6.	c	10.	a
3.	c	7.	b	11.	c
4.	a	8.	a	12.	c

Completion Questions

1. entrepreneur, zeal, ideas
2. Pure, dies, sells, franchise
3. entrepreneurship, innovation, expansion
4. perform, money, machines
5. higher, outside, self-expression, half
6. half, 18, overachievers
7. reasonable, odds, sure, high
8. compulsive, 60
9. achievement, self-renewing
10. investment, profit, competitive, reward, higher
11. high, entrepreneurship
12. group, failure
13. failure, emotional

© 1990 Houghton Mifflin Company. All rights reserved.

Chapter 3

True-False Questions

1.	T	14.	T	27.	F
2.	F	15.	T	28.	F
3.	T	16.	F	29.	F
4.	F	17.	T	30.	T
5.	T	18.	T	31.	T
6.	T	19.	T	32.	F
7.	T	20.	T	33.	T
8.	F	21.	T	34.	F
9.	T	22.	T	35.	F
10.	F	23.	F	36.	T
11.	T	24.	T	37.	F
12.	F	25.	F	38.	F
13.	T	26.	F		

Multiple-Choice Questions

1.	c	6.	a	11.	b
2.	c	7.	d	12.	c
3.	a	8.	b	13.	c
4.	a	9.	b	14.	d
5.	c	10.	a		

Completion Questions

1. products, two-thirds, three-fourths
2. middlemen, 80, caretakers
3. consumers, 50, Specialty
4. skills, easiest
5. big
6. small, General, Subcontracting
7. 15,000
8. venture, rent, risk
9. commercial, residential, developers, 25,000
10. five, 100,000

© 1990 Houghton Mifflin Company. All rights reserved.

Chapter 4

True-False Questions

1.	T	13.	T	25.	T
2.	F	14.	F	26.	T
3.	T	15.	T	27.	F
4.	T	16.	T	28.	T
5.	T	17.	F	29.	T
6.	F	18.	T	30.	F
7.	T	19.	T	31.	F
8.	F	20.	F	32.	F
9.	T	21.	T	33.	T
10.	T	22.	F	34.	F
11.	F	23.	F	35.	T
12.	F	24.	T		

Multiple-Choice Questions

1.	c	6.	a	11.	a
2.	a	7.	b	12.	d
3.	b	8.	a	13.	b
4.	b	9.	c	14.	a
5.	d	10.	c	15.	b

Completion Questions

1. entrepreneur, product, buy, start
2. bankers, less
3. fear
4. financial, adjustments, five
5. accountant, lawyer
6. earnings, asset, earning
7. capitalizing, yearly
8. personal, buyer's
9. assets, liabilities
10. less, profitable, guess
11. market, research, important
12. inventors, money, attorney

© 1990 Houghton Mifflin Company. All rights reserved.   408

Chapter 5

True-False Questions

1.	T	11.	T	21.	T
2.	F	12.	F	22.	F
3.	F	13.	F	23.	T
4.	F	14.	T	24.	T
5.	T	15.	T	25.	F
6.	T	16.	F	26.	F
7.	T	17.	T	27.	T
8.	T	18.	F	28.	F
9.	T	19.	T	29.	T
10.	F	20.	T	30.	T

Multiple-Choice Questions

1.	a	6.	d	11.	c
2.	b	7.	a	12.	c
3.	b	8.	b	13.	b
4.	c	9.	c	14.	c
5.	c	10.	a		

Completion Questions

1. franchise, franchisee, franchisor
2. 10, 34
3. $640
4. 4
5. royalty
6. riches
7. independent, sergeant
8. disclosure, federal, 20
9. contract, franchisee
10. one, five
11. franchise
12. working
13. Royalties
14. 900

© 1990 Houghton Mifflin Company. All rights reserved.

Chapter 6

True-False Questions

1.	T	12.	T	23.	T
2.	T	13.	T	24.	T
3.	T	14.	F	25.	T
4.	T	15.	T	26.	F
5.	F	16.	F	27.	T
6.	T	17.	T	28.	F
7.	F	18.	F	29.	T
8.	F	19.	F	30.	T
9.	F	20.	T	31.	F
10.	T	21.	T	32.	T
11.	T	22.	T	33.	T

Multiple-Choice Questions

1.	d	6.	c	11.	b
2.	a	7.	b	12.	b
3.	a	8.	d	13.	c
4.	b	9.	c	14.	c
5.	b	10.	a		

Completion Questions

1. rigorous, think, road
2. Outside, creditors, investors
3. process, substance
4. consultants, turnoff
5. 5, 95
6. sales, three, monthly, quarterly, yearly
7. selling, promotion
8. dollars, creditors
9. cash, sheets, income, profitgraph
10. two, beginning, end
11. sales, operating, loss
12. profitgraph, profit

© 1990 Houghton Mifflin Company. All rights reserved.

Chapter 7

True-False Questions

1.	T	13.	F	25.	T
2.	F	14.	F	26.	F
3.	F	15.	T	27.	T
4.	F	16.	F	28.	T
5.	T	17.	T	29.	F
6.	F	18.	F	30.	F
7.	T	19.	T	31.	T
8.	T	20.	F	32.	T
9.	T	21.	T	33.	T
10.	F	22.	F	34.	F
11.	F	23.	T	35.	F
12.	T	24.	T		

Multiple-Choice Questions

1.	b	6.	b	11.	d
2.	c	7.	c	12.	d
3.	b	8.	d	13.	c
4.	c	9.	a	14.	b
5.	a	10.	b	15.	a

Completion Questions

1. lawyer, business, *Hubbell*, small, personal
2. 71, Freedom, low, unlimited, continuity, raising
3. least, Uniform, voluntary, liability, partnership
4. limited, active
5. family, investment
6. artificial, Limited, personal
7. preferred, common, assets
8. certificates, directors, vote, dividends, sell
9. charter, most, legal
10. directors, debts, founders, stock
11. double, S, 35
12. 1244, $50,000, ordinary
13. federal, 90
14. productivity, technology, formation

© 1990 Houghton Mifflin Company. All rights reserved.

Chapter 8

True-False Questions

1.	T	10.	T	19.	T
2.	T	11.	T	20.	T
3.	F	12.	T	21.	T
4.	F	13.	T	22.	F
5.	T	14.	F	23.	T
6.	F	15.	T	24.	T
7.	F	16.	T	25.	F
8.	T	17.	F	26.	T
9.	F	18.	F		

Multiple-Choice Questions

1.	d	6.	d	11.	a
2.	a	7.	b	12.	d
3.	b	8.	d	13.	b
4.	d	9.	b	14.	c
5.	c	10.	c	15.	b

Completion Questions

1. geographical, city, area, specific
2. Census, 50,000, 4,000, 5,000
3. Buying, *Marketing,* retail, yearly
4. sales, manufacturing
5. high, affordable, Midwest, labor, cost
6. entrepreneur, 25,000, 4,500
7. enterprise

© 1990 Houghton Mifflin Company. All rights reserved.

Chapter 9

True-False Questions

1.	T	15.	F	29.	F
2.	F	16.	T	30.	T
3.	F	17.	F	31.	F
4.	F	18.	T	32.	T
5.	T	19.	F	33.	T
6.	T	20.	F	34.	F
7.	F	21.	T	35.	T
8.	T	22.	T	36.	F
9.	F	23.	T	37.	F
10.	F	24.	T	38.	T
11.	T	25.	T	39.	T
12.	T	26.	T	40.	F
13.	T	27.	T	41.	T
14.	T	28.	F		

Multiple-Choice Questions

1.	d	6.	a	11.	c
2.	a	7.	a	12.	c
3.	b	8.	c	13.	c
4.	c	9.	b	14.	d
5.	b	10.	d		

Completion Questions

1. cash, financial, creditors
2. operating, estimates, intangible
3. Fixed, current
4. renting, risking, investors'
5. repayment, interest, bankruptcy
6. Investors', dividend
7. rapidly, computer
8. 360, risks, equity, loans
9. invest, acquisition
10. equity, friends
11. unborn, erroneous
12. fast, short, one, liquidating
13. permanent, profits
14. independently, private, small
15. $150,000, fifteenfold, shares

© 1990 Houghton Mifflin Company. All rights reserved.

Chapter 10

True-False Questions

1.	T	15.	T	29.	T
2.	F	16.	F	30.	F
3.	T	17.	T	31.	T
4.	F	18.	T	32.	F
5.	T	19.	T	33.	T
6.	T	20.	F	34.	T
7.	F	21.	T	35.	F
8.	T	22.	F	36.	T
9.	F	23.	T	37.	T
10.	T	24.	T	38.	F
11.	T	25.	F	39.	T
12.	T	26.	T	40.	F
13.	F	27.	T		
14.	T	28.	T		

Multiple-Choice Questions

1.	a	6.	a	11.	d
2.	d	7.	b	12.	b
3.	b	8.	b	13.	b
4.	c	9.	c	14.	c
5.	d	10.	d		

Completion Questions

1. circular, entrepreneurs, important
2. organization, skills, could
3. accountant, lawyer, banker, insurance, computer
4. description, organizational
5. personal, above
6. chart, responsibility
7. single, hire, knowledge
8. line, staff, functional
9. organizational, once
10. Elected, legally
11. president, delegate, dividends
12. president, goals
13. salesmanship, preliminary, fees, low
14. 1953, SCORE, ACE, SBI, SBDC
15. 2,500, fraction
16. *Networking,* effective

© 1990 Houghton Mifflin Company. All rights reserved.

Chapter 11

True-False Questions

1.	T	13.	T	25.	T
2.	T	14.	T	26.	T
3.	T	15.	F	27.	F
4.	F	16.	T	28.	T
5.	F	17.	F	29.	T
6.	T	18.	T	30.	F
7.	F	19.	T	31.	F
8.	F	20.	T	32.	T
9.	F	21.	F	33.	F
10.	F	22.	F	34.	T
11.	T	23.	F	35.	T
12.	F	24.	T		

Multiple-Choice Questions

1.	c	6.	b	11.	b
2.	d	7.	b	12.	c
3.	d	8.	a	13.	d
4.	d	9.	c	14.	b
5.	a	10.	c	15.	d

Completion Questions

1. accountant, information
2. comparison, financial, low, minimize
3. entrepreneurs, small, certified
4. profit, three
5. operating, sales, two
6. *goods,* customers
7. control, goals
8. one, assets, financed
9. right, left
10. *position, condition*
11. cash, receivable, sales, paid

© 1990 Houghton Mifflin Company. All rights reserved.

Chapter 12

True-False Questions

1.	T	13.	T	25.	T
2.	T	14.	T	26.	T
3.	F	15.	T	27.	T
4.	F	16.	F	28.	T
5.	F	17.	T	29.	T
6.	F	18.	F	30.	T
7.	T	19.	T	31.	F
8.	F	20.	F	32.	F
9.	F	21.	T	33.	F
10.	T	22.	T	34.	T
11.	T	23.	F	35.	T
12.	F	24.	F	36.	T

Multiple-Choice Questions

1.	c	6.	b	11.	b
2.	d	7.	b	12.	d
3.	c	8.	a	13.	a
4.	b	9.	d	14.	b
5.	c	10.	a		

Completion Questions

1. circular, haphazardly
2. prebirth, acceptance, breakthrough, maturity
3. fast, inadequate, revenues, specialists
4. goals, workers, lead
5. immediate, employee
6. reward, higher, lower
7. strengths, skills, superior
8. management, skills, entrepreneurs'
9. employees, key
10. *control*, planned
11. centerpiece, dollar, planning, control
12. evaluate, performance
13. actual, budgeted
14. sales, investment
15. profitgraph, visual

© 1990 Houghton Mifflin Company. All rights reserved.

Chapter 13

True-False Questions

1.	T	13.	T	25.	T
2.	F	14.	T	26.	T
3.	T	15.	F	27.	F
4.	T	16.	T	28.	T
5.	F	17.	F	29.	T
6.	F	18.	T	30.	F
7.	T	19.	F	31.	T
8.	T	20.	T	32.	T
9.	F	21.	F	33.	T
10.	T	22.	T	34.	F
11.	F	23.	T	35.	T
12.	F	24.	T		

Multiple-Choice Questions

1.	b	6.	d	11.	d
2.	c	7.	c	12.	a
3.	c	8.	b	13.	c
4.	a	9.	a	14.	b
5.	b	10.	c	15.	c

Completion Questions

1. control, analyzing
2. accountant's, entrepreneur's
3. goals
4. *investment,* assets, equity, permanent
5. debt, capital
6. analysis, profitability, health
7. *margin,* profit, revenues
8. goods, inventory
9. liabilities, assets
10. assets, liabilities, 2
11. year, turnover, sales, receivable
12. payback, original, average
13. nonpaying
14. Commercial, consumer
15. promptly, application, report, bureau

© 1990 Houghton Mifflin Company. All rights reserved.

Chapter 14

True-False Questions

1.	T	15.	T	29.	F
2.	F	16.	T	30.	F
3.	F	17.	F	31.	T
4.	F	18.	T	32.	T
5.	T	19.	F	33.	T
6.	T	20.	T	34.	T
7.	F	21.	T	35.	F
8.	T	22.	T	36.	T
9.	F	23.	T	37.	T
10.	T	24.	T	38.	F
11.	F	25.	F	39.	T
12.	F	26.	T	40.	T
13.	F	27.	F		
14.	T	28.	T		

Multiple-Choice Questions

1.	c	6.	a	11.	a
2.	a	7.	b	12.	a
3.	b	8.	d	13.	b
4.	d	9.	d	14.	b
5.	c	10.	d	15.	a

Completion Questions

1. research, satisfy
2. undertaking, fail, markets, dangerous
3. fact, niches
4. beginners, professional, survey
5. *market,* segmentation, subgroups
6. related, geographic, psychographic, demographic
7. distribution, users
8. skimming, penetration
9. communicate
10. selling, customers
11. salespersons, seven
12. promotion, contests, samples, exhibitions
13. varies, competitors, profit
14. 5
15. unknown, distance, complex
16. marketing, Commerce, Commerce, foreign

© 1990 Houghton Mifflin Company. All rights reserved.

Chapter 15

True-False Questions

1.	T	13.	F	25.	T
2.	F	14.	F	26.	T
3.	T	15.	T	27.	F
4.	T	16.	F	28.	T
5.	F	17.	T	29.	F
6.	F	18.	T	30.	F
7.	T	19.	T	31.	T
8.	T	20.	F	32.	T
9.	F	21.	F	33.	F
10.	F	22.	T	34.	F
11.	T	23.	T	35.	T
12.	T	24.	F		

Multiple-Choice Questions

1.	c	6.	d	11.	c
2.	a	7.	c	12.	a
3.	c	8.	a	13.	b
4.	c	9.	b	14.	a
5.	b	10.	d	15.	d

Completion Questions

1. mainframes, minicomputers
2. personal, *desktop*
3. hardware
4. central, primary, output
5. *Software,* instructions
6. productivity, input
7. word-processing, printer
8. Database, data
9. desktop, prints, typeset
10. contract, computer, understand
11. software, first
12. entrepreneurs

© 1990 Houghton Mifflin Company. All rights reserved.

Chapter 16

True False Questions

1.	T	14.	F	27.	T
2.	F	15.	F	28.	F
3.	F	16.	T	29.	T
4.	F	17.	T	30.	F
5.	T	18.	T	31.	T
6.	T	19.	F	32.	T
7.	F	20.	T	33.	F
8.	F	21.	F	34.	T
9.	T	22.	F	35.	F
10.	T	23.	T	36.	T
11.	F	24.	F	37.	F
12.	T	25.	T	38.	T
13.	F	26.	F		

Multiple-Choice Questions

1.	b	6.	d	11.	d
2.	c	7.	c	12.	b
3.	a	8.	a	13.	a
4.	a	9.	b	14.	d
5.	d	10.	a	15.	d

Completion Questions

1. oppressive, benevolent
2. Participatory, social, better
3. circular, needs
4. individual, five
5. McGregor, X, Y
6. Mayo, Hawthorne
7. authoritarian, Likert
8. loyalty, blindly, job
9. innovate, niches, value
10. competitors
11. $50, Social, income
12. 33

© 1990 Houghton Mifflin Company. All rights reserved.

Chapter 17

True-False Questions

1.	T	11.	T	21.	F
2.	T	12.	F	22.	F
3.	F	13.	T	23.	F
4.	F	14.	T	24.	T
5.	T	15.	T	25.	T
6.	T	16.	F	26.	F
7.	T	17.	T	27.	F
8.	T	18.	F	28.	T
9.	F	19.	F	29.	T
10.	T	20.	F	30.	T

Multiple-Choice Questions

1.	a	6.	b	11.	b
2.	d	7.	b	12.	a
3.	a	8.	c	13.	d
4.	d	9.	d		
5.	c	10.	d		

Completion Questions

1. profits, purchasing
2. wholesaling, retailing
3. quality, quantity, time, supplier, price
4. estimating, supplier, negotiating, following
5. inventory, customers
6. forecasting, forecasts
7. average, purchases
8. less, stockouts
9. physical, book, immediately
10. pilfered, physical, receiving
11. carrying, 21, money, shortages

© 1990 Houghton Mifflin Company. All rights reserved.

Chapter 18

True-False Questions

1.	T	14.	T	27.	T
2.	F	15.	T	28.	F
3.	T	16.	F	29.	F
4.	T	17.	F	30.	T
5.	T	18.	F	31.	F
6.	F	19.	F	32.	T
7.	F	20.	T	33.	T
8.	T	21.	T	34.	T
9.	F	22.	F	35.	F
10.	T	23.	T	36.	F
11.	F	24.	T	37.	T
12.	F	25.	F		
13.	T	26.	T		

Multiple-Choice Questions

1.	d	6.	b	11.	b
2.	a	7.	b	12.	c
3.	b	8.	d	13.	d
4.	c	9.	a	14.	c
5.	c	10.	b	15.	c

Completion Questions

1. avoidance, evasion
2. lawyer, accountant
3. legal, profit, loss
4. tax, financial
5. cost, depreciate
6. corporation
7. limited, partnership
8. pipeline, losses
9. limited, *limited,* investment
10. FIFO, LIFO, LIFO
11. 1, planning
12. double, debtors, agents
13. random, inaccurately, incomplete

© 1990 Houghton Mifflin Company. All rights reserved.

Chapter 19

True-False Questions

1.	T	13.	T	25.	F
2.	T	14.	T	26.	F
3.	F	15.	F	27.	T
4.	F	16.	F	28.	T
5.	T	17.	T	29.	T
6.	T	18.	T	30.	F
7.	F	19.	T	31.	T
8.	T	20.	F	32.	F
9.	T	21.	F	33.	T
10.	T	22.	T	34.	T
11.	F	23.	F	35.	F
12.	F	24.	T		

Multiple-Choice Questions

1.	a	6.	b	11.	c
2.	b	7.	c	12.	c
3.	d	8.	a	13.	b
4.	c	9.	d	14.	b
5.	d	10.	a	15.	b

Completion Questions

1. financial, sales, operating, assets, liabilities
2. pure, speculative, impersonality
3. pinpoints, estimates, selects
4. insurance, avoid, absorb, prevent, transfer
5. Insurance, fee, contract
6. large, chance, measurable, severe
7. Property
8. Liability
9. key-person, partnerships
10. one-stop, independent
11. breadwinners, term, protection
12. whole, employee's
13. group, four, medical, lower
14. Income, 20, $30,000

© 1990 Houghton Mifflin Company. All rights reserved.

Chapter 20

True-False Questions

1.	T	9.	T	17.	F
2.	T	10.	T	18.	T
3.	F	11.	T	19.	T
4.	T	12.	T	20.	F
5.	T	13.	T	21.	T
6.	T	14.	F	22.	F
7.	F	15.	F		
8.	T	16.	T		

Multiple-Choice Questions

1.	c	6.	c	11.	d
2.	d	7.	b	12.	c
3.	b	8.	c	13.	b
4.	a	9.	a	14.	b
5.	d	10.	a		

Completion Questions

1. free, individualism, property, competition, government
2. social, equal, justice, health, air, survival, income
3. negative, students, low, 35, 3
4. entrepreneurs, materialistic
5. equal, bigotry
6. minorities, managerial
7. Americans, discriminates
8. handicapped, severe
9. consumerism, 1966, continent
10. private, care, institutions, educate
11. 12, customers, community

© 1990 Houghton Mifflin Company. All rights reserved.